Guide to America's Outdoors

Eastern Canada

Guide to America's Outdoors
Eastern Canada

By Marq de Villiers
and the editors of National Geographic Travel Books
Photography by Michael Lewis

NATIONAL
GEOGRAPHIC
WASHINGTON, D.C.

Contents

Cover: Canoe on Pickerel Lake, Quetico Provincial Park   *Page 1:* Maple leaf on the move,
Prince Edward Island   *Pages 2-3:* Descending Mount Albert, Parc de la Gaspésie, Quebec
Opposite: Geologic layering, Bay of Fundy, Nova Scotia

Treading Lightly in the Wild

Pink lady's slipper

FROM THE INLAND SEAS of the Great Lakes in the west to the dramatic landscapes of Newfoundland in the east and from the unpopulated grandeur of the Eastern Arctic to the rolling landscapes around Point Pelee, NATIONAL GEOGRAPHIC GUIDE TO AMERICA'S OUTDOORS: EASTERN CANADA guides you to the best wilderness adventures in a vast terrain.

Visitors who care about this region know they must tread lightly on the land. Ecosystems can be damaged or destroyed by misuse. Many have already suffered from the impact of tourism. The marks are clear: litter-strewn acres, polluted waters, trampled vegetation, disrupted wildlife. You can do your part to preserve these places for yourself, your children, and all other nature travelers. Before embarking on a backcountry visit or a camping adventure, learn some basic conservation dos and don'ts. Leave No Trace, a national educational program, recommends the following:

Plan ahead. If you know what to expect in terms of climate, conditions, and hazards, you can pack for general needs, extreme weather, and emergencies. Do yourself and the land a favor by visiting if possible during off-peak months and limiting your group to no more than four to six people. To keep trash or litter to a minimum, repackage food into reusable containers or bags. And rather than using cairns, flags, or paint cues that mar the environment to mark your way, bring a map and compass.

Travel and camp on solid surfaces. In popular areas, stay within established trails and campsites. Travel single file in the middle of the trail, even when it's wet or muddy, to avoid trampling vegetation. Be extra sensitive in boggy or coastal areas, and avoid stepping on mussels, sea stars, and the like. If exploring off-trail in pristine areas, have your group spread out to lessen impact. Good campsites are found, not made. Travel and camp on sand, gravel, or rock, or on dry grasses, pine needles, or snow. Stay at least 200 feet from waterways. On breaking camp, leave the site as you found it.

Pack out what you pack in—and that means *everything* except human waste, which should be deposited in a hole dug away from water, camp, or trail, then covered and concealed. When washing dishes, clothes, or yourself, use small amounts of biodegradable soap and scatter the water away from lakes and streams.

Be sure to leave all items—plants, rocks, artifacts—as you find them. Avoid potential disaster by neither introducing nor transporting non-native species. Also, don't build or carve out structures that will alter the environment. A don't-touch policy not only preserves resources for future generations; it also gives the next guy a crack at the discovery experience.

Firewood depletion harms the backcountry, so keep fires to a minimum (try using a gas-fueled camp stove and a candle lantern instead). A fire built on a beach should be situated below the next high-tide line, where the traces will be washed away. If you can't use existing fire rings, employ fire pans or mound fires. Keep your fire small, use only sticks from the ground, burn the fire down to ash, and don't leave the site until it's cold.

Respect wildlife. Watch animals from a distance, but never approach, feed, or follow them. Feeding weakens an animal's ability to fend for itself in the wild. If you can't keep your pets under control, leave them at home.

Finally, be mindful of other visitors. Yield to fellow travelers on the trail, and keep noise levels low so that the sounds of nature can be heard.

With these points in mind, you have only to chart your course. Enjoy your explorations. Let natural places quiet your mind, refresh your spirit, and remain as you found them. Just remember, leave behind no trace. ■

MAP KEY and ABBREVIATIONS

☐ National Park	N.P.
National Historic Site	N.H.S.
☐ National Forest	N.F.
☐ National Wildlife Area	N.W.A.
Bird Sanctuary	
Conservation Area	C.A.
Ecological Reserve	E.R.
Game Management Area	G.M.A.
Game Sanctuary	
Migratory Bird Sanctuary	M.B.S.
Réserve Faunique	R.F.
☐ Provincial Park	P.P.
Territorial Park	
☐ Indian Reservation	I.R.
☐ Air Base	

Canadian Heritage River

POPULATION

● **MONTREAL**	above 500,000
● **Thunder Bay**	50,000 to 500,000
● Midland	10,000 to 50,000
• Lewisporte	under 10,000

ADDITIONAL ABBREVIATIONS

Ch.	Channel
Cr.	Creek
Fk.	Fork
Gl.	Glacier
HWY.	Highway
I.-s.	Island-s
L.	Lake
MEM.	Memorial
Mt.-s.	Mount-ain-s
N.M.P.	National Marine Park
Pen.	Peninsula
Pres.	Preserve
Prov.	Provincial
Pt.	Point
R.	River
RD.	Road
Res.	Reservoir
Terr.	Territorial
TR.	Trail
Wild.	Wilderness

U.S. Interstate — Quebec Autoroute — U.S. Federal — U.S. State — Canadian Prov. Highways — Trans-Canada Highways — Other Road

81   40   1   27   3   2   436

Ferry   Trail   Canal

BOUNDARIES

STATE, PROVINCIAL or NATIONAL

FOREST   N.P.   N.M.P.   WILD.

☐ Point of Interest	⊣⊢ Falls
⊛ National Capital	◯ Glacier
⊛ State & Prov. capital	⚬ Swamp / Wetland
+ Elevation	△ Campground

GEOGRAPHIC TRANSLATIONS

ENGLISH	FRENCH
Bay	Baie
Island-s	Île-s
Lake	Lac
Mount-ain-s	Mont-s
Park	Parc
Reserve	Réserve
River	Rivière
Wildlife	Faunique

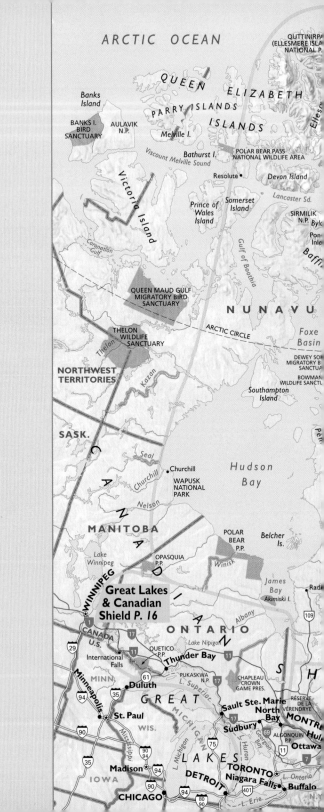

ARCTIC OCEAN

QUTTINIRPA
(ELLESMERE ISLA
NATIONAL P.

QUEEN ELIZABETH

PARRY ISLANDS

ISLANDS

Banks
Island

BANKS I.
BIRD
SANCTUARY

AULAVIK
N.P.

Melville I.

Bathurst I.

POLAR BEAR PASS
NATIONAL WILDLIFE AREA

Viscount Melville Sound

Resolute

Devon Island

Victoria Island

Coronation Gulf

Prince of
Wales
Island

Somerset
Island

Lancaster Sd.

SIRMILIK
N.P.   Byl

Pon
Inle

Baffi

Gulf of Boothia

QUEEN MAUD GULF
MIGRATORY BIRD
SANCTUARY

NUNAVU

ARCTIC CIRCLE

Foxe
Basin

THELON
WILDLIFE
SANCTUARY

Thelon

Kazan

DEWEY SO
MIGRATORY B
SANCTUA

NORTHWEST
TERRITORIES

BOWMAN
WILDLIFE SANCTL

Southampton
Island

SASK.

Seal

Churchill

Churchill

Hudson
Bay

Pen

WAPUSK
NATIONAL
PARK

Nelson

MANITOBA

POLAR
BEAR
P.P.

Belcher
Is.

Lake
Winnipeg

OPASQUIA
P.P.

Winisk

James
Bay

Rad

Akimiski I.

109

WINNIPEG

CANADA
U.S.

**Great Lakes
& Canadian
Shield P. 16**

ONTARIO

17

Albany

29

QUETICO
P.P.

Lake Nipigon

11

International
Falls

11

Thunder Bay

Minneapolis

MINN.

61

PUKASKWA
N.P.

17

CHAPLEAU
CROWN
GAME PRES.

RÉSERVE
DE LA
VÉRENDRYE

94

35

Duluth

GREAT

L. Superior

Sault Ste. Marie
North
Bay

St. Paul

90

MICHIGAN

MONTRE

Hull

94

WIS.

Sudbury

69

ALGONQUIN
P.P.

Ottawa

11

Georgian
Bay

7

35

Madison

94

LAKES

L. Michigan

L. Huron

TORONTO

401

Niagara Falls

L. Ontario

IOWA

90

DETROIT

Buffalo
N.Y.

CHICAGO

94

80
90

L. Erie

Mississippi

Eastern Canada

0 ——— miles ——— 400
0 ——— kilometers ——— 600

N

THULE
AIR BASE

GREENLAND
(KALAALLIT NUNAAT)
DENMARK

Baffin Bay

AUYUITTUQ
NATIONAL PARK

Davis Strait

Nuuk
(Godthåb)

Iqaluit

**Eastern
Arctic**
P. 226

*Labrador
Sea*

Ungava
Bay

Ramah

N E W F O U N D L A N D

Torngat Mts.

Caniapiscau

Ungava

George

**ATLANTIC
OCEAN**

Nain

QUEBEC

Labrador

Mealy Mts.

Cartwright

Churchill
Falls

500

Happy Valley-
Goose Bay

**The St.
Lawrence**
P. 74

L'Anse aux Meadows

St. Anthony

GROS
MORNE
N.P.

*Island of
Newfoundland*

TERRA NOVA
N.P.

Mts.

Sept-Îles

Île
d'Anticosti

Lewisporte

**St.
John's**

*Avalon
Pen.*

Baie-Comeau

Laurentian

Lawrence

Gulf of
St. Lawrence

138

Gaspé Peninsula

132

Newfoundland
P. 182

185

11

Îles de
la Madeleine

Québec

**NEW
BRUNSWICK**

P.E.I.

Charlottetown

Sydney

**Maritime
Provinces**
P. 126

2

Fredericton

2

104

105

104

Cape Breton I.

95

102

**NOVA
SCOTIA**

Halifax

Bay of Fundy

Sable I.

Portland

N.H.

BOSTON

The Geography of Remembrance

WHEN I CAME TO CANADA from the arid plains of South Africa half a life-time ago, I was captivated by the apparently endless bounty of my new home: springs and streams, creeks and rivers, tumbling cataracts and mighty waterfalls, ponds and lakes—lakes the size of small seas. And everywhere you looked, trees. The glorious maple woods of the southerly latitudes, the boreal forest stretching untold miles to the country where tundra began, the cedar thickets that nurtured the deer that sustained the wolves in their endless cycle of birth and death and renewal.

Every place in this book contains a trace of magic—that's why I've included them—but like any traveler I have certain images burned deeper into memory than others. One such is the winter's morning in Ontario's Algonquin Park. It had snowed heavily the night before but now the sun was out, the slanting rays glittering off the snow crystals, landscape like a jeweled mirror. In the fresh snow, the paw prints of a wolf, angling through the woods. Then, faintly, on the threshold of hearing, the excited yapping of wolf pups welcoming a parent home.

A day spent in Quebec's La Mauricie forest was every bit as haunting. It was a fall morning in early October, the air was crisp, and I was walking beneath a maple canopy that arched overhead, a rustling and technicolor tunnel. The trail debouched on the shores of a lake, and across the water, which steamed with morning mist, I saw a forest painted scarlet and brilliant orange and yellow as blinding as gold; and on the water a canoe, gliding quietly, as natural on these waters as a loon.

Just as powerful a remembrance is my first glimpse of Nova Scotia's rugged South Shore: a small cove with brilliant white sand, the plaintive piping of a plover, terns circling watchfully overhead, seals with their breathy and quarrelsome burping on the beach, the great swells of the Atlantic rolling in from unfathomable distances and crashing on the headland, the spray as white as a ghost and as evanescent.

The places profiled in this book are as diverse as memory itself. They range from tiny Point Pelee National Park, the birder's paradise north of Lake Erie, to the endless woodlands of La Vérendrye in Quebec, a park half the size of Belgium. They vary from the turf meadows and sheer cliffs of Bird Rock, at Cape St. Mary's in Newfoundland, to the awe-inspiring grandeur of the Penny Highlands on remote and ice-shrouded Baffin Island, where you can experience a land as elemental as it was before humans evolved.

If this guidebook helps you seek out and capture your own set of indelible wilderness memories—if it helps you love the lake and forest, cliff and fjord of my adopted land as much as I do—I will feel it has done its job. Perhaps these places will remind you, too, what a great privilege it is to sit in the silence of an unspoiled place, perhaps by a flickering flame, and hear nothing but the gurgle of water and the haunting cry of a loon echoing across a remote lake, until it is time to go home.

Marq de Villiers
Gros Morne Trail, Gros Morne NP, Newfoundland

St. Lawrence Islands NP

A Wilderness Rooted in Rock

AT FIRST GLANCE, no common thread links all the disparate fragments that make up Eastern Canada, a massive expanse of more than 2 million square miles. The lush peat marshes of northern Ontario, for example, are nothing like the desolate polar deserts of the eastern Arctic, while the vast wilderness of Woodland Caribou Provincial Park could not be more different from the wetlands and forests of Point Pelee in Canada's deep south. Even within the Maritime Provinces, the tame farmland of gentle Prince Edward Island contrasts radically with the toothy rockscapes of wild Nova Scotia.

Further compounding the difficulty of getting a handle on this region is its sheer size—nearly 60 percent that of the entire United States. Quebec alone is bigger than western Europe, while the territory of Nunavut—Canada's newest political entity, coined in April 1999—is twice as big as Quebec.

Take a satellite's-eye view, however, and you'll quickly see that four geologic ties bind eastern Canada together.

The first is the Canadian Shield (also called the Precambrian Shield), a vast bowl of metamorphic rock centered on Hudson Bay. The southern rim of this bowl takes in the northern Great Lakes, while its eastern rim sweeps up the north shore of the St. Lawrence River in the form of a 2,000-foot-high wall known as the Laurentide Scarp. The shield itself is a layer of ancient rocks that have been folded and twisted by mountain building and reduced by erosion to a rocky plain.

The second thread is the St. Lawrence River, which rises on the western edge of the region. The Ottawa St. Lawrence Lowlands are separated from Ontario by the Frontenac Axis, a narrow band of Precambrian rocks that link the shield to the Adirondack Mountains of New York, cutting across the St. Lawrence at the Thousand Islands.

The third cohesive string is the northward thrust of the Appalachian mountain chain, which extends in Canada from the eastern townships of Quebec through the Gaspé Peninsula to the Maritime Provinces—that is, New Brunswick, Prince Edward Island, and Nova Scotia—and from there to the Island of Newfoundland. This Canadian portion of the Appalachians forms the spine of a complex sequence of uplands: The Sutton Mountains and the Chic-Chocs in Quebec, the Chaleur and Miramichi Uplands in New Brunswick, and the Caledonia and Cape Breton Highlands in Nova Scotia. Finally, the northern Appalachians culminate in the Long Range Mountains, which extend the length of western Newfoundland island.

Glacial scarring is the fourth unifying strand in the geology of Eastern Canada. North America's last glaciation, which receded from most of the continent 10,000 or so years ago but is still retreating from the Canadian Arctic, left behind thin and acidic soils, myriad meltwater lakes, and a collection of curious formations known as drumlins—massive oval mounds of earth and stones deposited by a glacier. Visitors to Nova Scotia often marvel at the stubborn consistency with which area settlers built their farms atop hills. Yet the farmers were only heeding logic: These are glacial drumlins, and the hilltops are where the soil is.

A Land of Many Faces

With these four threads in mind, we have divided eastern Canada into segments that acknowledge both its geographic commonalities and its classic visitor patterns. We start with the Great Lakes and the nearby portions of the Canadian Shield—a territory of complexity and immense scope, with lush farmlands in the south, huge swaths of mixed and boreal forests in the center, and tundra and peat bogs to the north. From Lake Erie in the southwest to Superior in the north is a natural progression—the explorer's route to the interior. Visitors looking for a pristine forest experience, or for lake and river canoeing, will find prime opportunities in Quetico Provincial Park and easily accessible Algonquin Provincial Park.

The St. Lawrence follows the Laurentide Scarp, which stays on the north shore before dipping down to the Thousand Islands. Included here is the Gaspé Peninsula, which forms the southern shore of the St. Lawrence estuary. Quebec's far-reaching forests, protected in areas such as Gatineau Park, offer hiking and canoeing in

Young lobster

untrafficked wilderness; canoeists paddling through St. Lawrence Islands National Park, by contrast, may see more signs of civilization, but these are offset by opportunities to spy migrating whales and birds.

To the south, across Chaleur Bay, lie the Maritime Provinces—New Brunswick, Nova Scotia, Prince Edward Island, and the tiny Îles de la Madeleine (politically part of Quebec). Here you'll find ample chances to hike New Brunswick's boreal and mixed forests and explore its Bay of Fundy seashores; to cycle the length and breadth of Nova Scotia, capped by Cape Breton Highlands National Park; and to poke your way through the picturesque coves, inlets, and farmland of Prince Edward Island.

Despite sharing a somewhat similar perch in the Atlantic Ocean, the Island of Newfoundland—a bleak and beautiful place with the wildest weather in Canada—stands apart from the rest of the Maritimes. Here are tundra barrens, oceanside cliff hikes of hallucinatory splendor, and colonies of cacophonous seabirds—an Earthly paradise for sea kayakers.

Finally there is the Eastern Arctic and Labrador. The latter's Mealy Mountains, though not "true north" (they hold far too much boreal forest for that), are profiled in this section because most Canadians associate them with the classic northern wilderness experience. For the same reason we have included southern Hudson Bay, near the Manitoba border. Though challenging to reach, these immensities reward the extra effort.

From Delightful to Frightful

A word about the weather is in order. The southern ranges of eastern Canada enjoy long, warm summers and crisp, glorious falls. Some sites—among them Point Pelee, which shares a latitude line with northern California, and certain Gulf Stream-tempered pockets of Nova Scotia—boast mild winters that are over by early March. (This is no guarantee of sun sightings; fog is a spring tradition in Atlantic Canada.)

In the northern national parks, of course, it's an altogether different story. Winter temperatures there routinely plunge to minus 50°F and below, and July frosts are not unknown. The attractions of the north are simultaneously more austere, more elemental, and—in ways that visitors often struggle to articulate—more thrilling than those of the south.

The Pristine Chapel?

By almost any standards, eastern Canada is underpopulated. Does this mean the forces of modernization have yet to threaten its vast wilderness? Hardly. Much of the region's woodlands have been logged over, with clear-cutters still hard at work in many places. In Ontario you may hear the solitude-shattering whine of chainsaws even in remote parts of Algonquin Park, while the timber industry has so thoroughly denuded parts of Nova Scotia that the province's ugly scars are evident from the air.

Nevertheless, by the standards of almost anywhere on Earth but the great taiga of Russian Siberia, the visitor can still find true wilderness here: In some of the larger parks in Quebec and Ontario, you may canoe for a week or more without seeing a soul. ■

Early June sledding in Auyuittuq NP, Nunavut

Great Lakes and Canadian Shield

Canoe campers, Canoe Lake, Algonquin Provincial Park

Two NATURAL FEATURES DOMINATE Ontario, the Canadian
province that is a major focus of this chapter. One is the
"inland sea" of Lake Superior; the other is the Canadian
Shield, a vast bowl of metamorphic rock whose rim takes
in the northern Great Lakes and sweeps across the northern shore of the St. Lawrence River.

Although parts of Superior's shoreline are privately
owned, much of it is protected in a series of splendid
provincial and national parks such as Killarney, Superior,

Beach Trail, Pukaskwa National Park

Pukaskwa, and Sleeping Giant. Visitors to these parks will find truly wild land, places where amenities are as rare as human beings. This part of eastern Canada generally enjoys warm and sunny summers, but some of the waters—especially Georgian Bay and Lake Superior—can generate savage storms with little or no warning, and the water is very cold even in July and August.

The Canadian Shield contains places of superlative natural beauty, some of them just a few hours' drive north of Lake Ontario. The Muskoka lakes and parts of Georgian Bay have become "cottage country" for the well-heeled. But scattered throughout the area are dozens of small provincial parks with campgrounds and nature trails, as well as thousands of lakes where more humble cottages dot the shoreline.

The epitome of remoteness and grandeur is Woodland Caribou Provincial Park. Located in northwestern Ontario on the Manitoba border, the park is best reached by canoe. For those bent on more immediate wilderness gratification, many northern communities have floatplane operators who will happily drop visitors for a week on one of the park's secluded lakes.

Automobile-dependent visitors shouldn't despair, though; massive parks such as Algonquin, a three-hour drive north of Toronto, can easily be reached by car. Algonquin Park is still wilderness, but the park staff is wonderfully adept at introducing newcomers to the wild.

Winter in northern Ontario can be bitterly cold. That doesn't stop the locals from enjoying the outdoors, however. As a consequence, activities such as snowshoeing, ski-touring, and winter camping are growing in popularity. The region's attractions draw visitors the rest of the year as well: Spring and summer are best for fishing, while summer and fall offer hiking, camping, and canoeing nonpareil.

The lesser Great Lakes—Ontario, Erie, and Huron—are the pre-eminent features of the landscape of southern and southwestern Ontario. Though little wilderness still exists along the shores of these three lakes, this does not mean that nature (in the sense that wilderness lovers understand it) doesn't exist here. The Niagara Escarpment pushes up through some of the best farmland in Canada. The bucolic landscapes of Prince Edward County, to the east of Toronto, are peaceful and productive. and the corn fields of the southwest, around the Grand River and Windsor/Detroit, turn a lush and beautiful green in the summer, with their pockets of maple woods dappling the countryside a glorious scarlet in the fall.

Despite the relatively thick population and mature agriculture of the southern lakes region, many places merit the trip, and you'll find them profiled in this chapter. One is the birder's paradise of Point Pelee National Park, tucked between Detroit and Toronto. Another is the the Georgian Bay Trail in Bruce Peninsula National Park. A spectacular section of 300-mile Bruce Trail, the hike climbs up the Niagara Escarpment to Georgian Bay.

But you won't find Niagara Falls: Though still as magnificent as ever, the falls are so surrounded by development and tourist kitsch that their beauty—unlike the other places you'll read about in the pages ahead—can sometimes be hard to see. ◼

Point Pelee National Park

Point Pelee National Park

■ 3,840 acres ■ Southeast Ontario, between Detroit/Windsor and Toronto
■ Best seasons spring and fall ■ Bird-watching, canoeing, hiking, guided walks,
biking, cross-country skiing, wildlife viewing, wildflower viewing ■ Contact the
park, 407 Robson St., Leamington, ON N8H 3V4; phone 519-322-2365, 519-
322-2371 (recorded birding update). www.parkscanada.gc.ca/pelee

LOCATED AT THE END OF A LONG, narrow peninsula that juts 6 miles into
Lake Erie, Point Pelee National Park is for the birds. Or at least that's
what the birds seem to think. They come year-round, but particularly
during the spring and fall migrations, when hundreds of species drop in
here to rest up, feed, and prepare themselves for the long journey ahead.
And thanks to its boardwalk, which angles off from the park's only road
to snake through its cottontail marshes, Point Pelee (pronounced PEE-
lee) is for the birders, too.

The park's Marsh—it has no other name—is one of the last of its kind
in the region. Most other Great Lakes wetlands and marshes have been
drained and turned into arable land. The native peoples who lived in

Marsh boardwalk, Point Pelee National Park

these so-called "between lands" (neither land nor water) viewed them as vital sources of life—places to hunt, fish, and gather edible grasses and wild rice.

The Europeans who came here in the late 17th century took a different view of the Marsh: Mindful of ideas then current about healing and hygiene, they looked upon the marshes as noisome bogs and got rid of them whenever they could, transforming them into what they considered more productive farmland. It was European explorers who gave the area its name: Observing that the end of the peninsula was devoid of vegetation, they called it *pelée*, a French term meaning "bald" or "peeled." The name stuck.

Pelee's Marsh covers almost 70 percent of the park, and can be accessed either by foot along the boardwalk or by canoe. (You can bring your own or rent a canoe at the Cattail Café, 519-322-1654, on the boardwalk). A sea of cattails and bulrushes, the Marsh is home to a bewildering array of water creatures—reptiles, turtles, fish, muskrat, and waterfowl—and, during May and June, dragonflies, damselflies, and many other kinds of insects.

The rest of the park—a thin strip along the peninsula's western

The tip of the Tip, Point Pelee National Park

edge—is forest and beach. Three distinct kinds of forest grow here: The Carolinian forest is dense and dank with clinging vines of wild grape, Virginia creeper, and poison ivy, and it abounds with southern trees such as hackberry, black walnut, chinquapin oak, swamp white oak, tulip tree, red mulberry, blue ash, and sassafras. Species such as sugar maple, basswood, beech, oak, and white pine fill the more northerly areas of the park. The open fields are populated by the occasional red cedar, cottonwood, honey locust, or hop tree.

Despite its small size—just 8 square miles—Point Pelee National Park boasts more rare species of plants and animals than anywhere else in Canada. It contains more than 70 species of trees, 27 species of reptiles, 20 species of amphibians, and 50 species of spiders and insects not found in any other part of the country.

As for birds, Acadian flycatchers, Carolina wrens, blue-gray gnatcatchers, red-bellied woodpeckers, and yellow-breasted chats all make their home in the park, the northern extent of their breeding range. Small wonder, then, that Pelee—occupying the same latitude as northern California and the Costa Brava in Spain—is the southernmost and warmest part of mainland Canada, with vegetation found nowhere else in North America east of the Rockies.

Yet it's not so much the warmth that attracts those migrating birds as it is the shape of the land. Most migrants are hesitant to cross large bodies of water. In the fall, when they reach Lake Erie on their journey south, they turn to follow the shoreline, seeking a way around the water. This leads them down toward the end of the peninsula, a place known simply as the Tip (doubtless named by the same inventive soul who gave us the Marsh). Here they rest a while before striking out across the lake or continuing around Pelee's perimeter and along the Erie shore.

What to See and Do

Birding

Most of the 400,000 or so visitors who come to Point Pelee National Park every year come for the birds. And most of the birds who visit Pelee do so during the spring and fall migrations. To get your own eyeful of this avian abundance, take exit 48 from Hwy. 401 onto Hwy. 77 to Leamington. Turn left on Hwy. 20 and continue 1.2 miles to the Point Pelee sign.

Spring Migration

The total number of bird species recorded at Point Pelee is 370. All but 24 of these have been spotted in spring—the preferred time for photographers, when the birds' plumage is at its most brilliant. The spring migration can begin as early as February and continue well into May.

Big days for bird sightings occur during so-called ground-ings, when two weather fronts collide and make flying difficult. One such grounding in 1952 brought in 1,000 black-and-white warblers and 20,000 white-throated sparrows in a single day. Other groundings have resulted in large harvests of tundra swans (2,500), red-breasted mergansers (100,000), whimbrels (500), northern flickers (250), bank swallows (12,000), white-eyed vireos (50), hooded warblers (18), and Kentucky warblers (13). In 1978 on the **Tip** alone, staff and visitors recorded 80 yellow-billed cuckoos, 70 eastern wood-pewees, and 250 scarlet tanagers.

In spring the birds come in waves. February brings horned larks and great horned owls; in March, flocks of blackbirds, robins, geese, swans, ducks, gulls, and mourning doves. In April, the earliest insectivorous species arrive. Many of Pelee's winter visitors—the common merganser, rough-legged hawk, short-eared owl (rare), hairy woodpecker, common redpoll, and American tree sparrow—are still here at this time.

By the end of April, however, most will be gone. Even so, in May you can see more species than at any other time of year. This is when many of the long-distance, migrants arrive, some from Central (and even South) America. Most of the waterfowl migration is over by early to mid-May. Gone too are the numerous land bird migrants; 40 of North America's 50 species of warbler species have been recorded in one migration.

Fall Migration

Many of Point Pelee's passing avi-fauna lose their brilliant plumage by autumn. Perhaps exhausted by raising a family, they lose their songs, too. Nonetheless, most of

Prothonotary warbler, Tilden's Woods

Middle Island

In tones reminiscent of the War of 1812, the Canadian government announced in July 1999 that it had "successfully reclaimed Middle Island for Canada." However, the reclamation of Middle Island—which rises out of Lake Erie roughly midway between Point Pelee and Put-In Bay, Ohio—was an entirely peaceable affair. Though the 49-acre island was Canadian, it had been owned for 30 years by a family from Cincinnati, Ohio. When they decided to put it up for sale in 1999, the Nature Conservancy of Canada was ready to buy it back. The cost: $866,250. This new most southerly point in Canada was annexed to Point Pelee National Park in 2001.

the species found at Pelee have been recorded in the fall, not the spring, and in greater numbers—bird populations having swelled during the summer by breeding. Golden eagles, phalaropes, and falcons, for example, are hardly ever seen in the spring, but they are commonly spotted in the fall. Good days in fall have seen as many as 500 horned grebes, 100 great blue herons, 1,000 sharp-shinned hawks, 124,000 common terns, and 7,000 purple martins.

The park's visitor center has a variety of publications for sale, including checklists of all species known to inhabit the park. The center also maintains a book for visitors to report rare sightings.

Rarities are not all that rare at Pelee, however. This is partly because so many birders are constantly on the lookout and partly because the southerly extension of the peninsula captures a few southern species that overshoot the northern limits of their range.

Hiking

The **Marsh boardwalk** will guide you through the wonderland that is Point Pelee. The boardwalk is four-fifths of a mile long and has two parts: The southern end floats on the marsh; the northern end leads through the cattails. Interpretive signs can be found at frequent intervals, and an observation tower perches at each end.

A number of nature trails will take you through the park's varied vegetation. The **Centennial Trail,** for example, runs from the boardwalk past the visitor center—and on through hackberry forest to the picnic areas at **West Beach,** one of Point Pelee's four sandy beaches. The trail is about 2.5 miles long and a popular choice with cyclists. **Tilden's Woods,** off the northeastern end of the visitor center parking lot, is a favorite spot among bird-watchers. Only about half a mile in length, the trail passes through a variety of forest types on its way to **East Beach.**

Along with its other two beaches, **Northwest** and **Black Willow,** Point Pelee National Park offers visitors 15 miles of sandy strands. All are vehicle accessible, equipped with rest rooms and picnic tables, and—thanks to the location of the Pelee Peninsula—

Lake Erie, Point Pelee National Park

smiled upon by the warmest weather in this norther country.

Other Things to Do

Jack Miner's Bird Sanctuary *(322 Rd. 3 W, 3 miles N of Kingsville, off Division Rd. 29. 519-733-4034 or 877-289-8328)* is a waterfowl and migratory bird haven that was originally established to care for wounded Canada geese. Admission is free, and the sanctuary is open year-round.

The **Hillman Marsh Conservation Area** *(contact Essex Region Conservation, 360 Fairview Ave. W., Essex, ON N8M 1Y6. 519-776-5209)* is a 900-acre marsh located a few miles north of Point Pelee. Like the park, the conservation area is a birder's paradise, especially in spring when wading birds, shorebirds, and waterfowl are abundant. Bald eagles are frequently sighted here, too. A 2.5-mile nature trail leads visitors through the heart of the marsh.

Pelee Island is neither a park nor a conservation area, but a farming community and vacation center. Nevertheless, just as in nearby Point Pelee National Park, birds are abundant in spring and fall. Ferries cross from Kingsville and Leamington in Ontario, and from Sandusky in Ohio *(for schedules, call Pelee Island Transportation 519-326-2154)*.

Thirty-one miles east of Point Pelee is **Rondeau Provincial Park** *(R.R. 1, Morpeth, ON N0P 1X0. 519-674 1750)*, Ontario's second oldest provincial park. Its Carolinian forest is larger than Pelee's— and older, with many fine stands of tulip trees and sassafras. The 8,040-acre park is an important breeding ground for the prothonotary warbler. Of all Ontario and Great Lakes parks, this one has the most Southern—some would even say subtropical—air. ■

Migrating Monarchs

THEY COME IN ONES AND TWOS, fluttering across the swamp and through the forest, darting and dipping and dithering, yet always making their determined way southward along the Pelee Peninsula. A group of six or seven, then a few more solitaries, followed by another group—and eventually the air is alive with the golden-and-black palette of that most delightful of creatures, the monarch butterfly.

People travel hundreds of miles to see the annual migration of the monarchs. At the height of this lepidopteran hegira, thousands of butterflies roost in trees near the Tip, their delicate wings slowly opening and closing, waiting for a favorable wind to take them across Lake Erie.

Point Pelee isn't the only flight path of the monarchs; one year the migration crossed Toronto's western suburbs. But Pelee seems to be the preferred route, shortening the butterflies' hazardous venture across the open water. And there's another reason why they choose Pelee: This part of southern Ontario has abundant supplies of milkweed, the monarchs' only food.

Milkweed is an aggressive colonizing plant that invades farmers' fields, and it has been declared a noxious weed in Ontario. The plant contains poisons known as cardiac glycosides, as the local birds can attest: Because the monarchs accumulate so much of this toxin from the milkweed they eat, any bird that makes a meal of a monarch vomits up its dinner.

Point Pelee, then, is a way station on one of nature's greatest and most mysterious journeys—the migration of the monarchs from eastern Canada to Mexico, more than 1,860 miles to

the south. They go to Mexico, so the theory holds, because that's where monarchs and milkweed evolved together—and as the weed spread, so did the butterflies. In fact, so many millions of monarchs descend upon the evergreen forests in the volcanic mountains of central Mexico that they bend the branches of the trees with their weight.

Native legends have long described waves of monarch butterflies heading southward in the autumn. For thousands of years, their destination was unknown. Only in 1975 did the University of Toronto's Dr. Fred Urquhart officially discover their wintering grounds. Following reports of butterflies that had been tagged in Canada, Urquhart traveled to central Mexico and there discovered the monarchs.

The migratory cycle of the butter-

Monarch still life

flies remains enigmatic. Though adult monarchs don't always make the long trip themselves, they are able—through a mechanism imperfectly understood by scientists—to pass on to their offspring an understanding of the need for migration.

Monarchs mate in Mexico in early spring. They lay their eggs on fresh milkweed during the journey north, and the adults die some time thereafter. The generation produced somewhere in the southwestern United States can be found in Ontario each summer, from June onward.

Because butterflies grow from egg to adult in a mere 45 days, a couple of generations can go by before the southward migration resumes in the fall. If the weather turns cold on their way south, the monarchs alight in trees at the southern end of the Tip.

It's hard to predict just when the monarchs will arrive at Pelee, and there's no guarantee that you'll see them at all. Some people have visited the peninsula for years without ever seeing them.

When they do appear, the park's visitor center provides daily migration counts, and visitors can join a naturalist at the Tip to help tally the new arrivals. Throughout the fall, the park information line *(519-322-2371)* provides daily recorded monarch reports.

If you make it to Pelee, keep these monarch-watching tips in mind:

1) Large movements often occur in tandem with cold fronts.

2) Cold temperatures, southerly winds, or rain frequently delay the monarchs at Pelee.

3) Viewing is best from late August until early October; it generally peaks in September.

4) The Tip area is where most concentrations occur.

5) Roosting is best observed very early in the morning. ∎

Singing Sands, Bruce Peninsula NP

Bruce Peninsula National Park

■ 28,417 acres ■ Southeast Ontario, between Lake Huron and Georgian Bay
■ Best seasons spring-fall ■ Camping, hiking, scuba diving, bird-watching, wild-flower viewing, wildlife viewing, caving ■ Contact the park, P.O. Box 189, Tobermory, ON N0H 2R0; phone 519-596-2233. www.parkscanada.gc.ca/bruce

NAMED IN HONOR OF JAMES BRUCE, governor-general of Canada from 1847 to 1854, the Bruce Peninsula is one of the grand sights of southern Ontario. The grayish white dolomite cliffs; the stubborn and stunted cedars clinging to crevices in the rock; the sometimes green, sometimes azure waters of Georgian Bay—all are aspects of a beauty that draws visitors back year after year.

Not that all is well with this 80-mile finger of land between Lake Huron and Georgian Bay. The forests of the peninsula were long ago logged and stripped, and only now are they beginning to recover. Ironically, one of the great views over Georgian Bay is named **Halfway Log Dump:** Here foresters dragged freshly cut pine and spruce and tossed them into the waters 100 feet below—to be chained together in booms and towed or floated downstream to sawmills.

The Saugeen Ojibwa—whose ancestral lands these are—remain hopeful of making a recovery, too. They still live in two small reserves on the east and west shores of the peninsula, and have been seeking (so far unsuccessfully) to overturn the provisions of treaties they signed with the European settlers.

There is much to delight the visitor. The park's shoreline cliffs are part of Ontario's "Great Wall"—the Niagara Escarpment. The escarpment runs from Niagara Falls (which plunge over it) to Tobermory, where the park's reception center is located, right at the end of the peninsula. From there it ducks beneath the waters of Lake Erie before surfacing as islands in Fathom Five National Marine Park (see pp. 35-36).

Because of its geology, the Bruce Peninsula is a work in progress. Underneath its dolomite surface rock, the limestone is slowly eroding, and caverns and passages are opening in the rock. In the Cyprus Lake area of the park, just inland from Georgian Bay, park staffers have marked out a handful of sinkholes, dozens of caves, and even an underground river.

On the shoreline, the powerful waves generated by Georgian Bay's frequent storms have been further undercutting the dolomite cap to create grottoes in the limestone. One of the most exhilarating experiences in the park is to creep out onto **Overhanging Point,** a 90-foot slab of limestone that—thanks to the erosive powers of the water—projects out over the water. Farther out, you'll see the "flowerpots" of the bay's Flowerpot Island: These isolated stacks of eroded rock (in reality, they are stranded pieces of escarpment) belong to Fathom Five NMP.

The Bruce Peninsula boasts a wide range of habitats—cliffs, forests, rocky plains, wetlands, swamps—and a variety of wildflowers and plants that is unique in Canada. The plants most popular with visitors are the orchids. More than 60 species of orchid grow in Ontario, 43 of them on this small peninsula. The half-mile **Marr Lake** and the 3-mile loop **Cyprus Lake Trail** take visitors past many of the species. Almost half the

The Oldest Trees

While studying human impact on eastern white cedar trees along the Niagara Escarpment in 1988, the University of Guelph's Doug Larson came across a small cedar that was 511 years old. It was growing out of a cliff a couple of miles from Hwy. 401, Ontario's busiest thoroughfare. Since then Larson has discovered even older trees all along the escarpment—in Bruce Peninsula National Park, Fathom Five National Marine Park, and farther east, in Bon Echo Provincial Park. A stump he found on Flowerpot Island was from a tree that had died 1,500 years ago—at the age of 360. The oldest living tree found so far on the peninsula is more than 850 years old. These ancient trees are usually less than 5 feet tall, and are found growing in crevices and cracks in the cliffs, where no soil exists. Lack of rooting space and paucity of nourishment—together with strong winds, ice, rockfalls, and the glaring sun—cause the trees to take on their dwarfish and twisted shapes.

White cedar, Bruce Peninsula NP

Rock Garden

The ancient dwarf cedars of the Bruce Peninsula are just one part of a complex cliffside ecosystem. Mosses and lichen grow in profusion, too. But there's more here than meets the eye. Professor Doug Larson discovered that this is one of the few places in the world where the rocks are penetrated by cryptoendolithic—or "hidden-inside-rock"—life: fungi that actually grows inside the rocks.

world's dwarf lake irises also grow within the park, as do most of Canada's Indian plantain. The rare northern holly fern grows comfortably here, too, along with 20 other varieties of fern. You can see many of these plants at Singing Sands in Dorcas Bay, in the western section of the park, from which a short (unnamed) trail wanders through the marshlands and fens.

The usual small game of the region—raccoons, porcupines, squirrels, snowshoe hare, fishers—inhabit the peninsula, as do to white-tailed deer and black bears. However, Bruce Peninsula National Park is best known for one resident in particular: the eastern massasauga rattlesnake. This endangered species was once found throughout southern Ontario. Now Bruce Peninsula National Park is one of the creature's last protected habitats. Because the rattler is Ontario's only poisonous snake, hikers are advised to wear long pants or thick socks and boots—and always to watch where they place their hands and feet.

What to See and Do

Hiking

The most spectacular section of the Bruce Trail (see opposite) is **Georgian Bay Trail,** which lies north of Cyprus Lake. Between Halfway Log Dump and Little Cove it meanders along the cliff top, occasionally dipping down to sandy coves and passing by caves.

From **Halfway Rock Point** you can see Flowerpot and Bears Rump Islands. A little farther along, **Indian Head Cove** is popular with swimmers and divers for its wave-carved caves—the **Natural Arch** and the **Grotto.** You can wander into the cavernous Grotto and watch divers enter it from underwater. Of the Grotto's two entrances, neither one is difficult, even for beginning divers.

The **Horse Lake Trail,** less than a mile long, is a good way to see many of the park's natural habitats: It meanders through marshes, around lakes, through dense forest, and along the shore. The trail ends at a beach on Georgian Bay.

Camping

Cyprus Lake has 242 campsites in three campgrounds (reservations 519-596-2263), with fire pits, toilets, and potable water but no electricity. For something a bit more rugged and remote, try the campground at Storm Haven or the one at High Dump, each with nine campsites. Camping is not permitted anywhere else in the park. ∎

The Bruce Trail

■ 310 miles (main trail) ■ Southeast Ontario, from Niagara to Tobermory
■ Best seasons spring-fall ■ Hiking, backpacking, bird-watching, wildflower
viewing ■ Contact Bruce Trail Association, P.O. Box 857, Hamilton, ON L8N
3N9; phone 905-529-6821. www.brucetrail.org

CANADA'S OLDEST MARKED HIKING TRAIL, the Bruce Trail wanders for more
than 300 miles from the Queenston Heights overlooking the Niagara
River northward along the Niagara Escarpment to Tobermory, at the
northern end of Bruce Peninsula National Park (see pp. 30-32).

Covering such great distances in a heavily populated region, the trail
is bound to draw close to built-up areas. Indeed, it skirts some of southern Ontario's most highly industrialized regions, and for a stretch it
parallels one of the country's busiest highways—Hwy 401 between
Toronto and the U.S. border. For all that, much of the Bruce Trail still
wends its way through unspoiled woodland—past stands of coniferous

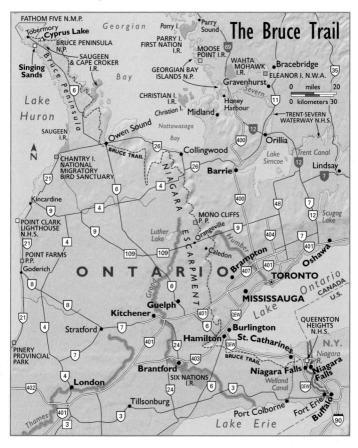

Bruce Trail, Bruce Peninsula NP

forest and deciduous hardwoods, as well as the delicate orchids of the
Bruce Peninsula, the ancient cedars of the cliff face, and the remaining patches of Carolinian forest. More than 300 species of birds, 55
mammals, 35 reptiles and amphibians, and 90 species of fish inhabit the
trail's environs.

The Niagara Escarpment itself has been declared a World Biosphere
Reserve by the United Nations. Like all escarpments, it rises gradually
on one side and terminates in cliffs on the other, which vary from 50 to
more than 200 feet. A number of waterfalls tumble over the escarpment,
the most notable being Niagara Falls itself.

The Bruce Trail is managed and maintained by nine volunteer trail
clubs comprising hundreds of volunteers. Working northward from the
Niagara River, the clubs are named Niagara, Iroquoia, Toronto, Caledon
Hills, Dufferin Highlands, Blue Mountain, Beaver Valley, Sydenham, and
Peninsula. Detailed maps and hiking guides are available from the Bruce
Trail Association. ■

Fathom Five National Marine Park

■ 71,776 acres ■ Southeast Ontario, north of Bruce Peninsula National Park
■ Best seasons spring-fall ■ Scuba diving, snorkeling, boating, bird-watching, guided walks ■ Contact the park, P.O. Box 189, Tobermory, ON N0H 2R0; phone 519-596-2233, 519-596-2503 (diver registration). www.parkscanada.gc.ca/fathomfive

THE TOBERMORY ISLANDS and the Georgian Bay waters surrounding them make up this marine park. The islands (20 in all) form a chain that is really an extension of the Niagara Escarpment—which, in turn, is part of a larger geologic formation that pushes northward through Manitoulin Island, eventually ending up on the western shores of Lake Michigan.

Though geologically similar to the Bruce Peninsula, the islands differ in significant ways from the mainland—and from one another. Distance from the mainland and from other islands has dictated each island's particular mix of plants and animals. Cove Island, largest of the Tobermories, is close to the mainland; not surprisingly, it has a mainland mix of species, including black bears and deer. Flowerpot Island is the most photographed of the chain and the most popular; located farther from the mainland, it is home to fewer species. There are no rattlesnakes on Flowerpot, for example, but there are many garter snakes (the latter are harmless to humans).

Boats have been visiting Georgian Bay for 200 years, but commercial shipping really began only in the 1850s, when vessels from the lower lakes started hauling away raw materials such as grain and ore and bringing in lumber to the towns growing up around the bay. A great many of these ships were wrecked in the unpredictable currents, sudden storms, and dangerous shoals of southern Georgian Bay. Though the number of wrecks diminished after lighthouses were built—on Cove Island in 1858, Big Tub in 1885, and Flowerpot in 1897—the debris from earlier wrecks is still here, giving divers a fascinating underwater world to explore.

Wrecks are not the only attraction for divers. They can also investigate a shoreline pocked with grottoes and caves, which—along with the crystal clear water—make for exceptional diving.

What to See and Do

Diving

Diving, indeed, is the park's most popular activity. The bay's geology features dozens of water-carved caves, grottoes, overhangs, and underwater ledges that present divers with plenty to do. The water is cold and—because there is so little sediment—amazingly clear. More than 20 shipwrecks lie around the shoals. Even divers with rudimentary skills should be able to reach a number of them without too much trouble.

The oldest wreck is the **John Walters,** a schooner that ran ashore in 1852. The remains of the vessel—the keel and the heavy timbers—rest in shallow waters, shallow enough for snorkelers to pay a visit. The barkentine **Arabia,** which foundered off Echo Island in 1884, lies in deep water with strong currents and is not recommended for beginners. Experienced divers will find the wreck in good condition; its bowsprit, windlass, and anchors are especially favorite subjects for underwater photographers. The **Wetmore** is popular with less experienced divers, and much of its wreckage is intact for exploring.

Divers who prefer the wonders of the natural world should visit the **Grotto,** on the Georgian Bay shoreline about 12 miles east of Tobermory. You can reach it over land via the Cyprus Lake Trail in Bruce Peninsula National Park (see p. 31), but divers prefer to explore the hidden underwater passages that lead in from the waters of the bay. This is a good site for all divers. Because it's a long walk to the grotto, however—and a tiring one if you are carrying your gear—everyone (of no matter what experience level) must dive from a boat.

Another site popular with divers is the **North Otter Wall.** You'll find it—and its underwater nooks, overhangs, and caves— about 40 feet beneath the surface and well worth a visit.

A note of caution: The waters of Georgian Bay are chilly, and the weather is unpredictable. Divers must register at the Parks Canada Diver Registration Office on Little Tub Harbour in downtown Tobermory.

For those who want to see the underwater world without getting their feet wet, a number of commercial operators run tours out of Tobermory in glass-bottom boats. Guides can take you out to the wrecks and to interesting underwater formations, where the clear waters invite you to peer deep beneath the surface of the bay.

Island Hopping

Back on terra firma, **Flowerpot Island** is the only island in the park with services such as rest rooms and a picnic shelter. The island offers several hiking trails, while half a dozen campsites overlook Georgian Bay at Beachy Cove. The "flowerpots" themselves are easily reached via a well-groomed **hiking trail** (almost 3 miles long).

Another **trail** and wooden staircase will take you to one of the island's caves; a lookout platform with guide panels shows you what's where. The **lighthouse** on the island's northeast corner has been restored by a local group of volunteers, who staff it in summer and are delighted to show visitors around.

Flowerpot and the other islands are easily accessible from Little Tub Harbour in Tobermory. Ferry crossings are frequent. An interesting sight-seeing side trip takes you via the car ferry **Chi-Cheemaun**—"Big Canoe" in Ojibwa—from Tobermory to South Baymouth on Manitoulin Island. The round-trip requires about four hours. Contact Ontario Northland (800-265-3163) for schedules and fares. ■

Georgian Bay Islands NP

Georgian Bay Islands National Park

■ 2,965 acres ■ Southeast Ontario, 59 islands in Georgian Bay ■ Best season summer ■ Primitive camping, hiking, guided walks, kayaking, canoeing, fishing ■ Access by boat from Honey Harbour ■ Contact the park, P.O. Box 28, Honey Harbour, ON P0E 1E0; phone 705-756-2415. www.parkscanada.gc.ca/gbi

AT LEAST 30,000 ISLANDS dot Georgian Bay, and 59 of them constitute Georgian Bay Islands National Park. Stretching for 40 miles along the coast from Honey Harbour to Twelve Mile Bay, the park's islands are rocky and can be difficult to reach. Easy landing sites are rare, as are sand beaches (although you'll find a few on the larger islands such as Beausoleil). Indeed, many of the islands are little more than rounded exposed stones, called "whalebacks" by the locals. Little or no wildlife lives on the islands, except for gulls and terns and the occasional turtle, although some host a few dwarf trees clinging to clefts in the rock.

The park is at its best at the height of summer, when the deep cobalt of the bay's astonishingly clear water is set off by the pink granite of the Canadian Shield and the dark greens of the spruces, cedars, and pines.

What to See and Do

You'll need a boat to get to the park. Many privately owned water taxis operate out of Honey Harbour. Canoeing and kayaking are recommended for experienced paddlers only.

The park's main facilities are on the largest of the islands, **Beausoleil,** which has campsites, overnight and daytime docking, education programs for children, a visitor center, and hiking trails. People in wheelchairs will find two accessible campsites at the Cedar Spring Campground; the Cedar Spring day-use area is also handicap accessible.

Beausoleil has a diverse history. Before the European settlement, the Huron used it as a hunting camp; then, about 150 years ago, it became an Ojibwa reserve. In 1856, however, the Indians were resettled on nearby Christian Island, and trappers, loggers, quarriers, and lumberers moved in. In 1929 the island, along with 28

others, was expropriated by the federal government as the nucleus of the new park. Little of the forest on the islands is old-growth.

The Georgian Bay islands are home to a variety of amphibians and reptiles, four of which—the eastern massasauga rattlesnake, the eastern hognose snake, the eastern foxsnake, and the spotted turtle—are threatened species. Though poisonous, the massasauga are shy; they have never accounted for a visitor death.

Hiking and Biking Beausoleil

Beausoleil's trails range from easy to moderate. Favorites include the **Dossyonshing Trail,** a loop of about 2 miles that wanders between wetlands on one side and dense hardwood forest on the other; and the 1.8-mile **Treasure Trail,** which leads to the picturesque shoreline of Treasure Bay. You can bike two others: the **Huron Trail** (5 miles) and the

Beausoleil Island, Georgian Bay Islands NP

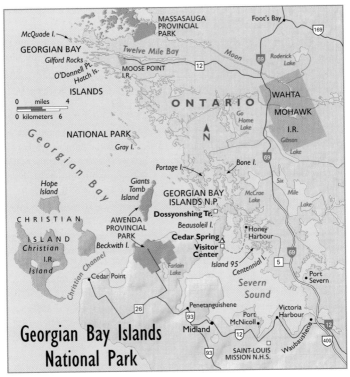

Georgian Bay Islands National Park

Christian Trail (less than 1 mile).

Beausoleil rewards the hiker with great views. **Blueberry Point,** at the north of the island, has extensive views of Beausoleil itself, as well as the open water of the bay. **Ojibway Bay,** in the northeast, is a cozy harbor surrounded by dense forests and rocky shores. And from **Papoose Lookout,** at the end of the island's 0.8-mile **Firetower Trail,** you can gaze out over Papoose Bay, sprinkled with islands. Most of these trails start near the Cedar Springs Visitor Center.

Camping

The park's three main areas for camping are Honeymoon Bay, on the northernmost point of the island; Cedar Spring, the park's largest campground, with sandy beaches, bay views, and 87 semi-serviced sites; and Touch Point, in the east-central part of the island, offering three small campgrounds connected by a hiking and biking bath. All campsites are accessible by boat and must be reserved ahead of time.

Sailing and Boating

With their coves and indented shorelines, the scattered islands are perfect for small boats and sea kayaks; flotillas of these craft swarm the open water in summer. Still, the currents can be unpredictable, the squalls sudden and ferocious. Charts are available at most local marinas, hardware stores, and sporting-goods stores. ■

Killarney Provincial Park

■ 119,842 acres ■ Southeast Ontario, north shore of Georgian Bay, northeast of Manitoulin Island ■ Best seasons summer and fall; winter popular for wilderness camping ■ Camping, hiking, canoeing, cross-country skiing, snowshoeing, wildlife viewing, wildflower viewing ■ Contact the park, Killarney, ON P0M 2A0; phone 705-287-2900. www.ontarioparks.com/kill.html

PICTURE-PERFECT KILLARNEY IS PROBABLY the only national or provincial park established at the urgings of prominent landscape painters, not at the behest of naturalists. The park's many beauty marks include the startling ivory-white quartzite ridges and striated red granites of La Cloche and Killarney ranges, as well as its string of lakes—many of them brilliantly azure and crystal clear—set in forested valleys. These attractions have lured artists here since the early days of the 20th century. They still do today.

No fewer than four members of Canada's so-called Group of Seven landscape painters painted in the Killarney area. It was one of that quartet, A. Y. Jackson, who pushed the Ontario government to establish Killarney as a reserve. A small one was created around Trout Lake in 1933, which soon afterward was renamed O.S.A. Lake—for the Ontario Society of Artists.

Throughout the 1950s the Ontario Society of Artists lobbied the provincial government to enlarge the protected area around O.S.A. Lake. Eventually, in 1964, a formal park was created. Jackson and two other members of the Group of Seven—Frank Carmichael and A. J. Casson— have had lakes in the park named after them. Casson's famous painting of La Cloche Ridge, "White Pine," is particularly striking. The painting is familiar to thousands of Canadian schoolchildren, whose classrooms were adorned for decades with copies of this and other Group of Seven paintings.

What to See and Do

Hiking

Starting at the George Lake Campground, **La Cloche Silhouette Trail** is a 62-mile loop that traverses much of the park. Along the way, it passes by lakes and secluded forests, as well as occasional lookout points that give spectacular views and much needed rest stops. The trail is strenuous and should not be attempted by the unfit or the unwary. For the experienced backpacker, this seven- to ten-day hike should provide all the challenge you need. A number of shorter trails also start and end at the campground, and sections of the main trail can be used as day hikes.

If you head northwest from George Lake along **La Cloche,** for example, you'll end up at Artist Lake, Bay Finn, and Threenarrows Lake. This day hike covers about 8 miles. A day hike to the northeast along La Cloche takes you up to

Canoe and kayaks on Chikanishing River, Killarney PP

Killarney's Clear Lakes

The brilliant clarity of many of Killarney's lakes is a sign not of their health, but of their frailty. In the 1950s and 1960s the lakes became increasingly acidic, lying as they do as close as 40 miles to the massive metal smelters in Sudbury and within a zone of high acid deposits, much of it generated in the United States. By the late 1970s the fish, crayfish, algae, aquatic insect, and plankton populations had gone into a steep decline, as had the waterfowl that depended on them for food.

In 1997, however, a species biodiversity survey showed that matters had substantially improved: Plants and animals were beginning to return to the water bodies from which they had been excluded, and emissions from most of the offending sources had been reduced. Even so, the survey also concluded that as many as 95,000 of Ontario's 250,000 lakes still suffer from some degree of over-acidification.

the shores of Georgian Bay itself.

Simpler and shorter trails include **Chikanishing Trail,** a moderate 1.8-mile loop that travels over pink granite outcroppings and through dense forest. Another is the **Granite Ridge Trail,** an easy 1.5-mile hike with interpretive signs and interesting looks at the park's varied geology.

Fall hiking is becoming increasingly popular. The spectacular colors at that time of year, set against the white pines and the dazzling white hills, make for an exhilarating visual display.

Canoeing

An interlinked network of small lakes, rivers, and short portages makes Killarney a paradise for canoeists. The campground at **George Lake** is the launching point for most of the one- and multiday trips, but other parts of the park are worth trying, too.

Nellie Lake, in the northwest, has the park's clearest water, with visibility of about 90 feet. A popular weekend trip is the one from George Lake through **Freeland** and **Killarney Lakes** and on to O.S.A. Dozens of longer routes take you deep into the park's interior. Most start either from George Lake or **Johnnie Lake** to the southeast, or from **Bell Lake** to the east.

Reservations for backcountry canoeing are a must. Detailed maps for routes and portages are available from the camp office. You can rent canoes and equipment from Killarney Kanoes (888-461-4446) or Killarney Outfitters (800-461-1117). Both keep canoes at the George Lake campground. ▪

Killarney Ridge and to the **Crack,** where the ridge has shattered and oddly square quartzite boulders have split off. A more ambitious, five-day backpacking trip leads beyond the Crack to **Silver Peak,** at 1,781 feet the highest point in the park. From here you can see a dozen small lakes ensconced in their forests, not to mention

Gargantua Harbour, Lake Superior PP

Lake Superior Provincial Park

■ 384,628 acres ■ Southeastern Ontario, lakeshore between Sault Ste. Marie and Wawa ■ Best months mid- to late May; July-Sept. Park facilities closed in winter but visitors allowed ■ Camping, hiking, kayaking, canoeing, fishing, snowmobiling, snowshoeing, bird-watching, wildlife viewing, pictographs ■ Contact the park, P.O. Box 267, Wawa, ON P0S 1K0; phone 705-856-2284 (information), 888-668-7275 (reservations). www.ontarioparks.com/lakes.html

A GOOD WAY TO GET a feel for the topography of this park before tackling any of its activities that involve foot or canoe travel is to take scenic highway 17—the famous Trans-Canada Highway. The highway takes you the full length of the park, from the Lake Superior shore inland past rivers and interior lakes. Lookout points and rest stops provide a chance to get out of the car, stretch your legs, and take in the views along the way. Several gravel roads provide access to backcountry hiking trails and canoe routes, including Mijinemungshing, Gargantua, and Frater Roads.

Three car campgrounds are located adjacent to Trans-Canada 17. The backcountry of Lake Superior Provincial Park is rugged, and many of its trails and canoe routes are demanding. The park staff maintains 11 hiking trails and 8 canoe routes. Some of the portages are long (the one to Gargantua Lake, for example, is 3 miles), but the effort is well worthwhile. The interior lakes are pristine, the water is generally clear, and the trout fishing is good. In some of the more remote areas, the chances of seeing a moose or a bear are as good as seeing another human.

What to See and Do

Hiking

The best way to see Lake Superior Provincial Park—indeed, the only realistic way if you're not a canoeist—is on foot. Approximately 75 miles of hiking trails are maintained, in varying lengths and degrees of difficulty.

The **Coastal Trail** is 40 miles one way—from Chalfant Cove in the north to Agawa Bay in the south. Access points include Gargantua Road, Orphan Lake Trail, Katherine Cove, Sinclair Cove, and Agawa Bay Campground.

The northern section from Gargantua to Warp Bay is an easy to moderate one-day hike; it goes inland over relatively flat terrain. A 2.5-mile side trail leads from Warp Bay to Devil's Chair. The southerly section from Garagantua to Agawa Bay (34 miles) is tougher: It takes four to seven days and can be a taxing struggle over hills, rocky headlands, and cobble beaches; slippery rocks and occasional windfalls add to the challenge. This section hugs the coast, and the views are stunning.

For those with a lower tolerance for strenuous effort—or simply less time—a variety of trails are available. **Agawa Rock** is a 15- to 30-minute hike from the highway to the giant rock overhanging Lake Superior (see sidebar). The **Orphan Lake Trail** (5 miles) offers hiking through boreal forest, as well as a lovely pebble beach, Baldhead Falls, and splendid views over Orphan Lake and Superior.

Trapper's Trail, only a mile long, features a floating boardwalk; keep your eyes peeled for moose, beavers, and wading great blue herons. Moderately difficult **Nokomis Trail** is a 3-mile loop that treats you to views of the 600-foot-high Old Woman Bay cliffs.

More challenging trails include the Peat Mountain and Towab Trails. **Towab** (15 miles round-trip) is best as a two-day hike, and autumn—with its scarlet and crimson sugar maples—is the best time to do it; you'll find a campsite below **Agawa Falls,** an 82-foot cascade on the Agawa River. The 7-mile **Peat Mountain Trail** includes a steady climb of 500 feet,

Stories in Stone

Animals. Canoeists. Warriors. The horned lynx and other mythical creatures. These are just some of the subjects painted by the Ojibwa Indians on Agawa Rock. Located along the shores of Superior 10 miles inside the park's southern boundary, the rock is reached via a short but rugged trail. To view the pictographs, visitors must walk along a rock ledge next to the lake. Extreme caution is necessary, and the site is accessible only when lake conditions are calm. No one knows the age of the pictographs, but they were probably created over the course of many centuries. The only image that gives us a clue is the horse: It must have been painted within the last 400 years, after arriving with the Europeans.

but the reward is a panoramic view. On clear days you can see Michipicoten Island to the west, Wawa to the north, and—to the south and east—lakes and rolling hills.

Canoeing

Eight maintained canoe routes cut through the park, some easy day trips, others longer affairs with frequent portaging; at least four may require shuttle services for boat pickup at the end.

The **Fenton-Treeby route** (*access via Trans-Canada 17*) is a 10-mile loop, good for a day trip or a relaxed overnight, especially for novices. The route has 11 portages, most of them short. **Belanger Lake** (*access via Gargantua Rd.*) is an 8-mile return day trip with four portages. This is a nice overnight trip for families. Brook and lake trout fishing is good.

Old Woman Lake (*access via Mijinemungshing Lake*) is a two- to three-day, 18-mile round-trip with 11 portages as far as the Sand River (one of them is 4,000 feet long). It offers interesting scenery, good brook trout fishing, and the chance to see moose.

Sand River (*access via Algoma Central Railway*) will take four to five days and has 29 portages in all. The Sand is a scenic river that runs from the northeast corner of the park. The scenery changes dramatically along the way, from lowland wetlands and woods to high cliffs and hardwood forests. The river drops about 600 feet over its 35-mile length from Sand Lake to Lake Superior. The upper half is mostly calm and meandering; the lower half has two significant drops, Calwin Falls and Lady Evelyn Falls, which must be portaged.

Of course, you can also canoe or kayak the shores of Lake Superior itself. This is not recommended for the beginner, however. Though there are many fine beaches, you'll also encounter sheer cliffs and rock shorelines— spectacular to look at but inhospitable in case you have to put in. In addition, the water is frigid, and the storms unpredictable and fast moving.

Canoes can be rented from the Rabbit Blanket Campground and the Red Rock park office. For Agawa Bay and Crescent Lake Campgrounds, rentals are through the Agawa Bay gatehouse from late June to Labor Day, otherwise through the Red Rock office.

Twilight Resort (*705-882-2183*), Northgate Service Center (*705-882-2159*), and Naturally Superior Adventures (*705-856-2939*) provide shuttle services and general outfitting services. You'll find campgrounds at Rabbit Blanket Lake, Agawa Bay, and Crescent Lake—249 sites in all, with an additional 174 sites scattered through the park interior. ∎

Red fox

Horseshoe Bay, Pukaskwa NP

Pukaskwa National Park

■ 464,000 acres ■ Southern Ontario, 13.5 miles from Marathon on Lake Superior's north shore ■ Best season summer ■ Camping, hiking, backpacking, white-water rafting and kayaking, sailing, canoeing, cross-country skiing, boat tours ■ Camping fee. Backcountry permit required ■ Contact the park, Hwy. 627, Hattie Cove, Heron Bay, ON P0T 1R0; phone 807-229-0801. www.parkscanada.gc.ca/pukaskwa

WITH ITS MIX OF ROCKY CLIFFS and pebble beaches, the Superior shoreline of Pukaskwa National Park can seem positively bucolic in the summer sunshine. But gales and storms are frequent here in spring and early fall, and can whip up waves 15 feet high.

Away from the shore, the park's terrain is scarred by mountain ridges and pocked with hundreds of lakes. The soil is thin, generally acidic, and often covered with a thick carpet of moss; from it grow spruce, fir, cedar, birch, poplar, red maple, and white pine, in a mixed boreal forest.

With logging to the north and east, mining to the north and southeast, and five marinas from Thunder Bay to Michipicoten, the park can seem to be under siege. Still, moose, wolf, black bear, and the usual array of small northern animals—red fox, lynx, otter, snowshoe hare, porcupine—continue to inhabit the park. It is also home (but just barely) to woodland caribou; whereas some 200 of the animals roamed the park at the beginning of the 20th century, as few as half a dozen may now remain.

Pukaskwa offers a number of services for visitors, including guided hikes, evening lectures on ecosystems and nature, and First Nations interpretive programs. The center for park activities, Hattie Cove, is 250 miles north of Sault Ste. Marie, 195 miles east of Thunder Bay.

What to See and Do

The only road access to Pukaskwa is at the north end of the park, near Hattie Cove. From Marathon, take Trans-Canada 17 east for 6 miles to the Hwy. 627 turnoff. Follow Hwy. 627 for another 9 miles, until you reach the park.

Hiking and Backpacking

The **Coastal Hiking Trail** is a difficult 37-mile trek that starts at Hattie Cove and winds south through the tangled boreal forest and rocky hillocks of the Shield. It ends at the North Swallow River. You'll find plenty of campsites along the way, most of them near the beaches.

For the less adventurous, three self-guided trails start near the Hattie Cove Campground. The **Southern Headland Trail** (1.25 miles) follows the shore and offers splendid views of the Superior shoreline. The **Beach Trail** (about the same length) meanders along three beaches on Lake Superior. And the **Halfway Lake Trail** (2.2 miles) tracks around a small lake in the hills of the interior.

The 4.7-mile (one-way) hike from Hattie Cove to the White River suspension bridge along the Coastal Hiking Trail is popular with hikers in search of something a little more demanding. The sights awaiting at the bridge are rich reward: Rushing along beneath your feet, the White River lives up to its name as it plunges down the Chigamiwinigum Falls to a waiting gorge.

All backcountry hikers must check in and check out with the staff at the park's administrative building or at the visitor center at Hattie Cove. The park strictly controls the number of backcountry campers at any one time, and group size is limited to a maximum of eight people.

Canoeing

The **White River route** is 61 miles long and should take skilled canoeists five days to complete. On this route, you'll be following in the paddle strokes of Ojibwa hunters and European fur traders, for whom the White River was an important waterway. The route, which can be paddled any time through the open-water season (*usually late May–Sept.*), begins at White Lake Provincial Park on Trans-Canada 17 and ends at the river's mouth in Lake Superior. From there, an hour's paddle north will take you to the Hattie Cove Visitor Center.

You can also try the **Pukaskwa River** itself, though only in high water, during the spring runoff in May and June. This trip will take at least eight days and is not recommended for the inexperienced. Start from Saniga Lake on Trans-Canada 17 and finish at the coast.

Driftwood, Lake Superior, Pukaskwa NP

If you prefer to be out on open water, try the **Coastal Canoe Route,** a 97-mile trip that typically takes 10 to 14 days to complete, depending on winds. This route demands a high degree of skill and fitness. Lake Superior's water is very cold, with an average temperature of only 39° F, so you must wear a wetsuit to canoe there. Out on the lake, weather changes can be startlingly quick and, when the water turns rough, safety (not surprisingly) is inversely related to distance from shore. Around the big sand dunes of the Pic River, onshore winds can gust up to 50 miles an hour and throw up 10-foot waves. The trip starts in the northwest corner of the park, near Hattie Cove campground, and ends at Michipicoten Harbor.

All paddlers must register with the park before setting out. Maps and guidebooks are on sale at the visitor center store. Canoes and kayaks can be rented from Naturally Superior Adventures in Wawa *(705-856-7107)* or Pukaskwa Country Outfitters in Marathon *(807-229-0265)*. If you don't want to paddle the shoreline but still want to get out on the lake, local commercial operators offer boat tours.

Camping

You'll find 67 serviced sites at **Hattie Cove,** as well as a range of unserviced backcountry campsites, especially along the Coastal Trail. No reservations are accepted at Hattie Cove. But you can reserve the backcountry sites *(807-229-0801, ext. 242)*, and it's a good idea to do so. No matter where you decide to pitch your tent, however, you must obtain a camping permit beforehand.

A word of caution about potential neighbors: Black bears are common in the park and can be aggressive, particularly in areas with plenty of wild berries or in the vicinity of a dead deer or moose. Park wardens will tell you about areas with unusually high bear activity; occasionally they close off sections of the park to prevent problems. ■

What's a Pukaskwa?

The alternative spellings of Pukaskwa (pronounced PUCK-a-saw) rival the competing theories as to what the name means. Apparently, it can mean anything from "cleaning fish" or "eaters of fish" to "something evil" or even "safe harbor."

The park that bears the same name contains a number of pukaskwa pits, which range from small, round depressions to rectangular, thick-walled structures, all floored with finer cobbles. Little is known about these pits, which the Ojibwa may have used for fires.

One Native American legend attributes the name to an Ojibwa man named Joe, who had a fierce fight with his wife and killed her. He burned her body in a fire, then threw her bones into the mouth of the Pukaskwa River. As a result, he was branded with the name Opaksu—"one who cooks marrow."

Perry Bay, Sleeping Giant Provincial Park

Sleeping Giant Provincial Park

■ 60,000 acres ■ Southern Ontario, east of Thunder Bay; take Rte. 587 south from Hwy. 11/17 ■ Best seasons summer and winter ■ Camping, hiking, backpacking, cross-country skiing, canoeing ■ Contact the park, Pass Lake, ON P0T 2M0; phone 807-977-2526. www.ontarioparks.com/slee.html

NAMED AFTER A LEGENDARY COLOSSUS who tried to keep white men away from the lands of the Ojibwa, Sleeping Giant Provincial Park now attracts rather than repels visitors. Most come to hike the park's 50 miles of trails, which cluster in and around the giant (from Thunder Bay, the southern peninsula in profile resembles a giant sleeping on his back).

The park sits at the southern tip of Sibley Peninsula, a rocky finger of land poking into Lake Superior. The surprisingly varied terrain harbors an exceptional mix of plant life. Arctic plants such as bistort and cloudberry are found here, hundreds of miles south of their usual habitats. Some 38 varieties of ferns and 24 varieties of orchids grow in the park, including the exceedingly rare adder's mouth. More than 190 species of birds have been recorded, as have wolves and lynx. The bird observatory at Thunder Cape is popular, particularly during the fall migrations, when —in addition to southern warblers and black-backed woodpeckers—exotics such as golden eagles and harlequin ducks often pass through.

Deep-cut valleys and fast-flowing streams typify the peninsula's landscape. Forests of pine and fir, aspen and birch still remain. In fact, Sleeping Giant was created to prevent the last mature stands of white and red pine from being clear-cut by lumberers.

The park is a good choice for backpackers and wilderness hikers but is equally suitable for families on a day outing or overnight camping trip. Park staffers conduct occasional nature walks and hikes up the easier routes to the giant's summit. An outdoor theater near the visitor center shows films about the park. Check with the center for current programs.

What to See and Do

Walking the Giant

A hike up to the giant's knees and chest provides wonderful views across Thunder Bay and out toward Lake Superior. Along the way you will pass Superior's highest cliffs, which drop almost 800 feet straight down. For hikes less strenuous than these, the park contains eight shorter trails, which range from a few hundred yards to about 1.5 miles. At least one of them, **Plantain Lane,** is accessible to wheelchair travelers.

A popular long-distance hike is the **Kabeyun Trail,** whose 21 miles run along the western shore and provide a number of access points to the giant itself. With 11 backcountry campsites along the trail, the decision of where and when to stop and rest is up to you. The trailhead is off **Lake Marie Louise Scenic Drive.**

Hiking the full length of the Kabeyun will take three to four days, though sections can be done as day hikes. You can follow the trail through old-growth forest to **Pickerel Lake,** for instance, or through wetlands and fens to **Middlebrun Bay.** The scramble up **The Chimney,** which takes you to the giant's knees, is challenging; it should be attempted only by the fit —and in wet weather not even by them. The trail climbs 800 feet in little more than half a mile, and the views from the top are tremendous.

A somewhat easier climb—but still a climb, not a hike—is to the giant's chest by the **Sawyer Bay Trail;** the views from the 820-foot cliffs over Sawyer Bay are well worth the effort. Easier still is the trip to the wooden viewing platform at the north end of the Kabeyun Trail, which juts out over a sheer 350-foot drop to the pine forest below. It is vehicle-accessible over a rather rough forest road.

Other Activities

At Sleeping Giant Provincial Park, the best canoeing is at **Pickerel Lake** and **Lizard Lake.** Another good choice is **Marie Louise Lake,** which has a long sandy beach.

The park is open for cross-country skiing in winter and offers 30 miles of groomed trails *(access via the visitor center).* Some seasonal ski events attract substantial numbers of visitors. Speaking of numbers prompts this word of caution: The park is close to several large urban centers and can become crowded in summer. Reservations at the main campground, at Marie Louise (190 sites), or at the 20 interior sites are essential. Contact the park for reservations. ■

Mountain biking the Kabeyun Trail

Kakabeka Falls

Kakabeka Falls Provincial Park

■ 1,235 acres ■ Southern Ontario, 17 miles west of Thunder Bay ■ Best seasons summer and winter ■ Camping, hiking, cross-country skiing ■ Contact the park, 435 James St. S., Suite 221, Thunder Bay, ON P7C 6E3; phone 807-473-9231. www.ontarioparks.com/kaka.html

WHETHER THE OJIBWA WORD *KAKABEKA* means "steep cliffs" or "thundering water" doesn't really matter: They're both here at **Kakabeka Falls,** where the **Kaministiquia River** plunges 130 feet into a gorge that melting glaciers carved from the Canadian Shield at the end of the last ice age. From the observation platform perched over the falls (as well as from others along the gorge), you'll get close-up views of the river roaring past and see why the hydroelectric potential of the Kaministiquia has been tapped since 1904.

When you've observed enough and are ready to move on, you can choose from among the park's seven nature trails (or, in winter, the park's 8 miles of groomed cross-country ski trails). The trails vary in length and interest, but the most striking is the 1.2-mile **Mountain Portage Trail,** which follows the ancient transportation routes of the Ojibwa and the first European explorers in portaging around the falls; it cuts through dense forests of spruce, poplar, and hemlock, always with the sound of the falls playing in your ears *(trailhead access via main parking lot).*

And when you've walked enough, you can retire to either of the park's two campgrounds—a total of 169 sites located in nicely wooded areas. From these convenient bases you can wake refreshed and ready to explore the rest of the park and the surrounding area. ■

Pickerel Lake, Quetico Provincial Park

Quetico Provincial Park

■ 1.2 million acres ■ Northwest Ontario, west of Lake Superior, 70 miles west of Thunder Bay off Hwy. 11 ■ Best seasons spring-fall ■ Camping, hiking, canoeing, swimming, fishing, cross-country skiing, snowshoeing, rock paintings ■ Contact the park, 108 Saturn Ave., Atikokan, ON P0T 1C0; phone 807-597-2735. www.ontarioparks.com/quet.html

QUETICO PROVINCIAL PARK and the neighboring Boundary Waters Canoe Area Wilderness of Minnesota may well be the finest canoeing locations in North America. The lakes are quiet and unspoiled. The rivers gurgle over rapids (clearly marked on the park's detailed maps) or wander through forested groves. And except for the occasional float boat, the sound of motors is nowhere to be heard.

There are hundreds of lakes in Quetico; no one knows precisely how many. Nor does anyone know the number of miles of pristine canoe routes. The park's network of interconnecting lakes makes for almost endless choices, and you could travel 1,000 miles of waterway without repeating yourself. Visitors to the Boundary Waters Canoe Area Wilderness often make their way into Quetico Provincial Park, which has far fewer people per square mile.

For the most part, campers and canoeists will be on their own in Quetico park, where slim indeed is the prospect of finding any particular lake "occupied" by even one canoe. This country has changed little since the Ojibwa daubed rock faces here with paintings of human figures, canoes, and animals such as caribou and moose. More than 30 such sites have been identified in the park. The largest of them, located near the Lac La Croix entry to the park, may date back 500 years.

The forest cover is largely boreal—spruce and jack pine, aspen, and birch. But there are also pockets of mixed hardwood forest and isolated stands of massive red and white pines in the interior, untouched by loggers. Thick carpets of fern moss often underlie the spruce woods, while the jack pine woods shelter Quetico's largest orchid, the moccasin flower.

Chickadees, woodpeckers, and jays live in the woods, as do the boreal and great gray owls and many other species. The most characteristic bird of the park, though, is the loon, whose haunting cry is heard on every lake at dusk. Black bears and marten are common in the park. The bears have seldom been a problem: Quetico sees so few visitors that the animals have not become habituated to humans—and usually retreat on sight.

What to See and Do

The park has six entry points, each with a ranger station that supplies maps and camping permits. Three are water-entry points from Minnesota; canoeists must apply (six weeks in advance) for a remote area border-crossing permit from the Revenue Canada Customs and Excise Office (807-964-2095). Only one entry point is reachable by car: the Dawson Trail Campground (807-929-2571), just off Trans-Canada 11 at French Lake. Dawson Trail has 107 camping sites for trailers and tents; its information center is a valuable resource for updates about park conditions.

Canoeing

None of the canoe routes or portages are marked. More than 2,200 backcountry campsites are scattered throughout the park, most of them nestled into quiet coves or occupying some isolated rocky island. Sand beaches are frequent.

If the idea of planning a completely free-form trip into the vast unknown is daunting, outfitters in Atikokan will help you design one suited to your abilities and interests. Most such operators can fly you into the interior. The park has an up-to-date list of outfitters who will tailor trips to follow the route taken by early explorers such as Pierre Radisson and Alexander Mackenzie; to visit Ojibwa rock paintings; or simply to visit some quiet lake well stocked with fish, there to spend a day or a week entirely on your own.

Hiking

Seven hiking trails radiate from **Dawson Trail**, varying from 600 yards to 6 miles. The **Pines Hiking Trail** (3 miles round-trip) is challenging, but the payoff is a view of magnificent stands of towering red and white pine and the chance to picnic on the sandy beaches of **Pickerel Lake**. For history buffs, the easy two-hour tramp along the **French Portage Trail** (1.6 miles one way) is worth a try. It once formed a leg in a longer trail used by the Ojibwa and later by the fur traders, pressing into Manitoba and the west. Consider, too, the **French Falls Trail;** only a loop of only three quarters of a mile, it follows the cascades of the picturesque **French River**. ■

Woodland Caribou Provincial Park

■ 1.2 million acres ■ North of Lake Superior on the Manitoba border, 370 miles west of Thunder Bay ■ Best seasons spring-fall ■ Primitive camping, canoeing, fishing, bird-watching, wildlife viewing, pictographs ■ Contact the park, P.O. Box 5003, Red Lake, ON P0V 2M0; phone 807-727-2253. www. ontarioparks.com/wood.html

IF YOU WANT TO WALK IN WOODS that have never been logged or paddle across lakes that have never been named, this park is the place for you.

The creatures for which the park is named are secretive, but more and more caribou are spotted by keen-eyed canoers every year—a sight that transforms an ordinary moment into a lasting memory. The cari-bou (there are about 130 in all) are most often seen in or near lakes and rivers. They share the park with moose, black bears, wolverines, river otters, great blue herons, and bald eagles.

Mushrooms, Woodland Caribou PP

Woodland Caribou is a walk— or more often a paddle—on the wild side. No campsites have been designated in the backcountry, but there are plenty of traditional campsites with easy landings for canoeists. Firewood is plentiful, and so is bare bedrock on which to build small fires; elsewhere thick beds of fragrant moss invite campers to pitch their tents. To lessen the impact that visitors have on the park's fragile boreal land, the occupancy at any campsite is limited to nine campers.

A limited park staff maintains a network of portages connecting many of the lakes. Countless other lakes remain to be explored. The staff attempts to clear a quarter of the portages each year.

Portages are marked by small blazes in the form of ax marks in the bark of mature trees. With the passage of time these blazes weather and fade, so wilderness travelers must remain observant and rely partly on their own navigational skills.

What to See and Do

Getting There

With no roads leading into Woodland Caribou Provincial Park, reaching the site can be an adventure in itself. All access points, even those by road, take you only to places where you can canoe into the park proper.

Most visitors reach the park through the western Ontario towns of Ear Falls and Red Lake, both located on Hwy. 105 north of Trans-Canada 17. At Red Lake the highway ends and the wilderness takes over.

The park has six traditional entry points for canoeists, five of which can be reached by driving along a forest access (logging) road from either Red Lake or Ear Falls. The road hugs the park's southeastern boundary and loops to connect the two towns. Although the road is navigable by two-wheel-drive vehicles, visitors must be cautious because they will be sharing the road with long-haul trucks. If your vehicle isn't up to it, take a ground shuttle offered by one of the canoe outfitters listed on page 58.

The sixth entry point is located north of Red Lake on the Upper Chukuni River. This option takes paddlers through crown land wilderness (meaning it is owned by the state) for three days before reaching the park boundary and the headwaters of the **Bloodvein River,** a Canadian heritage river. The river's 190-mile water trail conveys canoers on a 15- to 20-day journey through the heart of the land, eventually depositing them at the community of Bloodvein on the east shore of Lake Winnipeg.

The park can also be accessed by canoe from the Manitoba side at these four entry points: Oiseau Creek, Garner Lake, Wanipigow River, and Carroll Lake. Reaching the park from any one of these places entails a paddle of one to three days. Because the Bloodvein River is susceptible to high-water fluctuations, paddlers should ask an outfitter or the park offices about recent conditions before they venture out.

Long-distance Canoeing

It's possible to cross the park from east to west by canoe—a distance of about 40 miles as the crow flies but a good deal longer as the fish swims. Access to the Bloodvein River is interrupted by several portages at the end of Pipestone Bay or by the numerous but shorter portages along the Upper Chukuni and Sabourin Rivers leading to the Bloodvein. Many paddlers opt instead to fly within closer range of the river, be it to Olive, Bigshell, or Knox Lakes.

At any point along the Bloodvein, paddlers have the freedom to venture out on side trips. One such side trip is from Bigshell, where you can veer off onto unbeaten paths and aim for Burntwood Lake; from there a series of short portages lead to the Dutch River. The Dutch, in turn, makes its way to **Thicketwood Lake,** a long and eye-pleasing body of water that pours out through the Sabourin River into **Sabourin Lake.** Here you'll find an attractive main base lodge. From Sabourin Lake the

Following pages: Woodland Caribou Provincial Park

Leano Lake, Woodland Caribou PP

route joins the Bloodvein, which meanders placidly through wetlands and into Barclay Lake, Mary's Lake, and then Artery Lake on the western border of the park.

The Bloodvein is only one of two large river systems in the park. The **Gammon River** cuts the park roughly in two halves, eventually emptying into the Bloodvein River inside Manitoba. In common with the Bloodvein, the Gammon enables you to wander across large lakes with sharp drops in elevation between bodies of water.

The remainder of the park consists of countless smaller elongated lakes and creek systems, all bordered by typical Shield glaciated landscape: bedrock outcroppings, thin soils, and hardy but splendorous jack pine forests. This type of water drainage offers paddlers endless interconnected routes, which can be followed on two- or three-day journeys to weeklong adventures. The area also seems to invite more intimate views of the land, both its plants and its wildlife. For these reasons—together with the fact that it is easily accessed by road—the southern half of the Woodland Caribou Provincial Park attracts the majority of visitors.

Four canoe outfitters operate from Red Lake: Woodland Caribou Outfitters *(807-727-9943)*, Goldseekers Outfitting *(807-727-2353 or 800-591-9282)*, Woodland Caribou Canoe Outfitters *(807-727-2263)*, and Atikaki Canoe Outfitters *(807-727-2797)*. Each offers similar packages and can help you plot out a route, select and rent equipment, and coordi-

nate flight and shuttle services.

In country as wild as this, good maps are essential. For a detailed map of the canoe routes and large-scale topographic maps of the park, contact Northern Sporting Supplies *(807-727-2302)* or Four Seasons Sport Shop *(807-222-2200)*. The canoe outfitters listed above may also have these maps on hand. Not only does the park publish the canoe route map, it puts out an annual newsletter; call 807-727-1336 or 807-727-1388 for a copy.

Fishing

Spectacular sportfishing awaits anglers on almost any canoe foray into the park. Because many of the lakes are fished only a few times a year, the fish are plentiful—and hungry. The park supports some eagerly sought-after freshwater game fish species—walleye, northern pike, and lake trout. Fish are easily caught on lures; no bait is required. Indeed, park personnel prefer that no live bait be brought into the park lest it introduce new species into the water ecosystem.

Where to Stay

A number of lodges and outpost camps perch beside various lakes in the park, nearly all of them located along the Bloodvein and Gammon Rivers. The largest commercial main base lodge sits on Sabourin Lake; another occupies the shore of Douglas Lake, while a third is situated by Carroll Lake. Gammon and Donald Lakes are home to a pair of private lodges.

In addition to its lodges, the park features 15 outpost camps, with room for four to ten people. A handful of private cottages are available as well.

Access to all sites is by aircraft or canoe only. Contact the park for a list of commercial accommodations and phone numbers.

Pictographs

Woodland Caribou has some of the largest and best preserved Native American pictographs in the Canadian Shield. The Bloodvein River is steeped in history, having long been used as a major traveling corridor by the first inhabitants of this continent, then later as a secondary fur-trade route.

Along the stretch of the river within Woodland Caribou are six pictograph sites. Make sure to visit the site at Artery Lake: The writing on the wall here may date back to 900 to 1,200 years. Other pictograph sites can be found near **Bigshell** and on **Beamish, Aegean, Musclow, Hansen,** and **Hjalmar Lakes.**

Customarily drawn or painted on the base of a cliff, pictographs are an eloquent reminder of the Ojibwa peoples who have lived, fished, and hunted in this wilderness for almost nine millennia. The park is understandably protective of these sites, and visitors are urged to treat them with the utmost respect (that means don't touch them!).

Many Ojibwa still consider the pictographs to possess spiritual significance, so you may see offerings of tobacco, cedar, or coins tucked into cracks in the rock. Ask a park staffer for locations so you can include a visit to one of these rare renderings in your trip. ■

Chapleau Crown Game Preserve

■ 2 million acres ■ Northeast Ontario ■ Best season summer ■ Camping, white-water rafting and kayaking, canoeing, fishing, bird-watching, wildlife viewing ■ Contact the preserve, Ministry of Natural Resources, 190 Cherry St., Chapleau, ON P0M 1K0; phone 705-864-1710. www.township.chapleau.on.ca

LOCAL TOUR OPERATORS CLAIM that 94 percent of visitors to Chapleau encounter at least one black bear or moose. It's wise to be wary, but despite the preserve's ban on firearms no humans have yet come to harm from either animal. The area abounds with other large mammals such as lynx and timber wolf, as well as beaver, otter, and marten. Elk and eastern cougar are believed to live in the preserve, too. Common birds include eagles, ospreys, herons, and cranes.

Straddling the heights between the Arctic and Atlantic watersheds, the park is the logical starting place for 2,000 miles of canoeable rivers and lakes. This two-million-acre area was set aside in 1925 to protect and replenish bird and game populations in northeast Ontario. The borders stretch from the Algoma Central Railway (ACR) in the west to the Chapleau River in the east, and from the Canadian Pacific Railroad (CPR) in the south to the Canadian National Railroad (CNR) in the north.

What to See and Do

The town of Chapleau serves as the gateway to the preserve. Access is by gravel road from Chapleau to Racine Lake and Missinaibi Lake Provincial Park; by train on the ACR, CPR, or CNR lines; and by canoe or bush plane from Chapleau.

Canoeing

Canoeing is the most popular nature adventure in the preserve. Given adequate time, energy, and ambition, you could paddle all the way from Chapleau to the Arctic.

The most popular rivers are the **Missinaibi** and the **Chapleau.** On the Upper Missinaibi it's possible to run 40 sets of rapids, portaging fewer than ten times. The first 50 miles of the Lower Missinaibi are rife with riffles as well; the white water ends at the spectacular **Thunder House Falls,** where a splendid campsite perches 150 feet above the canyon. Below the falls it's an easy float downriver to the Cree villages of Moosonee and Moose Factory on James Bay.

The **Kesagami River,** which begins in the lake of the same name, is often described as Ontario's wildest paddling river. A demanding but exhilarating trip is the one from Kesagami Lake to James Bay—11 days of almost continuous Class II to Class IV rapids, chutes, and falls.

Camping and Fishing

Chapleau Preserve consists mainly of publicly owned land. Camping is permitted anywhere on this crown land, as long as you have a permit. **Racine Lake** is the largest in the preserve, and has two campgrounds along its shores. Contact Missinaibi Headwaters outfitters in Chapleau *(705-864-2065 in summer, 705-444-4480 in winter only; www.missinaibi.com).*

Fifty-five miles north of Chapleau in the center of the preserve lies **Missinaibi Provincial Park** *(705-234-2222 or 705-864-1710, ext. 214).* Walleye, northern pike, rainbow trout, splake, yellow perch, and smallmouth bass can be fished in the park, which offers 36 regular and 20 remote campsites. ■

Forest mushrooms

Algonquin Provincial Park

■ 1.9 million acres ■ Central Ontario, 160 miles north of Toronto ■ Best seasons spring and fall ■ Camping, hiking, backpacking, boating, canoeing, swimming, fishing, biking, cross-country skiing, snowshoeing, dogsledding, bird-watching, wildflower viewing ■ Contact the park, P.O. Box 219, Whitney, ON K0J 2M0; phone 705-633-5572. www.algonquinpark.on.ca

ONE MERE LIFETIME WOULD NOT SUFFICE to accomplish all the wilderness exploits on tap at Algonquin Provincial Park. Established in 1893 to protect the headwaters of the five major rivers that originate in the park—the Petawawa, Bonnechere, Oxtongue, Madawaska, and Amable du Fond—this is Ontario's best known and most beloved park. It rewards all sorts of visitors, from the long-distance paddler keen on savoring the melancholy call of a loon on a remote lake to the gregarious camper who wants to enjoy the great outdoors in the company of others.

Three separate Algonquins make this possible. First is the vast **"interior,"** as the backcountry is referred to here, and the only way to see it is on foot, by canoe, or through a combination of both.

The second and much less demanding Algonquin is the **Parkway Corridor,** a 34-mile section of Hwy. 60 that cuts through the park's southwest corner. This is where the amenities are: outfitters, the park's visitor center, two museums, restaurants, cottages, and campgrounds. First-time visitors expecting to find pristine wilderness are sometimes dismayed to see all this development within a provincial park, but its concentration in the corridor is deliberate; it keeps the interior free from all but rudimentary camps, the occasional four-person ranger's hut, and marked portages. The corridor is easily accessible for day-trippers. About one-third of the park's 300,000 annual visitors stay in nearby towns and enter the park only for the day, where they can pick from a menu of recreational options: walk a trail, have a picnic, visit a museum, or swim on a sand beach (in particular, the sand beaches of the Lake of Two Rivers).

The third Algonquin is what's becoming known as **Algonquin South,** a tongue of park protruding down into Hastings and Haliburton Counties, adjacent to the Haliburton Highlands (see pp. 70-71). Until 1998 this section of the park was relatively undeveloped, but hiking and camping facilities are now legion. Algonquin South is not as developed as the corridor, nor is it quite as inaccessible as the interior.

The park has inspired no fewer than 60 books, at least 1,800 scien-

Canoe ashore at Opeongo Lake, Algonquin PP
Opposite: Portage trail, Algonquin PP

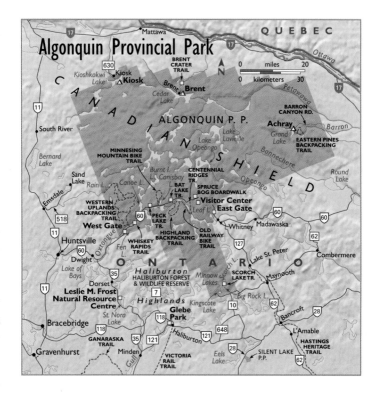

tific research papers, endless paintings by Canada's Group of Seven artists, and at least one symphony.

The park's landscape is typical of the Canadian Shield—a wild and beautiful place of lakes and streams, craggy granite hills, and seemingly endless forests. A boreal forest or spruce bog materializes here and there, but the typical woodland is maple forest that turns the park into a dazzling autumn palette of plum, scarlet, bright yellow, and deep gold.

Having been logged early in the 20th century, most of the park is second- growth forest. Yet considerable numbers of mature old-growth trees still stand, especially red and white pine up to 350 years old, a few hemlock groves, and some maple woods. Logging is banned on lakeshores, near portages, and on islands, but the practice persists in the northern reaches of the park.

Most central Ontario mammal species are found in Algonquin: moose and white-tailed deer, black bear, marten and fishers, porcupines and beavers. The park is also famous for its wolf packs (see pp. 68-69).

More than 250 bird species have been recorded in the park. The most looked-for local species are the spruce grouse and the gray jay. Warblers, thrushes, finches, and waterfowl join this avian chorus, but the most famous soloist is the common loon; it nests on virtually every lake, where its soul-stirring cry can be heard at dusk in spring, summer, and fall.

What to See and Do

Canoeing

The park staff has designated more than 1,300 miles of canoe routes. Many of the routes, such as **Lake Lavieille, Dickson Lake,** and **Lake Opeongo,** are appropriate for beginners; others, such as the **Nipissing, Petawawa,** and **Tim Rivers,** involve long portages that make them considerably more demanding. Those planning a trip should order the detailed map "Canoe Routes of Algonquin Provincial Park" in advance. It includes information about routes that require reservations, perimeter access points, natural and cultural history, and backcountry canoe trips. A less detailed preview version may be downloaded from the park's website.

Most of the interior is a connected network of lakes. Canoeists can—and frequently do—make their own way through the park without benefit of route markers, but this calls for considerable orienteering skills.

There are three major canoe routes in Algonquin South: a one-day trip to **Upper** and **Lower Minnow Lakes,** a one-day trip to **Big**

Northern leopard frog

Rock Lake, and a three-day trip to **Scorch Lake.** Access is through the Kingscote Lake Campground, 36 miles northeast of Haliburton and 32 miles northwest of Bancroft.

The **Scorch Lake Lookout Trail** is the reward for getting to the lake: Steep but short, it rises in less than a mile through hardwood forest to spectacular views over the lake and the woods beyond. Most of the routes in this area are designed for canoeists who want a slightly easier wilderness experience than the deep interior of the park proper.

Day Hikes

Sixteen interpretive walking trails of varying length and challenge have been laid out. All but three of them are accessible from the Parkway Corridor. Detailed hiking guides are usually tucked inside boxes at the trailheads.

The **Whiskey Rapids Trail** is a 1.3-mile hike along the Oxtongue River *(trailhead on Hwy. 60, 4.5 miles from west gate);* the 1.1-mile **Peck Lake Trail** *(trailhead 12 miles from west gate on Hwy. 60)* circumnavigates Peck Lake; the 3.4-mile **Bat Lake Trail** *(trailhead 19 miles from west gate)* passes through hardwood and coniferous forests and visits a substantial hemlock grove; the 6.2-mile **Centennial Ridges Trail** *(trailhead 23 miles from west gate)* offers spectacular views over the forests; and the 1-mile **Spruce Bog Boardwalk** loop *(trailhead 26 miles from west gate),* not surprisingly, passes through typical spruce bog. The 1.2-mile **Brent Crater Trail** *(accessible from*

Hwy. 17 on Brent Rd.) offers a view of a meteorite crater from an observation tower.

Backpacking

Three areas of the park encompass designated backpacking trails, with loops ranging from 3.7 to 55 miles.

The **Western Uplands Backpacking Trail** can be reached from two points: the corridor at Kilometer 3 near the west gate or the Rain Lake access point, 21 miles east of Hwy. 11 at the village of Emsdale. The trail has several loops, from 19 to 54 miles long. The **Highland Backpacking Trail,** which comprises 7- and 14-mile loops, is reached from the Parkway Corridor at Kilometer 29.7. The **Eastern Pines Backpacking Trail** begins at the Achray Campground on the park's eastern rim and features 8- and 22-mile loops.

Biking

Two trails have been laid out for cyclists, both of them along the Parkway Corridor. The **Minnesing Mountain Bike Trail** is moderately difficult, with four loops ranging from 2.9 miles to 14.5 miles. The **Old Railway Bike Trail** is a 6.2-mile trail (one way) that is suitable for families. Ask at the park about places to rent bikes.

Fishing

Algonquin has some of the best trout fishing in Canada. More than 230 lakes contain brook trout (**Welcome** and **Dickson Lakes** are particularly good), and 149 have lake trout (**Lake Louisa** and **Hogan Lake** are recommended). Many lakes are also stocked with splake, a hybrid of these two types of trout. Spring is the best season for trout, summer for bass. Purchase a fishing license at the park's information offices at the east and west gates.

Winter Activities

All 50 miles of groomed cross-country skiing trails in the park are along the Parkway Corridor, but possibilities for snowshoeing exist almost everywhere. Ski loops range from 3 to 18 miles. Check with the park and get a trail map before setting out. **Pine Tree Loop** at Leaf Lake and **Minnesing Trail** are the most challenging.

The Algonquin Nordic Wilderness Lodge *(705-745-9497)* sits by a secluded lake on the park's borders in nearby Cavan, Ontario, and requires a 1.6-mile ski-in from its parking lot. Maintaining 50 miles of groomed and wilderness cross-country ski trails, the lodge is an ideal spot for those who like a little well-being with their wilderness: The saunas after a long day on skis are justifiably popular.

Another winter activity is dogsledding. Excursions are available in three locations: two along the corridor and one in the northwest sector (accessible from the village of South River on Hwy. 11).

Camping

Approximately 1,200 campsites are available in eight campgrounds along the Parkway Corridor, while an additional 1,900 primitive campsites are scattered throughout the interior. The corridor sites have a range of amenities, including electrical hookups, flush toilets, and laundromats.

A few paddle-in campsites have

Winter meadow, Algonquin Provincial Park

been set up on **Canisbay Lake** for canoers seeking seclusion. Four "peripheral campgrounds"—that's park shorthand for no modern conveniences—are even more remote, yet they can still be reached by a drive over unpaved roads. Kiosk Campground is in the north end on beautiful **Kioshkokwi Lake;** Brent is located on **Cedar Lake,** one of the park's largest and a particularly good site for pickerel fishing; Achray on

Grand Lake is best known for its pine forests and sand beaches. The fourth campground, Algonquin South, capitalizes on the tranquil isolation of **Kingscote Lake.**

Winter wilderness camping is allowed in Algonquin Provincial Park, but the camp must not be within sight or sound of ski trails, on a summer campsite, or within 100 feet of any lake, trail, or portage. Winter camping almost always requires snowshoes. ■

Bay, O Wolf!

IT IS THE MOST THRILLING of all wilderness sounds: the long, mournful howl of a timber wolf echoing out of the blackness of the night. This call of the wild draws humans to Algonquin Park in fall for public "wolf howls" conducted by park naturalists. In addition to hearing wolf cries in a wilderness setting, park visitors are coached to imitate the rising and falling notes of an authentic-sounding wolf howl.

That wolves respond to human facsimiles of their calls has long been known. Less well understood is just *why* they do—especially to even amateurish and unconvincing human attempts to mimic their cries. Indeed, some Algonquin wolves have answered back to the sound of trucks changing gears on a distant highway.

Naturalist guides have conducted wolf howls in the park since the early 1960s. Once they have located a wolf pack, the guides lead an evening convoy of visitors—sometimes up to 1,000 people in 300 or so vehicles—onto the nearest logging or access road. At a radio signal from park headquarters, all engines are killed and all lights are extinguished. The guides then begin calling to the wolves with howls that strike most visitors as convincing approximations of the real thing. If the wolves respond, the lucky visitors will be treated to the wildest wilderness symphony of all: timber wolves in full cry.

That doesn't always happen, of course. The wolves may have wandered out of earshot, or for reasons unknown they may simply choose to ignore the intrusion. A number of visitors have come to the park year after year to hear the wolves, only to go home disappointed each time. Still, the 80 public wolf howls between 1964

and 1997 drew 102,160 people (an average of 1,277 per outing) and achieved a success rate of 71 percent.

Algonquin's chief naturalist, Dan Strickland, retired in 2000. Since conducting his first wolf howl in the 1960s, he has never lost the thrill of hearing a lupine reply. "The howling of wolves arouses deep emotions," he writes. "Perhaps it is the buried wish for the wild freedom of remote ancestors; the mystery of an animal that responds to us but which we almost never see; the thrill of direct communication with a legendary outlaw; or just the magic of a night in wolf country, including that tinge of fear carried over from childhood."

As a center of wolf research, Algonquin Park is charged with teaching the public about wolf habits and wolf ecology. The park's wolf howls help to accomplish that by dispelling many of the myths that continue to surround wolves. The animals are very social creatures that mate for life. Adult females cooperate to raise their young, and both parents are playful and tolerant, especially with the pups.

As wolf-howl participants learn, the animals bay neither at the moon nor at any other celestial body. Rather, they vocalize for social and territorial purposes. And that trebly yapping of their pups? This is thought to occur when the young—left at rendezvous sites while their elders are out hunting—howl as a way to stay in contact with the adults.

Another lesson learned by Algonquin visitors is that wolves are not aggressive: There is no record of an unprovoked attack by a healthy wolf on a human in North America. Yet the wolf's fiendish image—legacy of an era when rabies was a much more preva-

Timber wolf on the howl

lent threat than it is today—lives on.

The true nature of these creatures is a far cry from the stereotype. Upon entering wolf dens to tag youngsters, Algonquin naturalists have encountered nothing more threatening than a growl from the mother. Yet wolves are frequently shot when they stray beyond the boundaries of the park. The animals who remain steadfastly inside Algonquin and other designated areas throughout North America face a danger just as implacable: the shrinking habitat of the timber wolf.

Public wolf howls customarily take place at Algonquin Provincial Park on Thursday evenings in August. They are frequently canceled, though, for the unassailable reason that no wolf pack has been located in the vicinity.

Check with the park on the day of the howl, then assemble before dusk at the Pog Lake outdoor theater. After listening to a short talk about the procedure and etiquette of the wolf howl to come, you'll be treated, with luck, to theater of an entirely different stripe. ■

Walk in the Clouds, Haliburton Forest and Wildlife Reserve

Haliburton Highlands

■ 1.1 million acres ■ Central Ontario, 125 miles north of Toronto on Hwy. 35
■ Best seasons summer, fall, and winter ■ Hiking, guided walks, white-water
rafting, canoeing, swimming, mountain biking, dogsledding, cross-country skiing,
wildlife viewing, petroglyphs ■ Contact Haliburton Highlands Chamber of
Commerce, P.O. Box 147, Minden, ON K0M 2K0; phone 705-286-1760 or 800-
461-7677. www.haliburtonhighlandschamber.on.ca

SOME 50,000 ACRES OF THE Haliburton Highlands—a large region of lakes,
wetlands, and mountains bordering Algonquin Park to the south—are
taken up by the **Haliburton Forest and Wildlife Reserve** *(R.R. 1, Haliburton, ON K0M 1S0. 705-754-2198).* This privately owned property
boasts 50 lakes for swimming, dozens of rivers and streams for picnicking
or paddling, and almost 200 miles of trails for hiking or mountain biking. The reserve is also an educational facility offering some remarkable
attractions. One is a guided tour *(fee)* to a beautiful stand of old-growth
white pine—with a difference: This tour takes place above the ground, on
an elevated boardwalk called the **Walk in the Clouds.**

A third of a mile long and 65 feet in the air, the boardwalk provides a
bird's-eye view of forest and lakes. A park warden atop a platform high in
the trees explains forest ecosystems and checks your safety harnesses: The
boardwalk has rope handrails, but the walkway is barely 18 inches wide.
The Walk in the Clouds is part of a four-hour guided tour that includes
an orientation drive through the park's forest lands, a half-mile walk
along a meandering creek, and a boat ride across a wilderness lake.

Another attraction is the **Haliburton Forest Wolf Centre,** set up as a
research and educational facility in 1996. The center has a 15-acre enclosure that is home to a pack of gray wolves. An observatory at one end of
the forested enclosure—complete with one-way windows next to the

wolves' feeding area—provides a wonderful opportunity to watch the animals without their being aware of your presence. The center also houses displays and artifacts relating to wolves, and samples of wolf-based folklore from around the world.

Like the Haliburton Forest Wolf Center, the **Leslie M. Frost Natural Resource Centre** *(705-766-2451)* is primarily an educational facility for natural resource and environmental programs. It is located due west of the Haliburton forest, 7.5 miles south of the little community of Dorset, and has access to nearly 60,000 acres of crown, or state-owned, land.

Nestled on the shores of St. Nora Lake, the Frost campus offers courses in birding, geology, lake and forest ecosystems, and other subjects. The facility maintains a network of hiking trails and, in winter, some 13 miles of cross-country skiing trails. The 1.4-mile **Fox Trail**—fairly easy and the closest to the parking area—is a favorite. There is also a **Geomorphology Trail** and 6 miles of interpretive trails. More than 60 lakes are available for those who prefer to canoe or swim; the shoreline of all of them except St. Nora's is uninhabited.

Also located in Haliburton Highlands is the **Central Ontario Loop Trail.** This trail provides an uninterrupted hike of more than 250 miles in five separately managed sections. Within each section are multiple access points and numerous side trails, with enough choices to suit everyone. The trails pass through a mix of crown land and private property; in many cases they follow the beds of now abandoned railroads.

The main trail occupies an old railroad pathway from Haliburton village south to Kinmount. A number of others join it; among them are trails from the Frost Centre and several small provincial parks, including **Glebe Park** and **Silent Lake** *(call Haliburton Highlands Trails and Tours Network 705-286-1760).*

Pathways in profusion lace the neighboring counties as well. In Hastings County you will find the **Hastings Heritage Trail,** a 96-mile ribbon running from Lake St. Peter in the north to the Trent Canal system. The trail passes waterfalls, wetlands, and ghost towns such as Brinklow *(call Eastern Ontario Trails Alliance 705-778-3624).*

Northumberland County has two long-distance trails: The **Waterfront Trail** leads from Brighton to Port Hope along the shore of Lake Ontario, while the **Ganaraska Trail** winds from Port Hope through central Ontario to Lindsay in Victoria County. The Ganaraska eventually joins the Bruce Trail *(see pp. 33-34)* to the west *(call Ganaraska Trail Association 905-885-7376 or Northumberland County Tourism 800-354-7050).*

The **Victoria Rail Trail** is a 34-mile path from Lindsay through the village of Fenelon Falls and on to Kinmount and Haliburton *(call Victoria County Development Department 705-324-9411, ext. 233.)* A welter of trails in Peterborough County take hikers to **Petroglyphs Provincial Park** *(705-877-2552),* which contains the largest concentration of aboriginal rock carvings in Ontario, and to **Warsaw Caves Conservation Area** *(705-745-5791),* where visitors can explore seven extensive caves and listen to the Indian River as it flows underground. ■

Mazinaw Lake, Bon Echo PP

Bon Echo Provincial Park

■ 16,408 acres ■ Southeast Ontario, between Renfrew and Belleville on Hwy. 41 ■ Best seasons summer and fall ■ Camping, hiking, rock climbing, boating, canoeing, swimming, fishing, pictographs ■ Contact the park, R.R. 1, Cloyne, ON K0H 1K0; phone 613-336-2228. www.ontarioparks.com/bone.html

BON ECHO'S MASSIVE ROCK—dubbed the Canadian Gibraltar—is a sheer cliff that rises more than 330 feet straight out of Mazinaw Lake. But there's more to the rock than meets the eye—300 more feet of it, hidden beneath the waters of Mazinaw, one of Ontario's deepest lakes.

Clinging to the rock face are stunted cedars, some of them nearly 900 years old. But that's not what draws most visitors to Bon Echo. Neither is the (admittedly spectacular) view from atop the cliff. The main attraction—a Canadian National Historic Site—is the remarkable concentration of **Ojibwa pictographs** that stretch for a full mile along the cliff face between the waterline and a height of about 6 feet. More than 260 images have been cataloged—the biggest collection of drawings in the Canadian Shield.

Like such images elsewhere in Ontario (see pp. 44 and 60), the pictographs were painted using crushed hematite rock mixed with fish oil. Ojibwa lore is more colorful, though: It holds that the pigment is either turtle blood or a sacred liquid flowing from the fingertips of shamans.

Some of the pictographs are most likely a record of images experienced by shamans in vision quests and dream fastings. Others are more prosaic; they served as route markers or hunt counts. Certain images have been interpreted by modern Ojibwa, who see in them representations of the great water cat Mishipashoo; the legendary folk hero Nanabush; the turtle, a link between the physical and spiritual worlds; and the Maymaygwayshi, little people who live inside the rock itself.

You'll also find more recent images—of 1920s vintage, in fact. That's when one of the owners of the now defunct Bon Echo Inn—an admirer of poet/wanderer Walt Whitman—had the following lines from the great writer's 1855 *Leaves of Grass* carved into the rock in foot-high letters:

> *My foothold is tenon'd and mortis'd in granite*
> *I laugh at what you call dissolution*
> *And I know the amplitude of time.*

Drawing nearly 200,000 people a year to its 530 campsites, beaches, and trails, Bon Echo is a popular park. Public boat launches pepper its 13 small lakes, and a ferry crosses the waters of **Mazinaw Lake** to visit several of the pictographs.

The park staff has laid out 17 miles of hiking trails through a variety of forest habitats and along the shores of the lakes. The most popular is the mile-long **Cliff Top Trail,** which runs from the Mazinaw lakefront to the top of the **Rock.** Access to the lakefront is by ferry. At the other end of the trail, a steep staircase facilitates your climb up the Rock. The Cliff Top Trail ends at a viewing platform that commands miles of maple and oak forests.

The **Abes and Essens Trail** is a made up of three interconnecting loops offering a choice of 2.5-mile, 5.6-mile, or 10.6-mile hikes. The trailhead is located at the parking lot about 3 miles along the road to Hardwood Hill Campground. It takes 90 minutes or so to hike the first loop around **Clutes Lake.** A full four hours should be allocated to hike the first two loops, which take you around **Essens Lake** and back. Allow seven hours to complete all three loops, which together skirt five of the park's inland lakes. Overnight campsites *(reservations required)* are located on Little Rock, Abes, Essens, and Clutes Lakes.

A trail of another sort is the **Kishkebus Canoe Trail.** Its leisurely 13 miles take about six hours to complete, including the time required to negotiate its three short and one longer portages. The canoe trail starts and ends in Mazinaw Lake and treats you to both the pictographs and the Walt Whitman inscription.

Bon Echo's main campsites—Mazinaw Lake and Hardwood Hill, the latter located in a sylvan serenity of maple and beech—can be reached by car. Canoe-in sites (24 in all) also beckon at Joeperry and Pearson Lakes. ■

The St. Lawrence

St. Lawrence Islands National Park

DOMINATING QUEBEC on its northeasterly course through the province, the mighty St. Lawrence River curls around islands and pushes all before it—from canoes to cargo ships—on its way to the open sea. In its wake, the river embraces a host of parks and reserves offering livelihood, refreshment, and recreation to people, sustenance and habitat to wildlife.

Long before anyone had conceived of a St. Lawrence Seaway, with its series of locks and canals that allows

seagoing vessels to reach all the Great Lakes in their quest to bear wheat, ore, and coal to foreign ports, the river served as an access corridor to the North American interior. For centuries, Native Americans hunted its shores, and paddled and fished its waters. Europeans, calculating dominion and riches, explored its reaches for minerals, timber, and fur. Loftier bounty was sought by missionaries hunting the heathen soul. The river's shores offered the promise of a new life to early settlers and latter-day immigrants alike. Even armies bent on conquest negotiated its riffles and eddies. Today, the river's banks grow thick with human settlement. Montréal, Quebec's largest city, rests atop an island in the middle of the river,

while a couple of hundred miles farther downstream lies Québec, the provincial capital.

In the 21st century a different need for the river has emerged. Subduing nature and extracting her bounty no longer claim preeminence. Now there is a longing for solitude in which to see and hear wildlife, to feel the wind on your face, the warmth of the sun on your back—to stop and turn away for a few moments from the bustle and busyness of our quotidian existence. Here on the river's banks, you can observe wild creatures as they forage for food, shelter in forest or other fastness, and navigate the river. Even the great fin whales ply the river hundreds of miles upstream from the Gulf of St. Lawrence and the Atlantic Ocean. Shorebirds and migrating waterfowl nest and forage along the river's banks, sometimes in massive concentrations, as found in the marshlands of Cap Tourmente.

On the St. Lawrence's shores south of Montréal, the Eastern Townships stretch toward the Vermont border. Picturesque lakelands and farm country set amid rolling hills lure harried city folk in search of peace and recreation. The hills offer excellent hikes, particularly along the Estrie Trail—or Les Sentiers de l'Estrie, as it is known in French. The countryside grows more rugged as you approach the region called the Gaspé, where several wilderness parks, especially the beloved Parc de la Gaspésie, delight hikers and campers in all seasons.

Forests and lakes define the vast hinterlands of Quebec north of the St. Lawrence River. Much of this is still Canadian Shield—a massive area of ancient exposed rock. Deciduous forest blankets its southerly reaches, with boreal forest to the north, and finally tundra, as Quebec falls away toward subarctic regions. Although larger than western Europe, the St. Lawrence's north shore, north and east of the Ottawa River basin, has few people and hence few roads; most of the latter fetch up in some town that got its start in mining or timber. Little wonder, then, that wilderness parks here can afford to encompass so much land: Both the Réserve Faunique La Vérendrye and the Réserve Faunique des Laurentides hold more than 5,000 square miles of land. Other wildlife reserves in the region exceed even these two.

Despite the vastness of the terrain, excellent roads run to all the major wilderness parks. Appealing to the casual and serious adventurer alike, sections of the parks remain within easy distance of the automobile and its attendant comforts, while other parts, remote and difficult to access, require serious backcountry effort. Gatineau Park lies a few minutes' drive from Ottawa, Canada's capital. Two hours from Montréal rises the Mont Tremblant massif, while a 30-minute car ride from Québec brings you to the Réserve Faunique des Laurentides.

Many beautiful sites hug the river. The drive eastward from Montréal along the south shore of the St. Lawrence, or along the freeway from Québec to Rivière-du-Loup, provides a superb introduction to the region. Rich farmland shares the setting with magnificent views of the river, where you will see a glittering ribbon of water with the north shore looming beyond it, as well as dramatic mountains and cliffs and great gashes of fjord. At Rivière-du-Loup, "gateway to the Gaspé," a ferry crosses to St.-Siméon on the north shore. Then, an easy drive eastward brings you to the Saguenay and its fjord. Close by, to the west, you'll find Cap Tourmente, Mont Ste.-Anne, the Laurentides reserve, the Jacques Cartier conservation area, and Québec itself. Rather than return to Montréal along the expressway, more wilderness awaits along alternate Rte. 157 from Trois-Rivières to Shawinigan and on to La Mauricie National Park and Mont Tremblant. A two-hour drive from there takes you back to Montréal—and the 21st century. ■

St. Lawrence Islands National Park

St. Lawrence Islands National Park

■ 2,944 acres on 24 islands and 90 islets ■ Eastern Ontario, 240 miles east of Toronto, between Gananoque and Brockville via Thousand Islands Parkway ■ Best months mid-May–mid-Oct. ■ Camping, hiking, boating, kayaking, canoeing, biking, bird-watching, boat tours ■ Contact the park, 2 County Rd. 5, R.R. 3, Mallorytown, ON K0E 1R0; phone 613-923-5261. www.parkscanada.gc.ca/sli

COMPOSING ONE OF CANADA's smallest national parks, and the oldest east of the Rockies, these jewel-like islands and tufted rock islets resemble bits of cork expelled from Lake Ontario's northeast corner by the pressure of the St. Lawrence River. The native Huron call the islands Manitouana, "garden of the great spirit," in keeping with a legend that says the islands are petals of divine flowers scattered in the river.

More prosaically, the islands are the eroded hilltops of the Frontenac Arch, an isthmus joining the Canadian Shield and Adirondack Mountains. Some 10,000 years ago, retreating glaciers exposed the hilltops; glacial meltwater then engorged the St. Lawrence, transforming the hilltops into islands—approximately 1,825 of them, far exceeding the much

St. Lawrence Islands National Park

ballyhooed "thousand." Drawn by the moderating effects of the Great Lakes, which created protected microclimates, plants and animals colonized the area over the centuries. The vegetation that grows in the thin soil of these rugged islands clings tenaciously to craggy outcroppings.

The region's relatively moderate climate attracts species that would otherwise have reached the northern limits of their range farther south. These include the park's symbol, the pitch pine, a southern variety that makes its only Canadian homes here and in southern Quebec. Certain animal species rarely found in Canada thrive here as well, such as Canada's largest reptile, the black rat snake, which can grow to 8 feet. Eight other species of snake live in the park, as well as six species of salamander, five of turtle, and nine of frog or toad.

Vegetation on the islands is equally remarkable, boasting more than 800 species of flowering plants. Many islands have plant species found nowhere else in the archipelago. Grenadier and Hill Islands are two of the few islands in the park that sustain an interior wetland. Only Hill Island supports the wild calla, which flourishes in the isle's narrow ravines.

Few mammals make their homes in the park, but the birdlife, whether permanent or temporary, is impressive. During the spring and fall migrations, the islands attract canvasback ducks, scaup, and mergansers. You will undoubtedly spot blue herons winging low over the water as well as (in spring) ospreys nesting in the tops of pines or spruces. In winter, keep your eyes trained for bald eagles as they dive the river for fish or other prey. You may even surprise a few wild turkeys.

The park was created in 1904 when the Mallory family bequeathed a small piece of St. Lawrence shore to the Canadian government, stipulating that it be set aside as a park. Nine more islands already owned by the Canadian government were then annexed. Parcel by small parcel, the park has continued to grow over the years.

To a large degree the United States and Canada share the Thousand Islands (not the park, the islands themselves), and most of them have long been "colonized" by vacationers. Cottages, houses, docks, boathouses—and, not uncommonly, mansions, improbable in both size and opulence—virtually smother the little islands on which they perch. At the beginning of the 20th century the area was known as The Millionaires' Playground, local pride claiming a serious rivalry to Newport, Rhode Island. Tour boats still stop for visitors to gawk at what remains of Boldt Castle, located on American soil. George Boldt, then owner of New York's Waldorf Astoria Hotel, designed this 124-room palace as a tribute to his wife, Louise, and had his engineers reshape the island into a heart. Alas, Louise died before the work was finished, and Boldt never completed his dream.

In summer, hundreds of boats wander among the islands—runabouts, yachts of varying sizes, "motorized cocktail bars," canoes, kayaks, and, frequently, oceangoing freighters on their way up the St. Lawrence Seaway, bound, perhaps, for Toronto or Chicago. The mighty ships appear strangely hallucinatory as they pass among the tiny islands and small bobbing boats.

Despite areas of high activity, you can still find a small uninhabited island with a sunny rock outcropping to idle away a few hours, listening to little more than the soul-easing symphony of lapping water, croaking frogs, and whistling shorebirds.

What to See and Do

Driving Tour
The **Thousand Islands Parkway** follows the St. Lawrence for 22 miles between Gananoque and Butternut Bay, near Brockville. You can't always see the river from the parkway, but dozens of turnouts offer fine views. The skydeck atop the **Thousand Islands International Bridge** over Hill Island rises 400 feet, and comes complete with an elevator for non-stairmasters. From here, enjoy splendid views of both sides of the frontier dividing the United States and Canada.

Hiking and Biking
A paved bike path parallels the Thousand Islands Parkway and passes the Mallorytown Visitor Center, offering an alfresco alternative (and slower pace) to the driving tour. In May, wildflowers, including trillium, the provincial flower of Ontario, carpet the area. Near the village of Ivy Lea, the trail

Swimming at Mallorytown, St. Lawrence Islands National Park

reveals breathtaking views over Hill and Wellesley Islands as well as others. Many of the islands have hiking trails, some with interpretive signs. You can set out on the mile-long **Mainland Nature Trail** that starts at the Mallorytown Landing for a leisurely amble through mixed deciduous and evergreen forest.

Boat Tours

Many park visitors arrive in their own boats, but tour operators and boat rental outfitters at Rockport, Gananoque, and Mallorytown provide services, too. In summer, tour boats offer four- to five-hour cruises, departing daily from the town of Kingston *(call 888-855-4555)*. Cruises available through tour companies in Gananoque, Rockport, and Ivy Lea sometimes stop at Boldt Castle.

Camping

Commercial campgrounds and marinas are scattered all along the St. Lawrence. Primitive campsites with wells are available on 13 park islands. Grenadier Island and Mallorytown offer group camping and accept reservations *(call park office)*; all others are first-come, first-served.

Canoeing and Kayaking

"Paddle 1,000," a cooperative tourist and marketing venture *(www.paddle1000.com)*, has identified nine paddling routes of varying difficulty. One popular route departs from Gananoque for a 3-mile paddle past sheltered channels and secluded bays as it winds among the **Admiralty Islands** to Aubrey Island. Here, superb camping awaits under a canopy of oak, ash, and maple. The **Navy Islands route** departs from the town of Ivy Lea for a 2.5- to 3-mile float to Mulcaster Island (only two campsites), where you can hike woodlands of pitch pine, cedar, and juniper, and descend ravines of towering hemlock. ■

Les Sentiers de l'Estrie

■ 100 miles long ■ Between Kingsbury, Quebec and Vermont border ■ Best season fall ■ Camping, hiking ■ Contact Les Sentiers de l'Estrie, C.P. 93, Sherbrooke, QC J1H 5H5; phone 450-297-0654.

STRIKING OUT FROM MONTRÉAL and heading south across the St. Lawrence River, you'll discover Quebec's Eastern Townships, a bucolic agglomeration of peaceful valleys, prosperous farms, vacation homes of varying extravagance, lakes, forests, scenic small towns—and the rugged spine of the Appalachians, thrusting northeastward from Vermont. Along this high ridge of mountains, amateurs and enthusiasts achieved enough right-of-way agreements with hundreds of landowners to carve out the remarkable Estrie Trail, which traverses private land for almost its entire length.

The Appalachians are an ancient range, their summits usually worn and rounded with age. One of the range's higher Canadian peaks, Sommet Rond (Round Summit), just tops 3,150 feet. Covered in a luxuriant growth of mixed forest—maple, birch, beech, and oak—the slopes of the mountains and hills are shot through with scarlet and gold in the fall. Interspersed with winking blue lakes, valleys are dotted with farms—their fields, in season, gilded with tasseling corn, their orchards yielding crimson apples. It is a comfortable landscape, lush and forgiving, to which many Montréalers repair on weekends to swim, to play, or to hike the Estrie Trail. Numerous vantage points open onto scenes of unhurried peace and ease—perhaps the harvesting of crops from late-summer fields or the billowing sails of boats skimming the lakes far below.

Most hikers, on the advice of the trail association—the nonprofit Les Sentiers de l'Estrie Inc.—head north to south, no matter what section of trail they're on. The trail sections, however, are numbered southwest to northeast, since the trail will eventually extend farther north. As the trail continues south, it becomes wilder and more remote until the final two stages near the Vermont border, where it demands true wilderness savvy. Along many sections of the trail, the damage done by the horrific ice storm of 1998 is still visible, with broken trees struggling to rebound. Detailed topographic maps and a guidebook in English with a useful French glossary are available from the trail association.

Multiple access points and the trail's propinquity to many towns and villages allow visitors considerable flexibility in how far they hike. Shuttle services are not available, but there is usually ample parking at access points and, with permission, at nearby restaurants or motels. White and red blazes clearly mark the trail, but signs are in French—and read "Les Sentiers de l'Estrie" rather than "Estrie Trail." The initials SE are the French shorthand for the main trail itself.

Most visitors to the area spend a week or more and take time to explore a few of the villages and resorts in the valleys. There are a number of places to stay, ranging from elegant inns to rudimentary campgrounds. Nine campsites are available along the route, but they limit your stay to two nights and prohibit campfires.

What to See and Do

Hiking the Trail

Divided into eight stages with multiple access points, the trail includes seven continuous sections and one much farther north, numbered 30 in anticipation of stages 8 to 29, which will eventually come in between.

The **Kingsbury Section** (Stage 7) begins in the village of the same name and continues for 10 miles to its end at Hwy. 222, winding through a glacial valley called the Gulf and climbing a ridge with splendid views of the picturesque **Rivière au Saumon.** A 400-yard side trail leads to the river's banks, with pleasant meadows for picnicking amid a profusion of wildflowers and wild strawberries. Another side trail leads down to **Lac Miller.** Near the end of the section, a sharp ascent to **Lac La Rouche cliff** rewards you with views of Mont Orford, Mont Carré, Mont des Trois Lacs, as well as lakes Brompton and La Rouche. No camping is permitted in this section, but parking is available at both ends.

Traversing 8.8 miles of old forestry roads from the McKenzie Beach Campground on Hwy. 222, the **Brompton Section** (Stage 6) affords high vantage points for spectacular views and culminates in the magnificent lookout from **Mont Carré** (*accessed from a side trail*). After a climb of about 2,300 feet, you'll look down on Carbuncle Bay and the Monts Stoke. The next lookout a few hundred yards farther along reveals the Mont des Trois Lacs and Mont Orford.

Les Sentiers de l'Estrie

Clear-cutting along this part of the trail, however, has exacted a visual as well as an ecological toll. The section ends at Hwy. 220 near Lac Fraser Campground. No camping is permitted along stage 6.

From its trailhead at Lac Fraser Campground, the **Orford Section** (Stage 5) travels 16 miles to its end at a log bridge in a valley that lies hard against the southern flank of Mont Orford. **Milepost 8,** at the summit of Bear Mountain, affords a magnificent 360-degree panorama of the region. The trail passes through **Mont Orford Provincial Park** and intersects a network of more than 50 miles of other park trails, many of them offering generous views of **Mont Orford** itself. Side trails up Mont Chauve (1,900 feet) and to the Orford summit (2,798 feet) are

strenuous but will reward you with fine views of Lac Memphrémagog and the town of Magog, as well as the summits of Owls Head and Mont Giroux. The Lac Stukely Campground lies in the heart of the park.

The **Bolton Section** (Stage 4) takes you from Rte. 112 *(park at Ronde Point Motel, less than a mile east of trailhead)* along 18.3 miles of fairly new trail blazed through rocky terrain, including a few sharp scrambles past waterfalls and up streambeds. In the process, you'll cross the summits of **Mont Chagnon** and **Mont Foster,** where a fairly new observation tower enhances your view of the surrounding hills and lakes. Picnic tables here may encourage you to linger before striking out again. The Mont Glen ski area marks the end of the trail for this section. Camping along the trail is not permitted, but a campground at nearby Lac Trousers welcomes hikers.

Winding through the scenic **Bolton Pass,** the **Glen Section** (Stage 3) covers 8.1 miles between the Mont Glen ski area and Baker Talc Road, near its junction with Rte. 243 (it's safe to park on this road for several days). The trail follows a steep ascent up **Mont Glen,** where a wooden staircase helps you scale the worst parts. The descent is just as precipitous.

Beginning at the intersection of Rte. 243 and Baker Talc Road, the **Echo Section** (Stage 2) continues 10.1 miles through majestic stands of hardwood forest until it ends at a junction with the **Mount Echo Summit Trail.** You'll find several long vistas along the way, with Montréal dimly visible from one of them and the Green Mountains of Vermont from several others. A memorable hike through **Passe du Diable** (Devil's Pass) with its huge boulders and rocky overhangs evokes a dank and gloomy, if somewhat romantic, atmosphere.

The southernmost **Sutton Section** (Stage 1) crosses numerous small streams on its 13.8-mile trek from Mont Echo almost to the U.S. border. The landscape here is less tame, the wildlife less timid. Along the way, you'll pass through **Le Nombril** (The Navel), so named for its curious dimple shape—the junction point of three surrounding mountains. The **Nymphes Waterfall** area draws picnickers. Five miles farther along, you'll come to a shelter perched at 2,755 feet. The trail ends at Glen Sutton, 7.5 miles shy of Vermont.

The "exiled" **Chapman Section** (Stage 30) of the trail winds across **Monts Stoke** for about 6 miles, beginning and ending near the village of Stoke. Its highest point, the summit of Mont Chapman (2,148 feet), caps a small circular trail with views northeast to Mont Ham, southeast to Mont Megantic, and west toward the Mont Orford park. ■

Southern trailhead, Les Sentiers de l'Estrie

Ottawa River Valley from Huron Lookout, Gatineau Park

Gatineau Park

■ 89,661 acres ■ 7.5 miles northeast of Ottawa's Parliament Hill ■ Best months Feb., July, and Oct. ■ Camping, hiking, fishing, cross-country skiing, snowshoeing, wildlife viewing ■ Camping fee ■ Contact the park, 33 Scott Rd., Chelsea, QC J9B 1A1, phone 819-827-2020; or National Capital Commission, phone 800-465-1867. www.capcan.ca/gatineau/eng_index.html

STRADDLING THE EDGE of the Canadian Shield between the Ottawa and Gatineau Rivers, Gatineau Park comprises a triangle of forested hills and limpid lakes within sight of the confines of Ottawa, the capital of Canada. The park's impressive Eardley Escarpment, a 1,000-foot-high cliff that delineates the edge of the Canadian Shield, gives you extensive views of the Ottawa River Valley along its 18-mile length (best view: Champlain Lookout). And even though Ottawa's urban sprawl can be made out from some of the park's vantage points, you can spend a peaceful interlude by a quiet lake and not see a soul.

Some 50 lakes are found in the park, home to 40 species of fish, especially bass, yellow perch, and trout. Substantial populations of beaver (the national emblem) and of white-tailed deer live in the park as well. Wolves come and go, their haunting howls sometimes heard, their spectral presence seldom glimpsed. Gatineau's black bears tend to shy away from people and rarely create a problem.

Because of the park's proximity to Ottawa, sections have been preempted for government service and are either off limits to the public or hold historical relevance. Mousseau Lake (formerly Harrington Lake), the summer home of the prime minister, is something like a Canadian Camp David. A conference center now rises on the shores of Meech Lake and plays host to high-level political meetings. Open to the public, the Mackenzie King Estate on Kingsmere Lake served as the summer residence of Canada's prime minister during World War II. The grounds of the estate display a collection of artsy, imported ruins. After King's death, rumors circulated that he had held seances with his dead mother and that he had communicated with spirits through Pat, his pet terrier.

Gatineau counts almost 7.5 million visitors annually. Most people come in summer, when long lines may form at the entrance gates. Gatineau's crisp, cold winters bring reliable snowfall and many sunny days, making for superb cross-country skiing and snowshoeing. As the first frosts of autumn settle upon hillsides blanketed in mixed deciduous forest, blinding scarlets and brilliant golds sear the park. Counterpoint to the blaze of autumn, softly hued spring, which arrives in late April or early May, draws visitors seeking an end to the rigors of winter. Then the park comes alive with the calls of migrating birds and other animals raising their young (the resident baby porcupines are particularly enchanting). In spring and early summer, carry insect repellent to ward off the black flies; they won't relent until the heat of summer descends.

What to See and Do

Hiking

The park's 77 miles of hiking trails include **Pink Lake Trail,** a leisurely 1.5-mile amble around the lake's perimeter, from the parking lot off Gatineau Parkway. Along the way, mature forest, leafy and cool in summer, offers relief from the heat. The mile-long **King Mountain Trail** begins at its parking lot near Black Lake and leads past lovely views of the broad Ottawa River Valley. Follow mile-long **Champlain Trail** to the top of the **Eardley Escarpment,** where informative panels explain the cliff's unique geology. A 3-mile hike along the **Luskville Falls Trail** begins at the village of Luskville's picnic grounds and likewise leads you up the escarpment, whence the falls descend. Detailed maps of park trails are for sale at the visitor center in Chelsea, off Hwy. 5.

Pink Lake, Gatineau Park

Pink Lake

Bright green rather than pink, this body of water takes its name from Samuel Pink, who settled nearby in 1826 and cut blocks of ice from the lake to keep his food fresh in summer. But it is more than just a beautiful gem of a lake lying among lovely hardwood forests: It is one of the very few "meromictic" lakes in Canada, meaning its water does not circulate seasonally; instead, it remains stratified year-round.

Lake water typically mixes each spring and fall as surface and bottom temperatures reach equilibrium. The turnover replenishes oxygen and provides nutrients to plant and animal life in the lower depths. In Pink Lake, the water mixes only to 43 feet. Below that, a suspended layer of mineral particles and dissolved salts increases the water's density, preventing the two layers from melding. Essentially, the 43-foot upper column rests atop a 22-foot lower column of heavier water devoid of oxygen. This oxygen debt keeps organic material on the bottom from decomposing, enabling scientists to study vegetation, such as pollen grains, dating back to the period when the Champlain Sea covered the region.

Of evolutionary import, the lake's saltwater fish, the three-spined stickleback, has adapted to fresh water over the past 10,000 years.

Winter Activities

Gatineau's ski-trail network—one of the finest in Canada—includes easy and difficult sections. Close to 125 miles of graded trails wind through deciduous forests and gentle meadows. Some 90 miles of trail are groomed for classic Nordic skiing, while about 50 of these allow for skate skiing—a kind of energetic skating on skis that requires more room than the push-and-glide style of traditional skiing. Another 35 miles are designed for snowshoers and winter hikers.

You'll find heated shelters at intervals along many trails. Some are patrolled by park staff watching for skiers in trouble (temperatures may fall to minus 30°F in winter). The 20-mile-long **"Highway 1" trail** starts near the park's Chelsea entrance and runs deep into the interior. Contact the visitor center for trail maps, passes, and information about ski conditions.

Camping

The park is open to both winter and summer camping. Five winter campsites have been set up in the northern Philippe Lake sector of the park, a 2-mile ski or snowshoe trek from the nearest parking lot. The shelters are not heated, but firewood is provided and drinking water is available nearby (reservations required; per person, per night fee). In summer, three campgrounds are open in the park: Philippe Lake with 246 campsites; Taylor Lake (semiwilderness family camping) with 33; and La Pêche Lake (designed for canoe camping) with 35 campsites among 12 locations. (Fee; reservations accepted by phone from mid-May to mid-Oct. at 819-456-3016, by fax only rest of year at 819-827-1210) ■

Réserve Faunique La Vérendrye

■ 3.3 million acres ■ Western Quebec, 175 miles north of Ottawa via Hwys. 105 and 117 ■ Best season summer ■ Camping, canoe camping, hiking, canoeing, fishing ■ Contact Sepaq, R.R. 1, Montcerf, QC J0W 1N0; phone 819-438-2017. www.sepaq.com/en/

EVEN THE MOST STALWART outdoor adventurer would be hard-pressed to explore more than a fraction of the massive Réserve Faunique La Vérendrye. Nearly half the size of Belgium, it cradles more than 4,000 lakes. Hwy. 117 from Montréal to Val d'Or cuts northwest through the reserve, providing access to its considerable recreational activities. Even by the generous standards of La Mauricie (see pp. 100-103) or Laurentides (see pp. 104-106), where people are few, La Vérendrye is a sparsely populated sanctuary.

These are the traditional hunting and trapping grounds of the Algonquin Indians. In times gone by, they were also prime trading territory for the *coureurs de bois*—combination explorers, trappers, guides, and warriors—and European fur trappers, who exploited the area as a main source of beaver for the fur industry. The Grand Lac-Victoria Beaver Reserve, one of ten such reserves in Quebec in which aboriginal people are allowed to trap and hunt, encompasses about three-quarters of the reserve. Some 700 Algonquin still live here, making this the only reserve in the province with a permanent native population.

Indeed, their presence was one of the reasons the reserve was created, in 1928. About 40 Algonquin from the Lac Barriére Band and 30 from the Grand Lac-Victoria Band currently trap in the reserve, but you're not likely to see them at work; most of their traplines are far from recreational activities.

Named for the first European explorer to sight the Rockies—Pierre Gaultier de la Vérendrye—the reserve tends to attract the self-sufficient wilderness adventurer. But activities are available for the less hardy, and even for families.

The reserve's four reception posts are at the north and south entrances, at Lac Rapide, and at the reserve's main center, Le Domaine—a combination outfitter, rendezvous point, lodge, and family resort.

Chutes Roland, Réserve Faunique La Vérendrye

Lac Roland, Réserve Faunique La Vérendrye

....

What to See and Do

Canoe Camping and Boating

Literally hundreds of canoe routes traverse the reserve's lakes, ranging from short scenic paddles to strenuous, 30-day-long wilderness circuits. *(Visitors should be aware that leeches are common in northern lakes, and take appropriate precautions.)*

Located 34 miles from the southern entrance to La Vérendrye, east of Hwy. 117, Le Domaine rents equipment as well as canoes and powerboats (ask which lakes allow the latter). The expert staffers at Canot-Camping La Vérendrye at Le Domaine will help canoeists assess their abilities. Be-

sides providing instruction, they can outfit visitors with canoes, equipment, and supplies. The staff is also essential for keeping paddlers abreast of the latest trail information, including which portages are flooded in the spring. The facility is open from early or mid-May until Labor Day. The longest portage on all the 500 miles of marked routes and 880 miles of unmarked routes is about a mile; most are far shorter.

Beginners tend to start with the **Jean-Peré Circuit,** a fairly easy 15-mile loop that typically entails one overnight stay. Only a short portage interrupts this dreamy trip through placid lakes dotted with forested islands. A mile after you shove off by canoe from the lodge's busy summer grounds, the sounds of children and families at play recede, and the loudest noise you're likely to hear is the heart-stopping cry of a loon. Later on, if you're less fortunate, you may catch the disconcerting grating of a porcupine chewing on your paddle in the middle of the night.

The most popular long route—the 40-mile **Chochocouane River Circuit**—includes a section that descends the wild Chochocouane River. This is heavy going that demands several portages past precipitous rapids and ledges, giving you a vivid taste of hard-core wilderness travel. Try a seven-day guided river trip, featuring beginner to intermediate white water, with nine portages around a handful of Class IV and Class V rapids and one waterfall. (*Contact Great Canadian Adventure Company, 10190 104 St., No. 300, Edmonton, AB, T5J 1A7. 888-285-1676. info@adventures.ca.*)

Other routes start at the massive Dozois Reservoir, a bit overwhelming to beginners when young men from the Algonquin village race up and down the road or charge the lake in Seadoos. But the high energy is confined to the area around the launching point; beyond that it becomes much quieter. (*For information on canoe camping, call 819-435-2331, May-Sept.; 514-252-3001, Oct.-April.*)

Fishing

Le Domaine is known mainly for its fishing. Walleye, pike, and lake trout are abundant in many of the thousand lakes accessible from the lodge. Fishing packages range from simple accommodations with equipment rental to guided fishing expeditions on remote lakes reached by floatplane. You can fish just a few yards from the Le Domaine complex, on **Lac Jean-Peré,** or venture 87 miles north to **Lac Granet,** which abounds with fish. In the central part of the park, **Cabonga and Dozois Reservoirs** (both built in the 19th century as launching points for logging drives) draw anglers with the promise of walleye and pike.

Hiking

Short hikes with interpretive signs are available along many park trails. Try hiking the dark evergreen woods of **Mysterious Forest** from Lac de la Vieille Campground. An understory of soft, springy mosses and oddly out-of-place plants, such as Labrador tea, muffles your footfalls and adds to the air or intrigue. The trail leads you past Lac Glaçon, a depression thought to still hold leftover glacial meltwater. The 3-mile **Lac Roland Falls Trail** starts at Hwy. 117, passes the falls a few hundred yards from the trailhead, and continues past beaver meadows to pristine Lac Malléole. Once you've got your hiking legs, you may want to head for the wilderness on one of the seemingly endless trails.

Where to Stay

At Le Domaine, 28 cabins plus a restaurant and service station provide most amenities. Lac Granet has three more cabins, the Nadagam sector six more. Campers may choose from among 192 serviced and unserviced sites available at Lac de le Vieille, 57 serviced sites at Lac Savary, and an additional 45 at Lac Rapide. ∎

Misty sunrise, Mont Tremblant Provincial Park

Mont Tremblant Provincial Park

■ 375,000 acres ■ Southern Quebec, 87 miles north of Montréal via Hwys. 15 and 117 ■ Best seasons summer-winter ■ Camping, canoe camping, hiking, canoeing, mountain biking, cross-country skiing, snowshoeing ■ Contact the park, chemin du Lac-Supérieur, Lac-Supérieur, QC J0T 1P0; phone 819-688-2281 or -2336. www.sepaq.com/en/

ASK ANY QUEBECOIS, particularly a Montréaler, about Mont Tremblant and inevitably a discourse will follow about the ski resort, detailing its 92 ski runs (highest vertical drop: 2,106 feet; longest run: 2.3 miles), its 46 miles of ski trails, its many restaurants, its full-service hotels and condominiums. Likely left unmentioned, curiously, will be the provincial park of the same name on the other side of the mountain.

Here is a gateway to true wilderness, set in lovely rolling countryside an easy morning's drive from Montréal. Seldom crowded despite its proximity to the bustling city, Quebec's largest provincial park affords nature lovers a quiet and tranquil experience. Within the park's borders lie some 400 lakes, six rivers, and the endless roll of the Laurentides Mountains, most of them covered in a hardwood forest of maple and yellow birch—gloriously scarlet and gold in fall, often blanketed in a 40-inch mantle of snow in winter.

The Laurentian Mountains (the Laurentides) still harbor a reservoir of wild creatures, including black bears, foxes, and moose, as well as wolverines and fishers. White-tailed deer roam the park's southern reaches, their regrettably obvious tails raised as if in surrender. And rumors of cougar sightings have begun to circulate once more (see sidebar p. 97).

The park has three developed zones: **La Diable** in the west, closest to Mont Tremblant and Montréal; **La Pimbina** in the center; and **L'Assomption** in the east. The roads connecting the three are unpaved but easily negotiated, and all three zones have visitor centers and reception stations that furnish maps. La Diable sector hosts the highest number of visitors; it can become crowded in summer and on long weekends. The number of visitors declines as you move east; L'Assomption draws the fewest people.

The developed parts of the three sections cover but a fraction of the park's total terrain. True backcountry and wilderness forays can take visitors into areas rarely seen by humans.

What to See and Do

Hiking

The 51-mile **Grande Randonné Trail** crosses the park in an east-west direction, winding through maple and birch forests and traversing the softly modeled mountains of the Laurentides profile. Beginning at the Lac-Monroe Service Center, the trail includes an 8.7-mile loop to the Croches Falls, followed by a long trek to the St-Donat Reception Station. For this section of the trail, you may want to overnight in one of the four shelters located along the route.

Of several short hiking trails in La Diable sector (most can be accessed at or near the Lac-Monroe Service Center), the easy **Chute du Diable Trail** (less than 1 mile) holds the greatest appeal: Water tumbles beside it through a heavily wooded ravine that is ideal for picnicking.

Also less than a mile long, **Les Chutes Croches Trail** begins 3.5

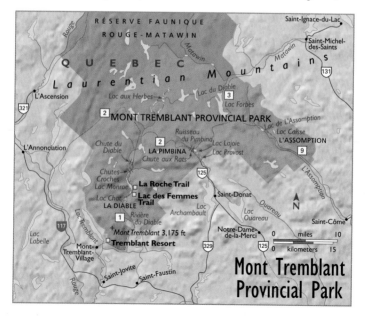

Mont Tremblant Provincial Park

Eastern cougar

Eastern Cougar

For decades the harsh screams of mating cougars have been absent from the eastern Canadian wilderness. Many believed the great cats were extinct here, even though only endangered elsewhere in eastern North America. In the 1990s, however, 11 sightings in New Brunswick and in the Abitibi and Bas-St. Laurent areas suggested that cougars may still make their homes in the more remote mountains of Mont Tremblant park. Despite the lack of a "smoking gun"—a plaster cast of a cougar track, a scat sample, or even a single collected hair—the sheer number of eyewitness accounts points to the animal's rebound.

Second in size only to the jaguar, the eastern cougar is one of the largest of America's great cats. The biggest ever found weighed 220 pounds and was 9 feet long (including the tail).

Protection from hunters and availability of prey—primarily white-tailed deer—do not appear to be crucial in re-establishing the eastern cougar. Instead, the best way to guarantee the great cat's return is to set aside large tracts of undisturbed habitat.

miles north of the service center and provides a relaxing stroll to a small bridge that affords a mesmerizing view of the falls. **La Roche Trail** winds for 3.1 miles through mixed forest and along a small brook, culminating in a startling panorama of the Lac Monroe glacial valley and the spine of Mont Tremblant. Depart from Le Chevreuil campsite for a day's outing along the manageable 10.6-mile **L'Ours Trail** with its fine views of the surrounding landscape. The slightly more difficult **Le Centenaire Trail** (5.7 miles) reveals splendid vistas of the River of the Devil and the Boulé Forest.

In La Pimbina, an inviting 6.2-mile trail follows the shores of lakes Provost and Lajoie until it heads inland to the Chute aux

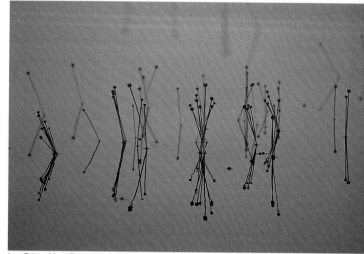

Lac Cabot, Mont Tremblant Provincial Park

Rats. Here Pimbina Creek somersaults 56 feet into a gorge set amid dense forest.

Six miles north of the reception station in L'Assomption sector, the 2.7-mile round-trip **Grandes-Vallées Trail** yields views of two picture-perfect valleys with azure lakes nestled in their centers. From the trail's pinnacle you can see for miles over Lac de L'Assomption and Lac Caisse.

Canoeing

Most people come here for the remote tranquillity of the deep woods; for that kind of experience, there's nothing quite like backcountry canoeing.

La Diable sector takes its name from the Rivière du Diable, or River of the Devil, which rises in Lac du Diable in the far northern part of the park. After exiting the park, it merges with the Rouge and then the Ottawa Rivers. No one knows for certain why the river bears such a sinister name: The

Chute du Diable is a dramatic enough site, and **Chutes Croches,** a series of cascades over glistening rocks, is admittedly turbulent. Yet for the most part the river charms rather than bedevils canoeists, unspooling before them in a series of sinuous S-bends that wind through dense hardwood forests before dropping into Lac Monroe. The **Diable canoe route** starts at the Lac aux Herbes Campground and covers 29 miles through rapids that range from Class I to Class IV, with a 4-mile portage halfway through around a series of waterfalls. (*To arrange for a shuttle, call 819-688-2281.*)

Far less developed than La Diable sector, La Pimbina promises fewer people and ideal paddling. Canoes may be rented at Lac Provost beach, where you can also cool off in the lake's cold, invigorating waters (*lifeguards on duty in summer*).

The canoeing in L'Assomption ranges from a peaceful drift down the sector's namesake river *(put-in at Lac de l'Assomption; some rapids follow)* to the spectacular **Six Lakes canoe route** *(put-in at Lac Crapaud).*

Mountain Biking

Choose from more than 35 miles of park trails—a mix of dirt roads and jeep tracks—the majority located in La Diable's **Lac Monroe area.** In La Pimbina, set out from the St-Donat Reception Station for the **Lac Cassagne** (10.5 miles) and **Descente** (4.8 miles) **Trails.**

Cross-country Skiing

More than 53 miles of patrolled and groomed cross-country trails lace the park in the sectors of La Diable and La Pimbina, beginning at the Saint-Donat Reception Station and the Lac Monroe Service Center. All trails are marked with a recommended skill level. Warming huts along several trails sleep eight people *(reservations required).* Skiers, bundle up! Temperatures can plummet to minus 40°F or lower.

For backcountry skiing, the main trail covers around 71 miles,

with four huts spaced from 6.2 to 13 miles apart along the way. You must reserve in advance, and check in with park officials on arrival. The park advises winter skiers to always travel in a group. *(For hut reservations, call Mon.-Fri. 819-688-2281.)* Visitors can rent cross-country skis and snowshoes at the Lac-Monroe Service Center or the Saint-Donat Reception Station.

Snowshoeing

La Diable's snowshoe trails start at Lac Monroe and include the La Roche Trail, which skirts Lac Monroe and Lac Chat on a 3.1-mile round-trip. In La Pimbina, try the 3.1-mile loop trail from the Saint-Donat Reception Station.

Where to Stay

La Diable provides 629 campsites and 178 canoe-camping sites. Eight lakeside cottages in L'Assomption, with showers and hot water, hold from 2 to 18 people (mid-May–mid-Oct.). L'Assomption also offers 86 campsites and 29 canoe-camping sites. La Pimbina has another 265 campsites. ■

Snowboarding, Laurentides Mountains, Quebec

La Mauricie National Park

■ 132,000 acres ■ Halfway between Québec (120 miles) and Montréal (125 miles) off Hwy. 55 ■ Best seasons summer-fall; only southern sections open in winter ■ Camping, canoe camping, hiking, canoeing, fishing, cross-country skiing ■ Contact the park, 794 5th St., P.O. Box 758, Shawinigan, QC G9N 6V9; phone 819-538-3232. www.parcscanada.gc.ca/parks/quebec/mauricie/en/index.html

ROLLING HILLS INTERSECT BROAD VALLEYS shimmering with peaceful lakes and rivers throughout this gently contoured land. Unlike the more dramatic Réserve Faunique des Laurentides (see pp. 104-06) to the east, La Mauricie conveys graciousness and placidity. Here visitors relax with tranquil hikes and lazy paddles, forgoing the ardor of strenuous back-country treks and the rush of white water offered elsewhere.

Most of the trees in La Mauricie's forests have been growing undisturbed for only 30 years or so. Around 1850, loggers and river men swarmed the area, cutting down forests of massive, 400-year-old red and white pine, followed by the felling of less valuable white spruce and birch. Around the beginning of the 20th century, the pulp and paper industry moved in on the area, and La Mauricie became the self-proclaimed "world capital of newsprint." Industry giant Consolidated Paper

Wapizagonke Lake, La Mauricie National Park

ruled over the territory until it was declared a national park in 1970; by then, however, more than half the original forest was gone.

Today the new forest shelters more mixed species than the old with fewer grand trees, yet it is still beautiful. Unimpeded by logging drives, its streams once again flow clear and free.

In about 1880, loggers began competing with wealthy American and Canadian businessmen who descended on the region to fish and hunt. Large private game clubs were formed—the Shawinigan in 1883, the Laurentian in 1886, the Commodore in 1906—and their ranks continued to grow until by 1970 some 16 operated in the area. Members were given dominion over vast tracts of land, and they adorned the shores of Lac à la Pêche with grand lodges (*maisons à folie,* according to the locals).

Two of those "houses of foolishness"—the Wabenaki Lodge and the Andrew Lodge—still stand, although they are now owned by the federal government and have been classified as "heritage buildings." The two lodges are open year-round, and they are furnished with heat, electricity, and running water—and even a room for waxing skis. *(Call 819-537-4545 for information and reservations.)*

Whereas the clubs are credited with protecting and preserving area wildlife, they regrettably introduced non-native species of fish. Many of these now thrive, harming the native brook trout.

Black-eyed Susans, La Mauricie National Park

What to See and Do

Canoeing

With more than 150 lakes, and at least 30 rivers and streams reachable from the parkway that follows the southern edge of the park from the St-Mathieu to the St-Jean-des-Piles Reception Centers, avid paddlers will be right at home here. One of the most popular lakes, **Wapizagonke** is long and twisty, its banks a tableau of beaches alternating with cliffs, marshy inlets, and crystal-clear streams. Paddling large canoes, park staffers conduct interpretive tours on the lake for older children.

Passing from Wapizagonke to **Anticagamac Lake** entails a long (1.5-mile) but worthwhile portage. A massive cliff overhangs the great bay where the portage ends; thereafter that, visitors will find water and meadows rich in wildlife.

For a 15-mile excursion that takes several days, put in at the Wapizagonke Campground, then paddle north to Lac Houle and

through Lac Dauphinais to the east. From there you can travel up to Lac des Cinq, La Mauricie's northernmost lake, or head south again to Lac Soumire and pull out at the parkway. A one-day excursion to **Waber Falls** involves a 5-mile canoe trip on Wapizagonke Lake, followed by a 3.7-mile hike. The hike is not difficult and yields many lovely views of the countryside. After your hike, cool off with a brisk plunge into the icy falls.

Fishing

Brook, or speckled, trout offers the best fishing in the park, accounting for almost 90 percent of the catch. Occasionally lake trout, bass, and pike may be fished on 30 of the park's lakes, including Dauphinais and Giron; permission is assigned by a daily drawing at 7 a.m. at the park's two reception centers, where you can purchase a one-day fishing license. The season runs from the last weekend in

May to the first Monday in September.

Hiking

An extensive network of hiking trails cuts through the park's varied topography. Opening onto scenes of a distant valley or a stand of red maples set against a backdrop of broken hills and black spruces, the trail vistas often appear to have jumped from an artist's canvas.

Among the more interesting hikes is the **Cascades Trail,** which loops 1.5 miles from the Shewenegan picnic area through mature maple forest before arriving at a waterfall. The loop connects to **Les Falaises Trail,** a 3-mile hike to the top of the escarpment above Wapizagonke Lake. **Les Deux-Criques Trail,** a steep but scenic 10-mile loop from the Rivière-à-la-Pêche Reception Center, reveals the magnificent falls of the **Ruisseau du Fou.** Also from the reception center, the new **Laurentian Trail** takes hikers on a 46-mile trek into rugged backcountry, where stands of maple share the forest with those of pine and fir, some of them first-growth. Unless you have arranged to have your car waiting for you, the trail concludes with 18 miles of highway hiking.

Cross-country Skiing

Regular snowfalls, heated shelters, and groomed trails make La Mauricie a popular place for Nordic skiing. Many trails start at Rivière-à-la-Pêche.

Where to Stay

Wapizagonke, Mistagance, and Rivière-à-la-Pêche provide a total

Réserve Faunique Mastigouche

Hugging the western boundary of La Mauricie and even more vast in scope, Mastigouche (800-665-6527) encompasses 607 square miles, 417 lakes, and 13 rivers and streams. Maple forest still blankets much of this wildlife reserve, now fully recovered after the droughts of the 1980s and the acid rain scare of the same decade.

Private hunt clubs held sway here until 1971, when Mastigouche was incorporated as a wildlife reserve. Today it lures visitors with the promise of fine canoe camping circuits and pleasant waterside cabins. While hiking to one of several picturesque waterfalls or canoeing the lakes, visitors may glimpse moose and black bears, or smaller mammals such as hare, mink, and porcupines. The speckled trout fishing here is considered superb.

of 517 campsites, some accessible by vehicle. For canoe campers, more than 200 backcountry sites are scattered among a dozen lakes. Although they're open year-round, not all have fireplaces, and campfires are prohibited in the park. Pit toilets and bear poles for storing food out of reach are provided. Make reservations for lodges and backcountry campsites with Info-Nature Mauricie (819-537-4555); for campground reservations, call 819-533-7272. ■

Réserve Faunique des Laurentides

■ 3.2 million acres ■ 30 miles north of Québec via Hwy. 175 ■ Camping, hiking, backpacking, rafting, kayaking, fishing, mountain biking, snowmobiling, cross-country skiing, snowshoeing, canoeing ■ Contact the reserve, 700 boul. Lebourgneuf, Suite 11, Québec, QC G2J 1E2; phone 418-528-6868 or 800-665-6527 (reservations). www.sepaq.com/en/

NOT TO BE CONFUSED WITH the Laurentians (Laurentides, in French) resort and vacation area associated with Mont Tremblant, the massive wilderness of the Laurentides reserve is one of Quebec's little-known treasures. This despite its proximity to the provincial capital—not much more than 30 minutes by car. The vast maze of woodlands, lakes, rivers, mountains, and valleys has been protected as a "forest area" since 1895 and as a wildlife reserve since 1981. Anglers and other outdoors people are drawn to the area by the abundant native brook trout that swim its lakes and rivers, as well as by the reserve's dependable and long-lasting mantle of snow, which ensures superior cross-country skiing.

The Laurentides reserve surrounds two parks and manages some of their services and facilities. The **Parc des Grands-Jardins** *(418-439-1227)*, a subarctic wilderness that is home to caribou, has been designated a UNESCO World Biosphere Reserve.

Also within the reserve's embrace is the **Parc de la Jacques-Cartier** *(418-848-3169)*, which includes most of the Rivière Jacques-Cartier. Here visitors will find the area's most spectacular scenery. The magnificent U-shaped glacier valley that holds the often turbulent Jacques-Cartier is a 1,800-foot-deep trench carved between two steep mountainsides. Owing in part to this exceptional canyon, in 1981 the national government in Ottawa nominated the Jacques-Cartier as one of Canada's great Heritage Rivers.

The reserve's landscape is very green and slightly mountainous. Covered in conifers and stands of white birch and balsam fir, the tallest peaks barely exceed 2,000 feet. The Parc des Grands-Jardins, in the far eastern section of the reserve, is more akin to taiga and tundra—dense, impenetrable forests of black spruce and acres of lichen and moss as thick as a luxurious carpet. The Laurentides caribou herd spends most of its time here, sustaining a stable population of wolves. Other mammals in large numbers share the reserve as well, and any foray on foot or by water is likely to reward you with a sighting of a moose, black bear, fox, lynx, beaver, or hare.

For those less confident of a solitary adventure into the Laurentides wilderness, the reserve will arrange guided, interpreted tours that feature wolf and black bear observations in the wild. Also available are guided canoe trips and hikes to explore and learn about some of the area's unique geological formations.

Pikauba River, Réserve Faunique des Laurentides

What to See and Do

Thanks to its extensive trail system and the canoeing opportunities along its river, the Jacques-Cartier park in the eastern part of the reserve is perhaps the most accessible. A detailed trail map for hiking, backpacking, and canoeing is available for purchase at the park's interpretation center.

Hiking

More than 40 miles of hiking trails have been laid out on either side of the **Jacques-Cartier River.** Many treat walkers to picturesque views of the water.

Although most of the area provides a mix of unpaved roads and easy hikes, some trails (notably **Les Loups**) wind through sharply steeper terrain that rewards you with spectacular vistas. Backcountry campsites lie along the river.

Boating

Advanced white-water kayakers will exult in the two-day, 25-mile stretch of the Jacques-Cartier River that begins where the river shoots through the 1,500-foot walls of the narrow **Taureau Gorge.** A far gentler 10-mile section below the gorge is suitable for beginners. For both trips, shuttles will take you and your equipment upriver from the park's interpretive center off Hwy. 175.

The park's southern end affords mild white-water rafting in the summer. For a wet and wild ride, try rafting below the park at **Tewkesbury.** Call Les Excursions Jacques-Cartier *(418-848-5969)* for information on all rafting.

Mountain Biking

The majority of the park's eight biking trails are easy to moderate, yet some sections are steep enough to give even the most experienced cyclists a major adrenaline rush. You can rent bikes at the park's interpretation center.

Cross-country Skiing

Miles of park trails are suitable for cross-country skiing. None are groomed, but the superb snow cover makes breaking new ground a treat. From ski headquarters at Camp Mercier, ski loops fan out for two- to five-day treks, with shelters situated at various points along the way.

Where to Stay

The reserve offers 110 cabins, some equipped with electricity and running water. Three campgrounds with 181 sites provide boats and access to specific fishing lakes and rivers. Jacques-Cartier park has many backcountry sites with pit toilets and picnic tables. ■

Understory, Réserve Faunique des Laurentides

Snow geese, Cap Tourmente National Wildlife Area

Cap Tourmente National Wildlife Area

■ 2,400 acres ■ North shore of St. Lawrence River, 31 miles east of Québec via Rte. 138 and Hwy. 360 ■ Best seasons spring and fall ■ Bird-watching ■ Contact Canadian Wildlife Service, 570 chemin du Cap-Tourmente, St-Joachim-de-Montmorency, QC G0A 3X0; phone 418-827-4591 (April-Oct.), 418-827-3776 (Nov.-March). www.qc.ec.gc.ca/faune/faune/html/nwa_ct.html

EMBRACING THE NORTH SHORE of the St. Lawrence River 31 miles east of Québec is **Cap Tourmente,** a strikingly beautiful confluence of river, mountain, and coastal marsh. The area was originally protected by private hunting clubs from Québec that were determined to keep anything from threatening the marshland habitat—and hence their quarry. The Canadian government took over the site in the mid-1960s, transforming it into a national wildlife area. Small portions of the reserve are still open to limited hunting today.

Cap Tourmente's vast marshland of American bulrushes attracts greater snow geese migrating from their breeding grounds on Baffin Island to the St. Lawrence River. The birds leave the Arctic by the beginning of September for their 2,000-mile flight, which they could probably accomplish in five or six days, yet they do not appear on the river until the first half of October. Apparently they pass those lost weeks somewhere on Quebec's Ungava Peninsula, but the precise location remains unknown. The snow geese generally hit the St. Lawrence near the mouth of the Saguenay River fjord, then travel upriver to their favorite tidal marshes to roost and feed. They stay at Cap Tourmente for a few days, gathering strength for the final leg of their flight, which takes them to wintering grounds in Virginia and the Carolinas.

The largest concentrations of snow geese—almost 100,000 birds, or one-ninth the global population—can be found at Cap Tourmente from about October 5 to 20. Smaller but still impressive numbers pass through during the spring migrations in April and May.

More than 10 miles of trails and boardwalks have been provided throughout the important viewing areas of the park. One of the best vantage points, 1,968-foot-high Cap Tourmente itself, overlooks a vast tidal marsh, where birds feed along more than 6 miles of muddy shoreline. Observation platforms have also been set up on the edges of the marsh. The wildlife area will rent binoculars to those unfortunate enough to have forgotten theirs.

In addition to the snow geese, more than 290 bird species live in the area, including peregrine falcons, a fairly recent arrival. Forty feeding stations sustain these nonmigratory species in winter. ▪

Parc des Hautes-Gorges-de-la-Rivière-Malbaie

▪ 56,215 acres ▪ 94 miles northeast of Québec via Rte. 138 ▪ Best months June–mid-Oct. Park closed in winter (but day use permitted for ice climbing only) ▪ Camping, hiking, kayaking, canoeing, mountain biking, ice climbing, boat cruising ▪ Contact the park, 4 Maisonneuve, Clermont, QC G4A 1L1; phone 418-439-1227. www.sepaq.com/en/

OVERPOWERING IN THEIR HEIGHT and sheer looming presence, rocky gorges rear above the **Malbaie River** as it twists and carves its way through the surrounding mountains. Thrusting skyward from the riverbed, the sheer cliff dubbed the **Acropolis** hangs 2,600 feet overhead. On the opposite bank, the impressive 1,310-foot-high **Golden Apple** beckons experienced ice climbers to scale its frigid walls. Hikes to the summits of Mont Élie, Mont Jérémie, and Maple Mountain (all just under 3,500 feet) treat visitors with long views of Lac Noir, Ruisseau du Pont, and the valleys of the Malbaie and Martres Rivers.

For naturalists, however, Malbaie Gorges Park holds another fascination: All the vegetation zones of Quebec—from St. Lawrence hardwood forests to mixed northern forests, boreal forest, and tundra—can be found within a very short, very steep distance. The park also draws visitors looking to unwind along bike trails and canoe routes or simply to relax on the boat cruises that ply the Malbaie.

At the confluence of the Malbaie and St. Lawrence Rivers, 94 miles east of Québec, lies the town of La Malbaie. From here an unmarked secondary road will take you to the picturesque village of **St-Aimé-des-Lacs**, about 8 miles distant, where the local school doubles as the home of the Charlevoix Historical Society. The collection holds a small archive of documents (in French, mostly) and photographs about logging in the area before the park's creation.

A **visitor center** is slated to open within the park in 2002. In addition to exhibits on area history, displays will shed light on the park's plants, animals, and geology. ▪

Pointe Noire, Parc Marin du Saguenay-St.-Laurent

Parc Marin du Saguenay-St.-Laurent

■ 70,080 acres ■ 185 miles northeast of Québec via Hwy. 175 or Hwy. 138
■ Best months May-Sept. ■ Camping, hiking, kayaking, bird-watching, whale-watching, boat tours ■ Contact the park, 91 Notre-Dame, Rivière-Éternité, QC G0V 1P0; phone 418-272-3008 or -1509. www.sepaq.com/en/

SOUNDING FROM THE RIVERS' DEPTHS, whales break the water of this marine park where the Saguenay River fjord meets the St. Lawrence. You may spot three or four species of these leviathans during a two-hour cruise. The animals come close to shore, feeding where the two great rivers merge and meld.

The crowd favorites are the 40 or so fin whales that return each year. Some visitors, too, come back season after season, greeting familiar whales as old friends. The largest creatures on the planet after blues, fin whales commonly weigh 50 tons and can reach 80 feet in length. They are easy to recognize by their habit of turning their heads sideways to feed; this allows them to take in massive amounts of krill and shrimp. They then expel the water in spurts through their baleen filters. Certain fin whales have been spotted in the park's waters for more than 30 years.

The growth of both whale-watching and industrial pollution in the area have sparked concern among marine biologists. At times, as many as 20 boats may vie for a sight of the same animals, and some of these craft are substantial: One carries 400 passengers. Additionally, the numbers of whales returning each year may be diminishing, leading environmentalists to speculate that the animals may abandon the area one day.

This joint provincial and national park lying along the Saguenay and the north shore of the St. Lawrence from Gros Cap à l'Aigle to Les Escoumins was originally established because of concerns over the water's high toxins, which were destroying the outstanding marine environment and poisoning the resident beluga whales. Today belugas calve in the river's center. Because Saguenay lies downstream from considerable heavy industry, however, pollution may pose a continued threat to the park's marine environment.

You'll find visitor centers at Tadoussac, Baie Sainte-Marie *(15 miles from Tadoussac)*, and at Baie Éternité, 21.7 miles up the Saguenay.

What to See and Do

Hiking

Apart from the whales, the park's main attraction is spectacular **Saguenay fjord.** Some 65 miles long and an average of 3 miles wide, the fjord boasts cliffs soaring 1,000 feet and higher. The water, frigid and clear, reaches depths exceeding 900 feet. A hiking trail leads from massive **Pointe Noire,** a short ferry ride across the Saguenay from Tadoussac, along the cliffs to Baie Éternité and beyond. This hike is long (more than 40 miles) but not difficult, with splendid views across the fjord. The view from Pointe Noire seems endless; a lookout fitted with telescopes has been constructed at its summit.

Cap de Bon-Désir, about 20 miles north of Tadoussac on Rte. 138, offers grand views up and down the St. Lawrence and fine whale-watching. Try the short 4-mile scramble along the rocky north shore from Tadoussac to the Baie de Moulin à Baude, or the 10-mile hike along the fjord's north shore from Tadoussac to **Pointe à la Passe Pierre,** a promontory often occupied by whale-watchers.

Bird-watching

Areas for watching nesting shorebirds include the tidal flats at **Baie Éternité** (south shore of the Saguenay) and **Baie St-Marguerite** on the Saguenay's north shore. **Tadoussac** has an excellent observation center for birds of prey. ∎

Canadian flag-emblazoned rock, Saguenay region

Réserve Faunique de Port-Cartier– Sept-Îles

■ 1.6 million acres ■ 360 miles east of Québec via Rte. 138 ■ Best season summer ■ Camping, canoe camping, hiking, fishing, wildlife viewing ■ Contact the reserve, 24 boul. des îles, Suite 109, Port-Cartier, QC G5B 2M9; phone 418-766-2524. www.sepaq.com/en/

SWATHED IN BOREAL forest and glinting with waterfalls, a thousand lakes, and 15 rivers, this splendid wilderness is little used by its native Quebecois. Perhaps they are spoiled by the surfeit of nature parks they have to choose from, but for the most part they have left this reserve to the Americans and Europeans—particularly the latter, who lack the luxury of endless acres in which to sate their desire for solitude.

Adding to its international appeal, the reserve combines wild countryside with a certain degree of comfort. Cabins at both Lacs Walker and Arthur include such amenities as propane stoves and refrigerators, but the services at Lac Arthur are more rudimentary. The Lac Walker site offers hot showers as well. If you're less of a hedonist, strike out for the reserve's backcountry, which permits camping in most areas.

Forest roads into the park are reasonably well marked, but it's wise to get a map from the reception office located at Port-Cartier off Rte. 138.

What to See and Do

The short **MacDonald** and **Carlos Trails** both lead from campgrounds to eponymous waterfalls, but the most popular activities by far are canoeing, canoe camping, and fishing. Most people combine canoeing and fishing expeditions, seeking out the serenity of more remote Lac Arthur, in the northern sector, and Lac Walker, near the southern end of the park. The latter is a jewel of pristine blue waters surrounded by high hills blanketed in black and white spruce, trembling aspen, balsam fir, and tamarack trees.

Canoeing

Small lakes and rivers entice paddlers in search of peaceful canoeing opportunities. The 32-mile circuit on Lac Walker almost always yields some of the park's abundant wildlife. Keep your eyes trained for black bears, wolves, lynx, foxes, beavers, porcupines, otters, and the many ruffed and spruce grouse.

Fishing

The reserve is a treasure for devotees of speckled trout, but if Atlantic salmon is your preference, stretches of the **Rivière aux Rochers** and **Macdonald River** will suit you better. The reserve's fishing packages include equipment, boat, and cabin rental. The fishing supervisor on hand assigns visitors to specific lakes or rivers; his job is to maintain the stock balance and direct you to areas that offer the fishing (and setting) you're after. ■

Migrating eider ducks

Getting Down

More than 20 islands stretch out along the St. Lawrence River between the towns of Kamouraska and Tadoussac. In an effort to protect the large number of seabirds that nest here, only a few of the isles are open to visitors. The largest islands are the 2,300-acre Île aux Lièvres, where cottages are available, and the Îles du Pot à l'Eau-de-Vie, where a former lighthouse now functions as a small inn. The five islands known as Les Pèlerins (the Pilgrims) were closed to visitors as of the summer of 2001.

The islands are well known as the nesting habitat for one of North America's largest populations of eiders, the biggest American ducks. Thousands of breeding pairs make their way here each spring, and their nesting season runs through early July. The eiders share the islands with double-crested cormorants, great blue herons, kittiwakes, guillemots, razorbills, and a variety of other birds.

Ornithologist Jean Bédard of Laval University in Québec devised various ways to purchase the islands so that they could be set aside as a sanctuary, including an innovative program for harvesting eider down, or *duvet*. Down-collecting still continues throughout the islands, which are now privately owned by the nonprofit Société Duvetnor—an organization committed to the protection of the islands' important seabird colonies.

Today, the eider population on the islands appears to have stabilized and may even be increasing.

Mingan Archipelago National Park Reserve

■ 108 miles long ■ 540 miles east of Québec via Hwy. 138 ■ Camping, hiking, kayaking, bird-watching, whale-watching, boat tours ■ Best month late June; open June-Sept. ■ Camping permit required ■ Contact the reserve, 1303 De la Digue St., Havre-St.-Pierre, QC G0G 1P0; phone 418-538-3285 (summer), 418-538-3331 (winter). www.parkscanada.gc.ca/mingan

MINGAN DRAWS A LOYAL CLUTCH of visitors who return year after year to immerse themselves in a nature experience that is hard to duplicate elsewhere. The archipelago's extraordinary landscape is wild and unspoiled, yet the islands lie only 1 to 2 miles from certain mainland towns. Remoteness combined with easy access to services add to Mingan's charms.

Barrens and peat bogs, rocky gullies, and eroded limestone sea stacks share the scene with sinkholes and bogs sustaining exquisitely fragile life-forms. Summer twilights—when the scarlet sunsets of the north Gulf of St. Lawrence shore glisten off island rocks—can be mesmerizing. Minke whales blow offshore, sometimes close enough to hit you with their spray, while gray and harbor seals bark hoarsely from the rocks. The tide gurgles in a rocky pool, and the whir of landing seabirds fans the sultry air.

Mingan lies between Rivière St.-Jean to the west and Aquanish to the east. Center for outfitters and boat operators, Havre-St.-Pierre is also the location of one of the park's visitor centers (the other is at Longue-Pointe-de-Mingan, whence boats also depart).

To protect Mingan's fragile ecology, the park carefully manages traffic. Several of the islands are closed to visitors from May until the end of August to protect the habitats of nesting seabirds. Park staffers will let you know which areas are off limits. Travel on the barrens of Île Nue (Naked Island) is not allowed at any time; access is limited to the shoreline and to areas around the campground.

Île d'Anticosti

Deer hunting in a remote setting is the main attraction of this two-million-acre, heavily wooded plug in the Gulf of St. Lawrence south of Mingan.

Celebrated French chocolate manufacturer Henri Menier bought Anticosti in 1895, then imported a small herd of white-tailed deer. Their numbers have since swollen to some 120,000 animals.

If hunting is not your thing, you can walk along the beach and explore the island's limestone geology, evident in its caves and grottoes. Later on, relax at one of the lighthouses that have been transformed into a guesthouse or restaurant. (For information, call 418-686-6313 or 800-463-0863.)

Humpback whale, Mingan Archipelago NPR

What to See and Do

Lodging possibilities in Mingan span a wide range of choices. While some visitors opt for the more elegant accommodations offered by the hotels and bed-and-breakfasts on the mainland, many enjoy camping at one of the park's 42 primitive campsites sprinkled over six islands. Permits for these sites are required.

Every summer the park presents a busy schedule of guided hikes, daily interpretive activities, and boat tours, as well as evening talks in the park's reception and interpretation centers.

Hiking

Thirty miles of hiking trails crisscross the Mingan Archipelago. Île Quarry's 3-mile **Petit Percé Trail** (*trailhead at island wharf*) loops through boreal forest, along steep cliffs, and through barrens and peat bogs. The island also boasts Petit Percé, a smaller version of the pierced rock at the end of the Gaspé Peninsula (see p. 124).

For erosion monoliths and a wide diversity of plant life, try visiting **Île du Fantôme,** named after the wreck of the schooner *Phantom* that went aground here in 1862. **Île du Havre** offers an 8-mile hike along lovely beaches and jagged cliffs. Near the beach, you can explore the vestiges of an old fox farm once run by the Hudson's Bay Company; a group campsite stands nearby. Perhaps most striking of all the islands in the archipelago, **Grosse Île au Marteau** includes splendid cliffs, beaches, shoals, and seabird colonies, all within a circumference of about 2 miles.

Bird-watching

The capelin-rich waters of the Gulf of St. Lawrence attract many species of seabirds, among them the Atlantic puffin (known locally as sea parrot or *calculot*, the calculator, for its habit of nodding frequently as though counting). Two colonies of puffins reside on

Île de la Maison; others live on **Île aux Perroquets** (Puffin Island) and **Île à Calculot des Betchouanes.** Arctic terns, kittiwakes, razorbills, gulls, and cormorants breed on some of the islands. Large eider ducks are found throughout the area.

Whale-watching

The turbulent waters of the Gulf of St. Lawrence circulate in a counterclockwise direction. While the St. Lawrence River stays close to the south shore, waters from the open ocean flow into the gulf along the north shore.

These cold waters and the upwellings they cause along the shore create the nutrient-rich environment responsible for breeding plankton and capelin, which attract many of the whales found throughout the archipelago. The whales, in turn, draw visitors eager to be in their presence.

Minke whales are the most common of the mammals that feed in the park's waters. The best time to see them is in June when they are close to shore, searching out the same capelin that entices the seabirds.

Ten other species of whales visit the area, including humpbacks and fins. Occasionally massive blue whales (the world's largest mammals) materialize, but they tend to remain far offshore, between Île d'Anticosti and the Mingan Archipelago.

Boating

The boat *Croisières Relais Nordik (800-463-0680)* links Havre-St-Pierre to the lower North Shore up to Blanc Sablon.

To reach the Mingan Islands, the park advises visitors to make transportation arrangements with private boat operators. An up-to-date list of local operators is available on the park's website, or you may call the park for a list. Reservations are recommended.

For additional travel information, contact the Duplessis Regional Tourist Association *(888-463-0808; www.tourismecote-nord.com).* ■

Mont Albert summit, Parc de la Gaspésie

Parc de la Gaspésie

■ 198,000 acres ■ 320 miles east and south of Québec, via Hwys. 132 and 299
■ Year-round ■ Camping, hiking, backpacking, canoeing, fishing, cross-country
skiing, snowshoeing ■ Contact the park, 900 Route du parc, Ste-Anne-des-
Monts, QC G0E 2G0; phone 418-763-7811 or 866-727-2427.
www.sepaq.com/en/

OF ALL THE WILD PLACES that grace the shores of the St. Lawrence River,
none is more deservedly described as spectacular and extraordinary than
this gem nestled in the heart of the Gaspé Peninsula. Here, the St. Anne
River Valley lies between the McGerrigle Uplands and an extension of the
Appalachian range known as the Chic-Choc Mountains. Hundreds of
square miles of high peaks and deep valleys, studded with more than 65
lakes, encompass a landscape that ranges from elegant birch forests and
dense boreal spruce to the lichens and mosses of subarctic tundra. Mont
Albert rises 3,786 feet, its summit a strange moonscape of more than
5 square miles. Also within the park's confines lies one of the most beautiful glacial cirques east of the Rockies, the Lac aux Américains, girded by
a massive glacier-carved horseshoe of rocky cliffs.

Coexisting in this extraordinary land are white-tailed deer, moose,
and caribou—the last remaining caribou south of the St. Lawrence/Great
Lakes system. At 200-strong, the carefully protected caribou herd splits
into three groups—one resides on Mont Albert, a second on Mont
Jacques-Cartier, and a few on the flanks of Mont Richardson. As a matter of fact, Mont Jacques-Cartier is closed in May and June for calving.

What to See and Do

Hiking

The park's 80 miles of hiking trails are designed to provide access to its astonishingly varied landscapes, from barren peaks and glacial cirques to deep ravines. During the summer months, park staffers lead interpretive hikes at the summits of **Monts Albert** and **Jacques-Cartier.**

The **Grande Traversée,** part of the International Appalachian Trail, winds for 60 miles from Mont Logan to **Mont Jacques-Cartier Campground,** crossing numerous peaks and passing through dense forest and tundra, as well as caribou habitat. It can be done in three sections or tackled all at once—a venture that requires about seven days to accomplish comfortably. Backpackers must use mountain huts (*reservations required; call park*). A baggage service is available for part of the hike but it varies with the season and the weather, so check with the park.

The first leg, a 30-mile hike from Mont Logan to Lac Cascapédia, traverses the northern slopes of the **Chic-Chocs.** The second leg continues for another 15 miles, crossing Mont Albert and ending up at the inn Le Gîte du Mont Albert. The final and most popular leg starts at the inn and traverses the **McGerrigle Uplands** to Mont Jacques-Cartier Campground, a trek of a little more than 15 miles. The first couple of miles offer an easy hike to a shelter at **Lac aux Américains,** which rests at the foot of imposing Mont Xalibu. Here the stunning glacial cirque

of the lake has been carved out of the surrounding rock, the water framed by Mont Xalibu's sheer cliffs and knife-edge ridges.

Guided treks include an eight-hour, 5-mile hike to the summit of Mont Jacques-Cartier, as well as a 2.5-mile jaunt one to the moose yards (moose habitat) of the Chic-Chocs. The guided 1.7-mile hike to the Lac aux Américains ends with a short boat ride.

Canoeing

Canoeing is limited to **Lac Cascapédia,** which is about 3 miles long, with views of the southern slopes of the Chic-Choc Mountains. Equipment and canoes are available for rent from the park at Lac Cascapédia.

Fishing

Catch-and-release salmon fishing is possible within the park's boundaries on the Rivière Sainte-Anne. Getting a license may be difficult and expensive, however; they are awarded by lottery the previous November.

Snowshoeing

Snowshoers can choose from six trails, ranging from 3 to 7.5 miles, in the Mont Albert section of the park. For the less adventurous, guided snowshoe trips cater to groups of four to eight people and are tailored to the abilities and desires of the participants.

Cross-country Skiing

With a total of more than 20 feet of snow in a normal season, the park offers superb cross-country

Following pages: Sunset, St. Lawrence River, Gaspé region

and telemark skiing. Trails are marked but not groomed, so skiers may occasionally find themselves breaking trail through fresh snow—inspirationally beautiful after a new snowfall. More than 118 miles of trails are available for backcountry skiing, and a network of 12 huts can accommodate 8 to 16 people each. Remarkably, a hut-to-hut baggage and food transportation service by snowmobile is available.

Park staffers recommend that overnight excursions in winter include a minimum of three people; winters are often severe, and the temperatures can plunge dramatically, with readings of minus 30°F not uncommon.

Telemark skiing is possible at several locations, most of them within a few miles of Le Gite du Mont Albert, the park's cozy country inn. Visitors should be aware that their cars can take them only partway to the slopes. After that, you must walk from the end of the road—a slog of 30 minutes to three hours—and conditions hardly improve once you reach the ski area: With no lift service, you have to herringbone uphill yourself, scaling inclines of 300 to 500 feet. Of the five locations, perhaps the most enchanting views can be seen from Mont Blanche-Lamontagne and Mont Hogs Back. Guided telemark excursions are also available.

Where to Stay

The park's delightfully luxurious country inn, Le Gite du Mont Albert *(418-763-2288)*, includes 48 rooms and 19 cabins; nine of the latter are winterized. Three campgrounds with showers, toilets, and firepits are available at Mont Albert, Lac Cascapédia, and in the Mont Jacques-Cartier sector.

The park also offers skiers 15 mountain huts *(3 accessible to vehicles)*, which are closed from October through December because of excessive snow and in May and June because of the opposite problem. Contact the park for reservations, weather conditions, and additional information. ■

Kayaking at sunset, St. Lawrence River, Gaspésie region

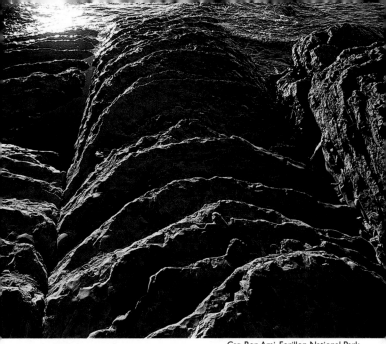

Cap Bon Ami, Forillon National Park

Forillon National Park

■ 60,500 acres ■ 435 miles northeast of Québec via Hwy. 132 at tip of Gaspé Peninsula ■ Best months June-Oct. ■ Camping, hiking, backpacking, boating, kayaking, cross-country skiing, bird-watching, whale-watching, wildlife viewing, scenic drive ■ Contact the park, 122 boul. Gaspé, Gaspé, QC G4X 1A9; phone 418-368-5505. www.parkscanada.gc.ca/forillon

THE GASPÉ PENINSULA does not thrust a smooth fist of land into the Gulf of St. Lawrence; rather, it rakes at the sea with small finger-like spurs. At the end of the northernmost spur lies the predominantly marine park of Forillon. Down the center of the park runs a ridge of rocky cliffs that roughly parallel the coast; these belong to the Appalachian Mountain system. Falling away to the St. Lawrence River on the park's north side, rolling hills covered in mixed deciduous forests gradually give way to boreal forest as the elevation increases. Dozens of narrow valleys carve their way from the central ridge down to the gulf, each with its own small torrent. Flatter reaches of these creeks are home to the park's important population of beavers. Along the coast, the ocean has sculpted terraces, high cliffs, coves, and grottoes. The plateaus of the peninsula's southern half slope toward the sea.

The park's bounty of flora and fauna draws naturalists keen on exploring its treasures. Nearly 700 plant species contribute to Forillon's complex botany. Among them are numerous communities of salt-marsh plants and dune flora, as well as many plants typical of a more northerly latitude (115 are arctic or alpine in nature). The topography provides a haven for wildlife that varies from beavers and porcupines to foxes, lynx, moose, and bears. Increasing numbers of the latter have prompted park

Cap Bon Ami, Forillon National Park

officials to post signs cautioning visitors to follow wise camping practices. More than 225 species of birds have been recorded at Forillon, including a breeding colony of kittiwakes several thousand strong and up to a hundred endangered harlequin ducks—a high percentage given that the total Canadian population of these ducks is only about a thousand.

The official theme of the park is "Harmony between Man, Land, and Sea," a reference to the period when early humans thrived here without spoiling the natural environment.

What to See and Do

Most of the park's highlights lie along the north shore of **Forillon Peninsula** from l'Anse au Griffon in the west to **Cap Gaspé** in the east. Some of this is accessible by car; Hwy. 132 parallels the coast as far east as Cap-des-Rosiers, then makes a U-turn and heads west around Gaspé Bay on its way to the town of Gaspé. The road does not take you to the peninsula's end at Cap Gaspé, but the 17-mile drive is a good way to get a sense of the land. The interpretive center, where many guided activities begin, is in the park's eastern sec-

tion on a small road a mile or so off Hwy. 132.

Hiking

Nine trails wend their way through Forillon, yielding beautiful views. More a short stroll than a hike, the 1.8-mile loop around the interpretive area reveals early human activity in the park.

One of the most interesting trails, **Les Graves** offers a 4.8-mile round-trip departing from l'Anse-aux-Sauvages and winding along the coast past a number of small coves and pebble beaches. The route takes you to Cap Gaspé, at the end of the Forillon Peninsula. **Mont St.-Alban,** a 5.2-mile hike from the beach at Petit-Gaspé (or 5.6 miles from Cap Bon Ami), offers a more difficult loop along the sea and its rugged cliffs. The trail climbs steeply for the first few miles and ends at an observation tower 928 feet above sea level.

At 11 miles one way, **Les Crêtes** runs through wooded mountains, passing numerous panoramic lookouts over the Gulf of St. Lawrence and Gaspé Bay. If you plan to use the two unserviced camping areas along the way, you must first register at a reception center. **Les Lacs Trail** passes a string of small lakes on its 9.8-mile route, which overlooks the grand Morris River Valley. This trail accesses the **International Appalachian Trail.**

Two trails are open to cyclists and horseback riders as well as hikers. **Le Portage,** a 6.8-mile trail, winds through woodlands and fallow fields in the southern part of the park. Visitors often see bears and small game along the way. Following the peaceful l'Anse au Griffon River on a 5.7-mile round-trip, **La Vallée Trail** offers a picnic shelter midway through its route.

Park naturalists conduct guided hikes in summer, including the popular **Underwater World** at Grande-Grave, which aims to help

L'Île Bonaventure

Presumably named by Jacques Cartier, who anchored in the bay on St. Bonaventure's Day in 1534, this 1,135-acre island 50 miles south of Forillon park has been declared a conservation area by the Quebec government. Bonaventure's northern gannet colony is the world's second largest. More than 200,000 gannets nest on the island; a viewing platform gets you within a few yards of the cacophonous birds. Colonies of black-legged kittiwakes, razorbills, and great cormorants roost nearby.

Several trails have been laid out on Bonaventure. All of them eventually lead to the gannet colony observation deck. Regular ferry runs and island tours operate out of Percé, 2 miles away. Contact Le Parc de l'Île Bonaventure-et-du-Rocher-Percé *(418-782-2240).*

Gannet colony, l'Île Bonaventure

Pierced Rock, Percé, Quebec

An Ocean Runs Through It

The town of Percé began as a Roman Catholic mission in 1670. Today it serves as a fishing port and summer resort that attracts people because it lies at the very end of the Gaspé Peninsula.

Many of them also feel a fascination for its great rock, tethered to the mainland at low tide by a mere sandbar. Rocher Percé, or "pierced rock," is a 290-foot-high sedimentary monolith eroded by the sea and pierced by a 60-foot arch. This dramatic geologic formation is a favorite of amateur photographers.

visitors understand the intricacies of the marine life that flourishes along Gaspé shores.

The area's complicated topography also lends itself to random hiking toward the central ridge, where you are unlikely to encounter anyone else.

Whale-watching

Seven varieties of whales swim off the Gaspé coast, including porpoises, blue whales, minkes, and fins. The best place to view them is along the **south shore,** from Grande-Grave to Cap Gaspé. During the summer months, boat cruises *(418-892-5500 for details and reservations)* leave Grande-Grave harbor daily in summer.

Bird-watching

The best place in the park to watch birds is from **Cap-des-Rosiers,** whose cliffs stretch toward Cap Bon Ami. Here, birders will almost invariably see thousands of kittiwakes on the cliff's narrow ledges.

Cross-country Skiing

More than 25 miles of maintained cross-country trails lace the park. Numerous shelters equipped with wood stoves, picnic tables, and dry toilets provide skiers with the basic comforts. **La Cédrière,** a 6.8-mile loop via **La Vallée, Le Ruisseau,** or **Le Portage Trails,** ushers skiers into the park's mountainous heights and through a magnificent 200-year-old cedar grove. ■

Parc de Miguasha

■ About 5 miles long by 1 mile wide ■ On Chaleur Bay, 200 miles south and west of Gaspé via Hwy. 132 ■ Open June–mid-Oct. ■ Hiking, walking, fossil viewing ■ Contact the park, 270 route Miguasha Quest, P.O. Box 183, Nouvelle, QC G0C 2E0; phone 418-794-2475. www.sepaq.com/en/

EMBRACING ONE 5-MILE-LONG CLIFF along the Restigouche River south of the Quebec Appalachians, Miguasha bases its reputation on the diversity and quality of its fossils. The park's extraordinarily well-preserved Devonian finds draw visitors touring northern New Brunswick or the various wilderness parks of the Gaspé Peninsula. About 40,000 tourists a year drop in; among them is a constant stream of paleontologists anxious to examine the park's fascinating collection.

The term "Miguasha" is a Mi'kmaq word meaning "red earth," an apt description of the area's overlying carboniferous rock. The site was discovered in 1842 by geologist Abraham Gesner. By 1892 the chiselers (in both senses of the word) were hard at work, and substantial numbers of fossils had been shipped off to museums in Europe and the United States. Over the intervening years, museums and collectors continued to chip off and cart away large numbers of fossils. Miguasha was declared a provincial park in 1985 and was placed on the World Heritage List in 1999. Today unauthorized digging has finally been brought to an end, and visitors are allowed to look but not touch.

Buried in the Paleozoic era of about 400 million years ago was the Devonian period, a stage that lasted about 57 million years. That's a trifle in geologic time, but the evolution of life during this span continues to reverberate throughout Earth's history. Dating from 370 million years ago, the fossils found at Miguasha reveal the transition of vertebrates from sea creatures to land creatures.

Of the eight groups of fishes known to have flourished during the Devonian period, six are found in Miguasha's cliff. They include the famous *Eusthenopteron foordi,* which many consider the "missing link" between fish and tetrapods—that is, vertebrates with two pairs of limbs. Scientists have also unearthed a number of invertebrate, plant, and spore fossils; more than 70 of the latter have been discovered. Together these relics have disclosed the crucial information that paleontologists needed to construct an accurate picture of Devonian life-forms.

The superb state of preservation of the Miguasha fossils allows scientists to study even soft body parts, such as gills, digestive tracts, cartilage, and blood vessels. Remarkable is the presence in the deposits of eight species representing the sarcopterygian ("fleshy fins") group, which gave rise to the first land vertebrate.

The **Museum of Natural History** at Miguasha offers bilingual guided tours that explain the fossil displays. A short film gives an enlightening overview of the many plant and animal fossil remains that have been dug up in the area. ■

Maritime Provinces

Prince Edward Island

As you might expect of a region nicknamed the Maritimes, the Atlantic Ocean dominates the landscape of this variegated area encompassing the three Canadian provinces of Nova Scotia, Prince Edward Island (PEI), and New Brunswick. Indeed, two fingers of the Atlantic dictate both the contours and the climate of the Maritime Provinces: The Bay of Fundy nearly turns the peninsula of Nova Scotia into an island, while the Gulf of St. Lawrence forms an immense funnel that pierces mainland

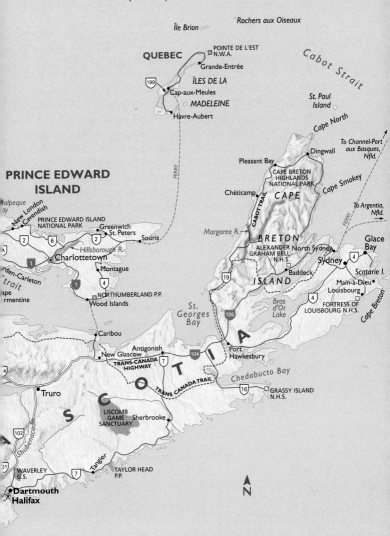

Gulf of St. Lawrence

Rochers aux Oiseaux

Île Brion

QUEBEC

POINTE DE L'EST
N.W.A.

Grande-Entrée

Cabot Strait

199

ÎLES DE LA

Cap-aux-Meules

MADELEINE

Havre-Aubert

St. Paul
Island

Cape North

To Channel-Port
aux Basques,
Nfld.

Dingwall

Pleasant Bay

CAPE BRETON
HIGHLANDS
NATIONAL PARK

Cape Smokey

Chéticamp

CAPE

FERRY

PRINCE EDWARD
ISLAND

alpeque
ay

New London
Cavendish

PRINCE EDWARD ISLAND
NATIONAL PARK

Greenwich
St. Peters

Margaree R.

BRETON

To Argentia,
Nfld.

2

6

2

Souris

ALEXANDER
GRAHAM BELL
N.H.S.

North Sydney

FERRY

Glace
Bay

Hillsborough R.

Charlottetown

Sydney

4

1

Montague

19

Baddeck

Scatarie I.

rden-Carleton

1

ISLAND

Main-à-Dieu
Louisbourg

rait

NORTHUMBERLAND P.P.

Bras
d'Or
Lake

4

ape
rmentine

Wood Islands

105

FORTRESS OF
LOUISBOURG N.H.S.

Cape Breton

Caribou

St.
Georges
Bay

New Glasgow

Antigonish

Port
Hawkesbury

4

TRANS-CANADA
HIGHWAY

7

104

Chedabucto Bay

TRANS CANADA TRAIL

Truro

16

GRASSY ISLAND
N.H.S.

102

LISCOMB
GAME
SANCTUARY

Sherbrooke

Shubenacadie

01

WAVERLEY
G.S.

7

Tangier

TAYLOR HEAD
P.P.

Dartmouth

N

Halifax

ATLANTIC   OCEAN

Sable Island

0   miles   50

0   kilometers   75

Swallowtail Lighthouse on Grand Manan Island, New Brunswick

Quebec and accounts for the sometimes turbulent and always changeable weather that affects the Maritimes, particularly PEI and New Brunswick.

Maritime Canada also includes the Magdalen Islands, or Îles de la Madeleine, a group of nine small islands about 60 miles north of PEI. Though geophysically similar to the Maritimes, politically they belong to the province of Quebec, some 150 miles to the west. Also sharing the Atlantic with the three main Maritime Provinces is the Island of New-foundland, yet it differs so radically from them—subarctic in flora and fauna, raw in geology, stark in climate—that it is covered on its own in Chapter 4 (see pp. 182-225).

Both the natural history and the character of Nova Scotia, Prince Edward Island, and New Brunswick stem from each place's degree of exposure to open water. On Nova Scotia, for example, you can experi-ence the windswept salt sprays of northern Cape Breton Island, which is capped by Cape Breton Highlands National Park and encircled by the scenic drive of the Cabot Trail. You can also explore the softer lake coun-try in the south of the island, tour the farmland of the Annapolis Valley and the Fundy shore (with its legendary tides), and noodle through the picturesque coves and rockbound fishing villages of the South Shore, whose harbors have turned out generations of boatbuilders and fisher-men. Visit Kedge's seaside adjunct, a South Shore landscape of protected beaches and sea meadows, and you will pass through fishing villages

where you are certain to catch these craftsmen in action. The spine of Nova Scotia is still almost entirely forested; a visit to Kejimkujik National Park, whose latitude is below that of Bangor, Maine, will give you a good idea of what the area looked like 500 years ago.

With its gentle farmland and rolling meadows and woods, Prince Edward Island displays an almost English character. Its endless miles of pristine sand beaches seem to invite strolling rather than hiking, making relaxation, not adventure, the core of the PEI experience. Smallest of Canada's ten provinces, PEI can be crossed by car in an hour or so.

Northern New Brunswick shares many natural traits—mixed and boreal forest, pristine lakes and rivers—with the Gaspé Peninsula, which overhangs it. Indeed, rivers seem to emblematize the Brunswick landscape. The province's four best known watercourses—from north to south, they are the Restigouche, the Miramichi, the St. John, and the St. Croix—are not only its prettiest but also its most accessible.

Southern New Brunswick consists of two distinct parts: The eastern shore is shielded from the brunt of Atlantic gales by PEI, while the southern shore offers visitors a chance to witness the extraordinarily high and fast tides that wash in and out of the Bay of Fundy. Although shipyards and pulp mills dominate New Brunswick's capital, St. John, the Fundy shore boasts long stretches of pristine coast, and the interior of the province still harbors spruce forests by the millions of acres. ■

Cape Breton Highlands National Park

■ 234,880 acres ■ Northern tip of Cape Breton Island ■ Best seasons summer and fall ■ Camping, hiking, sea kayaking, swimming, fishing, cross-country skiing, bird-watching, whale-watching, wildlife viewing, scenic drive ■ Adm. fee; camping fee. Fishing permit reqd. ■ Contact the park, Ingonish Beach, NS B0C 1L0; phone 902-224-2306. www.parkscanada.gc.ca

A RUGGED COAST POCKED by plunging gorges, long ocean views, and steep cliffs where eagles hunt below scenic overlooks is the blurred impression you might take away from a daylong drive through Cape Breton Highlands National Park. It's also a fairly typical one, for the blacktop skirting the park (the Cabot Trail) provides the area's only road access. To see the highlands' dramatically stark and brooding interior, you'll have to leave your car behind and strike out on foot.

Sandwiched between the picturesque coves of the Atlantic Ocean to the east and the massive cliffs of the Gulf of St. Lawrence to the west lies Nova Scotia's largest wilderness—a lofty tableland of forests, bogs, barrens, and river gorges, some of them nearly 1,000 feet deep. More than 90 miles of trails offer hiking options that range from scenic walks that can be done in a morning or afternoon to overnight hikes of two or three days.

Geologically speaking, the park is a high plateau comprising several wide-open but sparsely vegetated tracts of land: the Rocky Barrens to the southwest, the Everlasting Barrens to the south, and the North Barrens to the southeast. All three of these are studded with typical taiga vegetation—dwarf black spruce and fir, lichens, sheep laurel, and blueberries.

The highlands are dotted with dozens of small lakes and areas of "mire," or taiga-like wetlands. From these rise the Chéticamp, MacKenzies, and Grande Anse Rivers, which flow into the Gulf, and the Black Brook, Warren Brook, and Aspy River, which empty into the Atlantic. Vegetative dyes make the waters of all six typically brackish. The river valleys are lowlands carpeted with glorious stands of sugar maple, yellow birch, and beech, which consort with white birch and cherry at higher elevations.

What to See and Do

Wildlife Viewing

For birders, the coastal cliffs, especially **Middle Head** on the Atlantic side, are good places to look for seabirds such as guillemots, terns, and gulls. The best spots to spy these birds along the Gulf of St. Lawrence are on the 5.4-mile **Skyline Trail** loop or on the 2-mile (round-trip) **Benjie's Lake Trail.** Access to both hiking paths is from the **Cabot Trail** (see pp. 138-39) between Corney Brook and Fishing Cove.

Finback and minke whales often pop up in the waters offshore between May and September, as do porpoises and seals; the Skyline

Opposite: Tandem cycling through Cape Breton Highlands NP
Following pages: Margaree River, along Nova Scotia's Cabot Trail

Coastal highlands

Trail and **MacKenzies Mountain Overlooks** give you the best chance of spotting them. For close-up views, charters are available from Chéticamp *(call Whale Cruisers 800-813-3376 or 902-224-3376)*, from Bay St. Lawrence north of the park *(call Captain Cox's Whale Watch 902-383-2981 or 888-346-5556)*, and from other points of departure such as Dingwall, Ingonish, and Pleasant Bay.

Moose and bear are common at higher elevations, and lynx can be found along hiking trails.

Hiking

Cape Breton Highlands National Park abounds with hiking trails—26 in all, totaling 90 miles. Grand Anse Valley, paved with sugar maples, turns a flamboyant scarlet in the fall. To take in the spectacle, seek out the half-mile **Lone Sheiling Trail** loop. At higher eleva-

tions, the mixed woods give way to boreal forest of black spruce, birch, and fir. These make ideal summer hiking spots, seemingly custom-designed for cool, tranquil picnics.

The 6-mile **L'Acadien Trail** leads from the Chéticamp Information Center at an elevation of just 50 feet and then climbs through the boreal forest beside **Roberts Brook** before topping out at 1,200 feet. Pause here to catch your breath before it gets taken away again by the summit views of the Gulf of St. Lawrence to the west. To the northeast you'll get a clear and equally scenic look at the park's interior taiga barrens—bleak, mist-shrouded places where plants hug the ground to survive the furious winds, which have been known to gust up to 155 miles an hour. (A typical weather forecast, say local wags, goes like this: "Winds on mainland Nova

Scotia moderate, gales in Cape Breton....") From this vantage point the trail swings east and winds its way downhill to the start.

Fishing Cove Trail is a 5-mile (one way) jaunt that begins on the Cabot Trail north of Chéticamp on French Mountain. The path snakes down a rather steep slope in **Fishing Cove River Valley,** ending at **Fishing Cove**—a village abandoned in 1912. Near the cove's cobbled beach you'll find the park's only seaside wilderness campground, but you'll need a permit (available from park information centers at either end of the Cabot Trail) to stay there. In summer, hikers swim in the river and in the cove itself, where rough footpaths trace the shoreline. Catch your own supper of brook trout from **Fishing Cove River.**

The demanding but rewarding **Franey Trail** is a 4-mile loop that leads from Ingonish Center to the top of 1,405-foot-high Franey Mountain and some thrilling views of the Atlantic. From the summit you'll be able to spot Middle Head and Cape Smokey to the east, Money Point to the north, and the Clyburn Valley spreading out below.

The 2-mile-long **Broad Cove Mountain Trail,** which starts a little north of Ingonish, is just as steep, but still quite manageable —even for the inexperienced. It winds to the top of a 590-foot-high massif that overlooks the ocean, giving you superb views in several directions.

At 6.6 miles in length, the **Coastal Trail** is a longer but flatter and, therefore, much easier hike. It begins at **Black Brook Beach,** north of Ingonish, and passes through lush mixed forest of jack pine and spruce trees to the tidal pools at a cove called Squeaker's Hole. The trail climbs several forested headlands, dipping into stone-beach coves and small bays, then ends at the mouth of Halfway Brook.

For views of the St. Lawrence Gulf, the best hike is the Skyline Trail, which begins north of Chéticamp at a parking lot along an abandoned portion of the Cabot Trail leading up French Mountain. The trail winds through evergreens and hardwoods to the top of a dramatic cliff at Jumping Brook Mountain—a 5.4-mile loop hike. The clifftop is a favorite whale-watching spot; pilot whales breach offshore from May through September. Binoculars will help you enjoy the long vistas, which may include bald eagles riding the thermals above the headland.

On the park's northern border is the moderately strenuous 5.6-mile **Aspy Trail** along the **Aspy Fault,** a striking escarpment that runs from Cape North deep into the highlands. The trail starts near Beulach Ban Falls with a difficult stream crossing, then winds past jagged cliffs and gentle streams.

Swimming

Ingonish Beach is natatorially conflicted: Its long sandy strand allows ocean swimming on one side and freshwater swimming on the other. Only a barachois (natural breakwater) divides the two waters. For another splendid beach, visit the **North Bay area.** On the gulf side, the swimming is good at **Corney Brook** and Fishing Cove.

Scenic Drive: The Cabot Trail

CLOCKWISE OR counterclockwise? That is Cape Breton's longest running good-natured debate, and it concerns the best way to travel the Cabot Trail —a perimeter route around Cape Breton Highlands National Park that is often hailed as one of the most scenic drives (or pedals) in North America.

Parks Canada, for example, recommends driving the Cabot Trail in a clockwise direction. This allows you to use the Chéticamp Information Center's panoply of maps, whose guided tours happen to be laid out that way. Cyclists, too, usually travel clockwise, for the simple reason that it turns the prevailing westerlies into tailwinds. Carbound—er, carborne—tourists often drive the Cabot Trail counterclockwise, saving the most dramatic scenery for the final stretch along the Gulf of St. Lawrence coast.

Although the Cabot Trail measures 144 miles in its entirety, the middle portion that arcs through the park is only 65 miles long. It can, therefore, be cycled in a day. Experienced travelers, however, make at least one overnight stay. If you want to fully explore the side roads and walk a few of the many hiking trails that branch off the trail, four days is not too much. If you're not camping, good accommodations can be found in Ingonish (check out the Keltic Lodge, the grande dame of the Cabot Trail), Cape North, Chéticamp, Dingwall, and Margaree Forks.

The following scenic drive takes off from Ingonish Beach, the southeast entrance to the park. Just before you enter the park on the Cabot Trail, the highway climbs Cape Smokey, a 1,200-foot-high headland that offers an Atlantic vista extending as far as Glace Bay, some 100 miles to the southeast.

The highway clings to the Atlantic shore, cresting headlands and swooping down into small coves. At Lakies

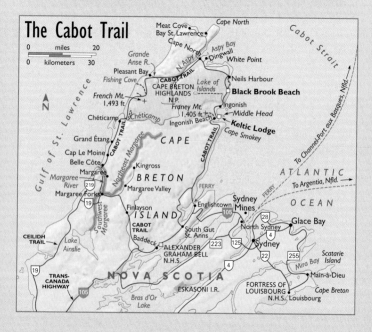

French Mountain, Cabot Trail

Head about 9 miles from your starting point, a scenic overlook provides a telescope for whale spotting.

From Neils Harbour about 17 miles farther on, the highway jogs northwest toward Cape North, which lies well outside the boundaries of the park. About 6 miles from Neils Harbour, a side road leads west to Paquette Falls —a worthwhile detour for its views of the open, windswept barrens.

From Cape North, take another detour: Head due west on Bay Road Valley to Meat Cove at the tip of Cape Breton Island, a 15-mile excursion through a landscape as dramatic as anything the park has to offer.

Back on the Cabot Trail, the road veers southwest and picks up the North Aspy River. Shortly before you reach the base of North Mountain, 7 miles beyond Cape North, watch for signs to Beulach Ban Falls, a lacy, 50-foot-high cataract that tumbles out of the highlands.

The Cabot Trail then descends sharply into the valley of the Grand Anse, meandering along the river lined with 300-year-old hardwood forests to Pleasant Bay on the Gulf of St. Lawrence. From there south you'll see dozens of startling gulf vistas, punctuated by steep headlands, 1,000-foot cliffs, and storm-lashed coves (if you're a novice kayaker, this part of the coast is not the place to float your boat). The road does a dogleg inland to climb MacKenzies and French Mountains, reaching elevations of nearly 1,640 feet—unusual for the park's eponymous highlands—before descending Jumping Brook Valley to reach the sea.

Although Cape Breton Highlands park ends at the Chéticamp River, the Cabot Trail continues south and then southeast, passing the Acadian communities of Chéticamp, Grand Étang, Cap Le Moine, Terre Noire, and Belle Côte. After Margaree Forks it threads the Margaree Valley—famous for its fall colors and salmon fishing—and then joins the Trans-Canada Highway south of Baddeck, site of the Alexander Graham Bell museum.

If you have the time, take the secondary road north from Margaree Valley to Kingross—as far into the Cape Breton Highlands as the Cabot Trail ventures. ∎

Cross-country Skiing

The park grooms seven trails along the Atlantic coast for beginners and intermediates *(for trail conditions, call 902-285-2549)*. The trailhead at Black Brook, 6 miles north of North Ingonish, accesses five of the trails (and warming huts nearby). If you're up to it, the **Sunrise** and **Mary Ann Falls Trails** lead 3.4 miles to **Mary Ann Falls,** where you can warm your hands and feet in a hut before skiing another 4 miles to **Warren Lake.** From the lake it's about 2 miles back to your starting point. Keep your eyes peeled for moose, deer, and otter tracks—and perhaps the animals themselves. Two other trails leave from Broad Cove Campground.

Sea Kayaking

One of the world's most exotic sea kayaking routes threads the steep cliffs, sea caves, and jagged coast of Cape Breton Island's northern tip. Expect to see bald eagles soaring above you and to have seals, porpoises, or pilot whales as paddling companions. Most sea kayaking voyages—supported by an outfitter or pack-and-paddle-it-yourself—depart from Pleasant Bay, Cape North, or Ingonish. ■

Scatarie Island

■ 6,100 acres ■ Opposite Main-à-Dieu, northeast tip of Cape Breton Island ■ Bird-watching ■ Contact Nova Scotia Department of Tourism and Culture, P.O. Box 456, 1800 Argyle St., Halifax, NS B3J 2R5; phone 902-425-5781 or 800-565-0000. explore.gov.ns.ca

BIRDS, BIRDS, AND MORE BIRDS are the big attraction of tiny Scatarie Island, which hosts a rich and diverse population of pelagic species, including scads of Leach's storm-petrels. From July to September, whimbrels and buff-breasted sandpipers drop in by the thousands to feast on the island's blueberries, cranberries, and bakeapples (the latter grow in bogs and resemble large yellow raspberries). About 25 nesting pairs of rare Bicknell's thrushes reside here—a significant number for a species whose global population may be only 5,000.

Scatarie may be visited by boat from Main-à-Dieu, the fishing village opposite the island; head for the town wharf and ask a lobsterman to ferry you across the short distance to the island, or contact local luminary Fraser Kennedy *(902-733-2309)* to arrange a day tour in advance. ■

Blueberries

Blomidon Provincial Park

■ 1,875 acres ■ 15 miles north of Hwy. 101 on Hwy. 358 ■ Best months June-Oct. ■ Hiking, mountain biking ■ Contact the park, 136 Exhibition St., Kentville, NS B4N 4E5; phone 902-582-7319. parks.gov.ns.ca/blomidon.htm

SICKLE-SHAPED BLOMIDON PENINSULA, culminating in Cape Split, separates the Minas Basin from the Bay of Fundy. With sea cliffs soaring to heights of 500 to 600 feet, it is known far and wide for its spectacular ocean views. That's where Blomidon Provincial Park enters the scene: It is a coil of interconnected hiking trails *(all are accessed via campground near park's entrance)* designed to carry you to those views.

The best hike is the 3.7-mile **Joudrey Trail** circuit, which winds through a forest of beech and maple while skirting the cliffs of the Minas Basin. Almost as scenic is the mile-long **Lookoff Trail,** which affords views 15 miles across the bay to the headlands of Five Islands Provincial Park.

Another worthwhile walk awaits at **Cape Split,** reached by following Hwy. 358 to the parking lot a mile beyond Scots Bay. From here a 4.3-mile (round-trip) trail climbs steadily from sea level through spruce woods to an open field at the top, which yields impressive views of the mouth of Minas Basin to the east and Minas Channel and the Bay of Fundy to the west. Caution: This trail is popular with mountain bikers, who like to bomb down the hill; not all of them have mastered trail etiquette. ■

Brier Island

■ 3,800 acres ■ Southwest Nova Scotia, 40 miles southwest of Digby on Hwy. 217 ■ Best seasons spring-fall ■ Bird-watching, whale-watching ■ Contact Tiverton Tourist Bureau, P.O. Box 694, Tiverton, NS B0V 1G0; phone 902-839-2853

WHALE-WATCHING AT ITS BEST awaits those willing to venture to the tip of Digby Neck, a long finger of land that extends like a tail from southwestern Nova Scotia. You'll need to take two ten-minute ferry rides to get here— one from the end of Digby Neck to Long Island and a second from Long Island to Brier Island. Both ferries operate on the hour, 24 hours a day.

Several outfitters operate boats from the town of Digby, at the head of the peninsula, and from Westport, which occupies Brier Island itself. Among them is Brier Island Whale and Seabird Cruises *(902-839-2995)*, whose resident scientists are so familiar with the returning humpback and right whales that they can identify each by name. Ocean Explorations Whale Cruises *(902-839-2417)* operates out of Tiverton at the north end of Long Island.

More and more visitors seek out Brier Island for its birds. Spring is the best season for migrating seabirds and nesting pelagics, summer for breeding terns. Migrating hawks make a spectacular autumn display. ■

Stepping-stones in the Mersey River, Kejimkujik National Park

Kejimkujik National Park

■ 147 square miles, including Kejimkujik Seaside Adjunct ■ Best seasons late spring-fall ■ Camping, hiking, backpacking, canoeing, swimming, biking, bird-watching, wildlife viewing, petroglyphs ■ Contact the park, P.O. Box 236, Maitland Bridge, NS B0T 1B0; phone 902-682-2772. www.parkscanada.gc.ca

REMOTENESS AND ACCESSIBILITY CONVERGE in Kejimkujik National Park and National Historic Site, a wilderness that is easy both to reach and to get around in. "More bobcats walk our trails than hikers," goes a local saying. That's a surprise, given the park's lush network of canoe routes and gentle hiking trails, which wind their way through sunny groves of birch and maple and dark, secretive stands of 300-year-old hemlocks. In the fall, the park's maples and oaks turn intense shades of scarlet and orange, framed by an ebony backdrop of spruce.

Kejimkujik occupies a warm climatic pocket within colder peninsular Nova Scotia. The park's growing season lasts 200 days—unusual for Nova Scotia—and summer temperatures frequently hit 85°F or higher. This explains the startling diversity of plants and animals found here. Twenty plant species, collectively known as the coastal plain flora, survive at the extreme northern limit of their range on the lake shores of Kejimkujik. These include water-pennywort and tiny yellow- or purple-flowered bladderworts.

With lake water temperatures only a few degrees cooler than the surrounding air, summer swimming is delightful. Of the 46 lakes that dapple the landscape of Kedge (the park's nickname, pronounced KED-gie), the best for swimming is Kejimkujik Lake itself, which has lifeguards and facilities, and Peskowesk Lake. Winters in the park are short *(Dec.-Feb.)* and mild (temperatures seldom drop below 20°F), with meager snow cover.

Kejimkujik lies athwart a traditional "canoe highway," in use for at least 4,500 years, that connects the Bay of Fundy with the Atlantic. The nomadic Woodland Indians used it as their main means of getting around the peninsula in summer. The present-day Mi'kmaq are their direct descendants.

Few signs remain of traditional Mi'kmaq life. For example, the park's petroglyphs—showing tantalizing glimpses of a vanished way of life, including scenes of hunting and fishing—date only from the 18th and 19th centuries because they were inscribed on soft, easily eroded slate. Understandably, the area where they are located is closed to general access by the public. During the summer months, however, Mi'kmaq interpreters lead tours to view the petroglyphs and explain their culture's ties to the landscape.

Although the park's lands were granted to farmers in the 19th century, the soil was too acidic and shallow for cultivation. Ruined sawmills through the park testify to bygone logging operations. Visitors can also hike the 2-mile interpretive **Gold Mines Trail** to view the remains of a small gold mine (*trailhead access via park road near turnoff for McGinty Lake*). Alas, Kejimkujik always yielded more lore than ore.

What to See and Do

Camping
Hundreds of campsites for smaller parties can be found at Jeremy's Bay, while larger groups can camp nearby at Jim Charles Point. Forty-seven wilderness campgrounds are situated at numerous points throughout the park (*off-site camping is not permitted*). Designated wilderness campsites have fireplaces, outhouses, and graveled tent pads. Firewood is available. With the number of campers at most of these remote campsites limited to six to minimize impact, reservations through the park are a must.

Hiking
Kejimkujik park has laid out 15 day hikes covering 21 miles of marked trails. These range from modest riverside strolls suitable for young children to half-day hikes. The park's longest day hike is the 16-mile (round-trip) **Channel Lake Trail,** whose trailhead is at Big Dam Lake Campground in the northern part of the park. On the return many worthwhile detours present themselves, all well sign-posted along the trail. Among these are the **Hemlocks and Hardwoods Trail,** which passes through a towering but nonetheless young stand of hemlock trees.

Peter Point (*1.8 miles round-trip*) is a pleasant walk that starts a mile past the Grafton Lake access point. The trail takes you to a low promontory overlooking Kejimkujik Lake that is ideal for bird-watching. To double the distance, bear left on the trail that branches off a few hundred yards from the trailhead; this offshoot takes you to **Snake Lake,** a breeding area for Blandings turtles.

There is also virtually limitless backcountry hiking (*backcountry guidebook and map available at visitor center*) on trails that will take you two to six days to negotiate. These wind through mature

Kejimkujik National Park

forests of hemlock or maple, fording brooks, skirting lakes, and occasionally leading you through acres of waist-high ferns. You'll find hiking options year-round, but try to hit the trails during the dry, comfortable weather of late summer and fall.

Canoeing

With no mountains or deep gorges to create white water, Kedge offers some of the most tranquil canoeing in Nova Scotia. Dozens of navigable streams and small lakes—notably **Kejimkujik Lake** and its countless islands—invite paddle-powered exploration. Watch out for submerged logs—relics of 1950s-era logging drives. Portages range from 160 to 2,000 yards.

There's no need to bring your own canoe—you can rent one at the Jakes Landing canoe concession *(call Wildcat River Outfitters 902-682-2196)*. Camping gear can be rented just outside the park gates. If you're not paddling one of the marked loops that bring you back to your starting point, you can arrange with the canoe concessionaire for return transportation to your car. Consult the park's backcountry guidebook *(available at visitor center)* for information on portages.

Biking

Biking is permitted on all secondary roads in the park. It's also allowed on a few multipurpose trails. One such path, the 5.9-mile-long **Fire Tower Road,** starts from the park's main road just beyond the Mersey River crossing and meanders through magnificent stands of sugar maple and yellow birch. Another, the **Mersey River Trail,** is a 2-mile loop that parallels the river north from Jakes Landing, where you can rent bikes.

Swimming

Swimming is possible in the warm waters of Kejimkujik Lake from late June to Labor Day. The sandy beach at **Merrymakedge** has lifeguards, changing facilities, and a snack bar. Swimming is also allowed (though unsupervised) at any of the lake's other beaches, as well as in the park's other lakes.

Children's Programs

Park interpreters lead bike hikes for kids, starting from the Jeremys Bay Campground and exploring nearby trails that lead through woods and beside waterways. They also operate a voyageur canoe—large enough to hold eight children—that explores a shallow, sheltered stretch of the Mersey

Canoes for rent in Kejimkujik NP

River. Each night at dusk, an interpreter presents a 45-minute program on Kejimkujik's natural and human history in the outdoor theater. Check the visitor center and park bulletin boards for information on interpretive programs.

Wildlife

Animals in the park are prolific, diverse, and easy to spot. That's because Kedge's microclimate makes it a haven for wildlife found nowhere else in Nova Scotia. Outside southern Ontario, for example, Kedge is the only place in Canada that provides habitat for the northern ribbon snake. Look for this 2-foot-long reptile—a species of garter snake—along lake shores and in shallow water. It can be identified by its single bright longitudinal yellow stripe on a velvety black skin.

Nearly all of Nova Scotia's rare Blandings turtles—about 150 adults—live in Kejimkujik park. Visitors lucky enough to spot one (look for a yellow spotted shell and yellow chin and neck) are urged to report the sighting to a park naturalist; this information will then be used to help track the population. Kedge is the turtles' only outpost in Canada; in the U.S., their northernmost range is Pennsylvania.

Considerably more common are black bears, white-tailed deer, porcupines, beavers, coyotes, and American marten. The latter were reintroduced here in the 1980s.

Bird-watchers will delight in the chance to view some 200 species. Here are a few you're most likely to see: loons, barred owls, warblers, woodpeckers, and waterfowl such as black ducks and mergansers.

Fishing

Kedge's fishing season lasts from April 1 to August 1; the daily limit (and maximum possession) is five. Many Kejimkujik lakes and rivers are naturally acidic, a condition exacerbated by acid rain. The park's 12 fish species, therefore, occur in sparse populations.

Being shallow, Kedge's lakes are warm, limiting brook trout to rivers and streams, and only in spring. The warmth-tolerant yellow perch is the park's most abundant fish. ■

Kejimkujik Seaside Adjunct

■ 5,400 acres ■ Southern shore of Nova Scotia, 15 miles southwest of Liverpool ■ Best seasons late summer-fall ■ Hiking, bird-watching, wildlife viewing ■ Contact Seaside Adjunct Warden Office, phone 902-683-2585; or Kejimkujik National Park, P.O. Box 236, Maitland Bridge, NS B0T 1B0, phone 902-682-2772. www.parkscanada.gc.ca

ITS BUREAUCRATIC NAME NOTWITHSTANDING, the Kejimkujik Seaside Adjunct—a non-contiguous landholding of the national park—boasts craggy coves, white-sand beaches, lagoons, a pristine headland, and distant views across the open ocean to Little Hope Island and beyond. Harbor seals are a common sight. Although most people recommend the fall as the best time for a visit, late summer is also good. Hikers gravitate here to walk on wild winter days—an exhilarating experience.

Two trails lead into the area. The first and more rustic, from South West Port Mouton, is a 5-mile, 90-minute trip to the shore at **Black Point;** look for harbor seals when you get there. The other trailhead—located at a parking lot 3 miles up the gravel road leading from Port Joli to the small community of East Side Port L'Hebert—leads to a 2-mile **boardwalk.** This is a more leisurely walk of about 35 minutes. It starts out in mixed woods that soon devolve to dense thickets of alder, holly, wild cherry, and huckleberry. As you approach the open ocean, these are replaced by cranberry and bog rosemary, juniper and foxberry; lichens grow on the rocks, while pitcher plants fill small, wet, trailside depressions. Rare purple-fringed orchids flourish in damp meadows.

Once you reach the shore, the path forks and you have two options: Head left (east) and you'll come to **Harbour Rocks** at the western end of **St. Catherines River Beach,** yielding a hike of 3.5 miles round-trip from the parking lot. Head right (west) to make a circuit of the exposed peninsula known as **Port Joli Head,** resulting in a loop hike of 4.3 miles round-trip from the parking lot.

The shore itself features rugged headlands and small white beaches. Eider ducks, cormorants, and other waterbirds feed in the ocean; sandpipers, yellowlegs, and piping plover dart about on the shore.

Indeed, the adjunct is a breeding area for the piping plover—a small, elusive bird that wound up on Canada's endangered species list in 1985. Within the next ten years, the number of nesting pairs at the adjunct had at least doubled. To protect the birds, the wardens close some beaches in nesting season, which lasts from May until early August.

The Kedge adjunct protects more wildlife than birds and seals. Deer visit the shore to eat fresh seaweed now and then; you may also see them along the boardwalk trail. On the beaches you may be treated to a sighting of a mink or a black bear (the latter are timid and rarely approach humans). This stretch of coast has a reputation for rogue waves, so hikers should keep their distance from the water if walking along the rocks. ■

Wood Islands ferry, PEI

Northumberland Provincial Park

■ 76 acres ■ Southeast Prince Edward Island ■ 1.8 miles east of Wood Islands ferry terminal ■ Camping, hiking, bird-watching ■ Contact Parks Division East, Box 370, Montague, PEI C0A 1R0; phone 902-962-7418 or 902-652-8950 (in winter)

HEAD EAST AFTER DRIVING OFF THE FERRY that carried you across Northumberland Strait to Prince Edward Island from Caribou, Nova Scotia, and within a few short miles you'll discover a park that is deservedly popular with families. They are drawn to Northumberland Provincial Park by its safe, supervised beach *(on Rte. 4, behind visitor center)* and by its warm (70°F) ocean water. Armed with small shovels and pails, dozens of family groups can be seen working their way along the shoreline in summer, digging up fresh clams for that night's dinner. Indeed, with a laundromat, hot showers, rest rooms, playground, kitchen shelter, dump station, and camp store *(902-962-7418)* all nearby, this park is probably about as far as you can get from Outward Bound.

From the park office, an interpretive **nature trail** meanders 1 mile through a mix of forests and meadows that display the flora and fauna native to PEI. A spectrum of shorebirds and waterfowl will have birders scrambling for their life lists. In addition, cliff swallows are a frequent sight; they nest in burrows along the shore.

At the ferry docks, another small picnic park, **Wood Islands,** offers a beach, changing facilities, a playground, and rest rooms for campers. ■

Prince Edward Island National Park

■ 29 miles long ■ Northern shore of Prince Edward Island ■ Best season summer ■ Camping, hiking, sea kayaking, canoeing, swimming, cross-country skiing, bird-watching, sand dunes ■ Contact the park, 2 Palmers Lane, Charlottetown, PEI C1A 5V6; phone 902-672-6350. www.parkscanada.gc.ca/pei

PRINCE EDWARD ISLAND NATIONAL PARK is a tenuous rainbow of coastline divided between the park proper and the Greenwich Extension, a collection of sand dunes 30 miles to the east. A sliver of red sandstone cliffs, pink sand dunes, olive-green marram grass and marine marshes, white- and red-sand beaches, and green tide pools, it clings to the island's north shore like a wilderness mirage that could disappear at any moment. Such evanescence is the product of powerful forces of nature.

Because the dunes migrate, slight changes in seasonal weather patterns can have a significant impact on their composition—and thus their survival. The shifting dunes allow coastal erosion to occur at the rate of about 3 feet per year.

Two types of people visit the park. The first are summer vacationers who come here to swim, golf, or play tennis. Drawn by gulf beaches that purportedly offer the warmest swimming north of the Carolinas, nearly 1.5 million people visit PEI National Park each year. Their base of operations is likely to be a campground *(contact park for camping brochure or call 800-414-6765 for reservations)* or perhaps even the splendid old mansion of Dalvay-by-the-Sea *(902-672-2048)*, now operated as an inn. High on this group's list of see-worthy sights is the farmhouse at **Green Gables House Heritage Place** *(902-566-7050)*. The site commemorates Lucy Maud Montgomery, a designated "person of national historic significance"

Cooking gear hung out of reach   *Following pages: Orby Head, Prince Edward Island NP*

Blue herons, Covehead, Prince Edward Island NP

whose now famous 1908 novel, *Anne of Green Gables,* vividly evoked a young girl's life on Prince Edward Island. The late 19th-century farmhouse was the real-life home of David and Margaret Macneill, cousins of Montgomery's grandfather, and inspired the setting in her novel.

The second type of PEI visitor is ecotourists eager to learn more about the island's fragile marine and dune ecology. Many interpretive activities (such as guided walks along the multiple hiking trails) have been provided for this group; if you count yourself among them, you'll find a wide range of options.

What to See and Do

Hiking

Hiking trails take you through all of the park's most characteristic landscapes—the dunes, the marshes and ponds, and the woodlands. Glacial erosion of the island's distinctive red sandstone gave rise to the park's unusual dunes. Today's dunes—loosely anchored by marram grass and thus easily disturbed—seem to be constantly on the move, either advancing toward the sea or retreating from it. Wind is the engine of this mobility. When the marram grass dies—often from excess foot traffic—the wind succeeds in carving small hollows, called blowouts, in the sand. Too many blowouts turn stable dunes into shifting sands.

Among the more distinctive features of the park, especially in Greenwich, are high, mobile,

parabolic dunes with a series of concentric dune ridges called Gegenwalle, or counter ridges. Parabolic (U-shaped) dunes are rare in the Americas; outside this park, they are found only southeast of Lake Michigan and in the Pacific Northwest. To see parabolic dunes firsthand in Greenwich, take the easy 2.6-mile stroll to the ocean along the **Greenwich Dunes Trail.** You'll find the clearly marked trailhead east of St. Peters on Hwy. 313, by signs and a parking area. Nearby is the Greenwich Interpretive Center.

The dunes are too fragile for walking or climbing; visitors must stay on the marked paths and boardwalks. In summer, staffers are on hand at the Cavendish and Dalvay Visitor Centres to answer questions; fact-packed lectures are presented at these two centers from time to time *(call park for schedule)*.

Among the more interesting dune areas is the **Cavendish Sandspit,** located at the western end of the park and accessible from the Cavendish Visitor Centre. It consists of old, stable dune ridges with marram grass vegetation, mobile dune systems in less stable areas, and intertidal deposits of sand and silt within washover channels. The half-mile **Cavendish Dunelands Trail** provides close-up views of the dunes from a boardwalk beginning at the eastern end of Cavendish Beach. Because this area is critical breeding habitat for the piping plover, an endangered species, it is closed to visitors at nesting time *(May–early June)*. At all other times, however, it is open. You'll also see common terns here.

The **Brackley dune system** in

the center of the park is one of the best examples of dune landforms within the park. The primary dunes, with marram grass and colonizing bayberry, are dominant, but secondary echo dune ridges occur nearby.

Bird-watching

Most of the park's many ponds, home to a diverse collection of wildfowl, are *barachois* ponds—saltwater bays that changed to fresh water after encroaching dunes cut them off from the ocean.

The salt marshes are low, grassy, muddy areas along the sheltered shoreline. Their role as "the ocean's nurseries"—the park's most productive habitats of all—make them favorite hiking and birding destinations for knowledgeable visitors. The salt marshes are also, to put it charitably, aromatic—a consequence of hydrogen sulfide gas that escapes from the mud. Aptly named **Brackley Marsh,** an open saltwater and brackish water system north of Brackley Bay and Covehead Bay, is home to thousands of birds, notably black ducks, red-breasted mergansers, and juncos. Thanks to its unique thickets of rushes and its patches of sea lavender and cordgrass, it is also the target of intense scientific scrutiny.

The best way to see the ponds is to take the **Reeds and Rushes Trail,** which starts on the Gulf Shore Parkway 1.5 miles west of the Dalvay Visitor Centre. The trail, just over half a mile long, features a boardwalk extending much of the way across a barachois pond, which abounds with a rich collection of water plants such as bladderworts and bulrushes, to say nothing of its diverse bird population comprising grebes, ospreys, and flycatchers. Topping it all off is the occasional glimpse of a muskrat or otter. At one point along the Reeds and Rushes Trail, an offshoot path a few hundred yards long takes you through a spruce forest mixed with aspen and maple.

Swimming

Although PEI National Park contains its requisite quota of corrugated Maritime coast—small bays and rocky shores—much of its length is in fact white-sand beach. Six beaches are supervised *(lifeguards in summer only),* but visitors can swim basically anywhere. In summer you won't find any beaches deserted—this is a deservedly popular park—but the crowds seem to congregate around those nearest the two park entrances: **Cavendish Beach** west of the Cavendish entrance, and **Stanhope Beach** just west of the Dalvay entrance. If you prefer more solitude, **Brackley Bay,** north of the Brackley Visitor Centre, is worth a try. So is **North Rustico Beach;** north of Rustico Harbour, it can be reached from the Cavendish Visitor Centre on Hwy. 6. Visitors with children should not be lulled by the warm Gulf waters (high 60s and low 70s in summer); rip tides are common.

Camping

Although PEI park can be reached in a 20-minute drive from the provincial capital of Charlottetown, many visitors prefer to camp on-

Cross-country skier, Prince Edward Island

site. Campgrounds have been set up at Cavendish (west of the park), Robinsons Island, and Stanhope *(near Dalvay-by-the-Sea inn).* The latter, only a few hundred yards from wheelchair-accessible Stanhope Beach, is the most popular. Campsites fill up rapidly in summer, so reserve in advance *(800-414-6765).*

Canoeing and Kayaking

Most of the park's ponds are open to canoers and kayakers *(motorized craft not permitted).* You can also kayak along the Gulf of St. Lawrence shore, whose warm waters and generally placid summer weather make for some easy paddling. A popular if slightly more ambitious destination for sea kayakers is the barrier islands that hem in Malpeque Bay; together they constitute a 20-mile-long sandspit seldom frequented by humans. If you haven't brought your own kayak, rent one from Outside Expeditions *(902-207-3899)* at North Rustico in the western part of the park.

Cross-country Skiing

Though PEI National Park doesn't get as much use in winter, some trails are groomed for cross-country skiing when snow conditions permit. Check with the park first, because not enough snow falls to justify trail preparation in some years. A popular choice is the **Woodlands Trail,** an easy 3-mile loop that begins just a few hundred yards west of the Dalvay entrance station. Another is the **Green Gables Trail,** a 7.5-mile loop that starts from the parking lot of the Green Gables homestead and meanders through mixed woodlands and alongside tidal marshes. ■

Windsurfing boards, Île du Havre aux Maisons, Îles de la Madeleine

Îles de la Madeleine

■ 55 miles northwest of northern Nova Scotia ■ Best season summer ■ Hiking, swimming, biking, bird-watching ■ Access by air from Montréal or Halifax; by daily car ferry from Souris, PEI; or by weekly passenger vessel from Montréal. Limited English-speaking facilities ■ Contact Bureau of Tourism Information, P.O. Box 1028, Cap-aux-Meules, Îles de la Madeleine, QC G0B 1B0; phone 418-986-2245. www.ilesdelamadeleine.com

WHEN THE SUMMER SUN SHINES and the weather is placid, this 40-mile-long archipelago belonging to the province of Quebec forms a vision of how islands should be: green-hilled meadows, red sandstone cliffs, and beaches whose golden or white sands stretch for miles (186 of them, to be precise) between rolling surf on one side and sleepy saltwater lagoons on the other. Despite ocean water that typically hits a toasty (for Canada) 63°F at the height of the summer season, it's rare to find another soul within several hundred yards of your spot on the beach.

This is not a wilderness untouched by human endeavor, yet the seascapes and coastlines of the Îles de la Madeleine possess a classic maritime beauty that makes the islands ideal for those seeking solitude, sea air, and picture-perfect fishing villages. And did we mention the seafood? Dozens of cafés and small restaurants in the Magdalen Islands (as they are called by the 800 or so Anglophone residents) serve such local delicacies as snow crabs, scallops, and blue mussels. And with 80 percent of Quebec's lobsters caught in the surrounding gulf waters (the local season starts in May), the islands take justifiable pride in their lobster dinners.

The Îles de la Madeleine remain one of Quebec's best kept secrets. Birders, especially Americans, are drawn by the chance to spot a variety of seabirds and migrants. Almost 200 species have been cataloged on the islands, ranging from great blue herons to tiny golden finches.

The archipelago is shaped something like an inverted quotation mark. The ferry from Souris on Prince Edward Island docks at **Cap-aux-Meules.** The town of the same name serves as a commercial center of sorts. Due south, along the Dune du Havre aux Basques, is the second largest of the Madeleines, **Île du Havre Aubert.** To the north, also along a skinny dune, the road passes over the most beautiful spot on the archipelago, **Île du Havre aux Maisons,** which offers sinuous roads, lofty headlands carpeted with lush turf, and endless beaches. After reaching the tiny **Île aux Loups,** continue farther north still along the skinny Dune du Nord to the last two of the large islands, **Grosse Île** and **Île de la Grande Entrée.**

The latter island is largely given over to the **Pointe de l'Est National Wildlife Area,** a sanctuary for common and gray seals. Two splendid hikes start at a place called **Old-Harry,** at the northeast end of Grande Entrée, near the fishing village of the same (but hyphenated) name. You can wander northeast up 8-mile-long **Grande Echouerie Beach,** with seal sightings virtually guaranteed, or make your way north along the 12-mile biking trail that parallels the Grande-Entrée harbor, savoring the views of the bay and its islands. Most hikers end their trek at Grosse Île lagoon, but it's possible to continue 5 miles or so to Pointe-aux-Loups.

For those who'd like to stay a little longer, houses are available for rent by calling Le Berceau des Îles *(418-937-5614).* ∎

Fundy National Park

■ 51,200 acres ■ Southeast New Brunswick, on Chignecto Bay ■ Best seasons summer and early fall ■ Camping, hiking, backpacking, swimming, mountain biking, cross-country skiing, scenic drive ■ Adm. fee ■ Contact the park, P.O. Box 1001, Alma, NB E4H 1B4; phone 506-887-6000. www.parkscanada .pch.gc.ca

HOW WOULD YOU LIKE TO WALK on the ocean floor? At Fundy National Park—specifically, Alma Beach—you can.

At high tide, Alma Cove is a sheltered harbor like any other. By low tide, however, the ocean is more than 1.5 miles away, exposing the floor of the cove: a tidal flat of cobblestones, sand, and mud.

Don't be embarrassed if you find yourself passing an entire afternoon staring at your feet: The flats harbor a universe of marine life, including soft-shell clams, burrowing seaworms, tiny mud shrimp (as many as 40,000 in a few square yards), and a raft of other creatures that attract sandpipers and shorebirds. There's the clam worm, for example—a rainbow of glistening pinks, browns, and iridescent greens—as well as the bamboo worm, which passes its life inside a tiny tube. A tide pole marks the high and low water levels; nearby are a telescope and an exhibit on ocean tides. Park naturalists lead interpretive walks across the tidal flats in summer. Call the park to learn the schedule or sign up for one of these excursions.

The Bay of Fundy's famously high tides—they rise as much as 52 feet in six hours and 25 minutes—are caused by resonance, or the synchronization that occurs as tons of bay water slosh back and forth at roughly the same periodicity (about every 13 hours) as the rising of the tide (about every 12 hours and 25 minutes). The shape of the bay also serves to funnel and magnify the extraordinary tides. In the nearby town of Moncton, about 20 miles inland, the tidal bore—a 2- to 12-inch-high wave pulse caused by the incoming tide—roars up the Petitcodiac River with the noise of a freight train, making it a local tourist attraction.

In addition to being high, the Bay of Fundy tides are fast. You'll have to take extra care not to get stranded in a cove or on a sandbar as the tide rises; you'll also need to ascertain that your return path will not flood. On the day of your visit, seek out the advice of park rangers—then follow it.

What to See and Do

Hiking

More than 75 miles of marked trails thread the park. These range from easy half-mile loops to a demanding 30-mile loop, the **Fundy Circuit,** that requires three to five days to hike but is also a great way to see the entire park. The series of linked trails takes you around lakes, through forests, and along river valleys, inlets, and coastal cliffs. The park's trail network connects to longer and more strenuous hiking options outside

Dickson Falls, Fundy National Park

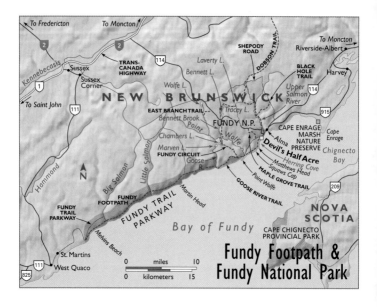

To Fredericton
To Moncton
To Moncton
Riverside-Albert

2 **2**
TRANS-CANADA HIGHWAY **114**
Sussex
Kennebecasis
Sussex Corner
1
To Saint John **111**

Laverty L.
SHEPODY ROAD
BLACK HOLE TRAIL
Harvey

Bennett L.
DOBSON TRAIL

Wolfe L.
Upper Salmon River **114**

N E W   B R U N S W I C K

EAST BRANCH TRAIL
Tracey L.
915

Bennett Brook Point
FUNDY N.P.
CAPE ENRAGE Cape Enrage

Chambers L.
Wolfe
CAPE ENRAGE MARSH NATURE PRESERVE Chignecto Bay

Marven L.
FUNDY CIRCUIT
Devil's Half Acre
Alma

Goose R.
Herring Cove
Matthews Head
Squaws Cap
MAPLE GROVE TRAIL

Big Salmon
Little Salmon
Point Wolfe
GOOSE RIVER TRAIL

Hammond
N

FUNDY FOOTPATH
Martin Head

FUNDY TRAIL PARKWAY
209

FUNDY TRAIL PARKWAY
N O V A   S C O T I A

Melvins Beach
Bay of Fundy CAPE CHIGNECTO PROVINCIAL PARK

St. Martins
111
West Quaco
825

0 miles 10
0 kilometers 15

Fundy Footpath & Fundy National Park

the park. The **Fundy Footpath** (see pp. 162-63), for example—part of the planned **Trans Canada Trail**—joins the Fundy Circuit at the southeastern border of the park. The circuit also links up with the **Dobson Trail** (see pp. 162-63)—a Canadian national trail—on the park's northern border.

If you lack the time to trek the whole route, try one or several of the Fundy Circuit's six constituent segments, described below.

The 6.3-mile **Coastal Trail** starts from the swimming pool at park headquarters west of Alma and heads southwest. The first part of the trail is an up-and-down trek with ridge top views. The Coastal Trail then drops to the shore at **Herring Cove** and its renowned tidal flats. From there the path climbs **Matthews Head,** giving you sweeping views over the bay; on a clear day you may even be able to distinguish the outline of the Nova Scotia shore. After crossing two

short boardwalks that bridge boggy patches, you'll have a view of the isolated sea stack known as **Squaws Cap.** The last mile or so of the Coastal Trail passes through old-growth red spruce to the deep inlet of **Point Wolfe River,** another estuary that empties at low tide.

The second leg of the Fundy Circuit, the **Marven Lake Trail,** is a 5-mile uphill amble along a grassy cart track to Marven and Chambers Lakes, two wilderness campsites.

From Marven Lake, the 4.8-mile **Bennett Brook Trail** takes over; be ready for some difficult patches. The adventure begins along a grassy road before descending a steep, rock-strewn hill. About 2 miles farther on, two fords cross the Point Wolfe River and Bennett Brook. Though relatively shallow, these streams lack stepping-stones, so prepare for wet feet. After some sharp, steep switchbacks leading up from the rivers, you'll have an easy hike (follow the old logging road and then the dry streambed) to Bennett Lake.

The Fundy Circuit's fourth segment, the 2.6-mile-long **Tracey Lake Trail,** skirts the western shore of Bennett Lake to Tracey Lake, where you'll find some more undeveloped campsites. The moist, sodden ground along this section makes for hard slogging.

From Laverty Lake, the trail follows an old road for 1.25 miles. It then joins the 2.1-mile-long **Forks Trail,** which leads to 30-foot-high curtain cascade tumbling over a steep rock face.

The loop's sixth and last stretch is the **Upper Salmon River Trail,** a difficult hike of 5.5 miles that passes by steep valleys and craggy cliffs, waterfalls and gorges, and potholes. At the trailhead of this segment, a steel cable imbedded in andesite (a volcanic rock) helps hikers ford the Salmon River. You'll also have to cross several lesser creeks and brooks, but the passage through the beautiful mixed Acadian forest makes the wet boots worth the trip.

Near the end of the circuit lies the popular **Black Hole,** a deep pool filled with cool water. Negotiating this penultimate portion involves some scrambling up steep rocks, but steel rungs help you cross the most massive boulders. You then join a park road for a final leg of 1.5 miles that completes the loop.

Mountain Biking

Biking is allowed on the following trails: **Goose River,** Marven Lake, **Black Hole,** Bennett Brook, **East Branch,** and **Maple Grove.** Except

Restoring the Woods

Mi'kmaq and Malmeet Indians lived in the area of present-day Fundy National Park for centuries, but European settlement did not occur until about 1825. By the late 1800s, however, logging for wooden boats denuded the area, clogging and polluting its streams. To begin repairing the damage, Fundy park was set up in 1948.

Substantial efforts have been made since then to restore the park's Acadian forests and clean up its streams. Moose and deer have returned in large numbers to the park, but their populations fluctuate annually. Beavers, porcupines, and coyotes are all thriving as well. Peregrine falcons have been successfully reintroduced, as has the American marten.

for a few climbs on the Goose River and Marven Lake Trails, most routes are easy. Ask the park staff before you set out whether any trail sections are closed.

Swimming

Swimming is popular in summer at a heated saltwater pool off Point Wolfe Road. Many visitors swim at **Bennett Lake** and **Wolfe Lake beaches;** hikers often succumb to the temptation of a dip in whatever brook or river their path happens to cross on a hot day.

Cross-country Skiing

Two systems of groomed trails are

These Trails Were Made for Hiking

HARDY HIKERS TAKE HEART: You don't need to climb in a car to visit Fundy National Park. If you wish to strap on a pack and spend a few days enjoying superb coastal wilderness, two long-distance trails lead to the park. The **Fundy Footpath**, a 23-mile-long strenuous journey, leads from the Big Salmon River to join the park's trail network at Fundy's southwestern border. If you're north of the park, the **Dobson Trail** begins in the Moncton area and intersects the park's northeastern border.

For a truly epic hike, drive the **Fundy Trail Parkway** (509-833-2019. Mid-May–mid-Oct.; toll) from St. Martins to the Big Salmon River Interpretive Center at the north end of the road. Behind the interpretive center a suspension bridge crosses the Big Salmon River and you begin your wilderness trek on the Fundy Footpath West. At Little Salmon River the west branch of the trail connects to the Fundy Footpath and on to the park. You'll traverse forested hills of dark spruce forest and mixed stands of maple and birch and negotiate breathtaking traverses along shoreside cliffs 490 feet above the surf with inspiring coastal scenes from the headlands. Excursions along short side trails lead to waterfalls such as Tweedle Dee Tweedle Dum Falls on Brandy Brook near Martin Head.

At times, seemingly endless switchbacks cross rocky gorges—up to 500 feet deep—riven by streams. When the tide is out, the gorges provide access to the exposed

Matthews Head

shoreline, where you'll fight for space with tens of thousands of birds combing the nutrient-rich flats for food. Over 245 bird species have been recorded in the area including great blue herons, cormorants, semipalmated sandpipers, and semi-palmated plover along the water and various warblers, white-winged crossbills, and pileated woodpeckers along the forested stretches.

Hikers on the Fundy Footpath should keep in mind that this is a three- to five-day hike and there are no facilities of any kind so be prepared with food, clothing, and a first-aid kit. Several stream crossings can be forded only at low tide so anticipate some reflective time sitting streamside in the woods. As with any wilderness hike in the area, remember that untreated water is unsafe to drink, and early morning fog along

the cliffs is common so use caution. At the Fundy National Park border the footpath connects to the 5-mile **Goose River Trail.**

The Dobson Trail, another long-distance hiking trail to Fundy National Park, departs from Pine Glen Road in the town of Riverview *(S of Moncton on Hwy. 112)*. This 36-mile-long track begins on the south bank of the Petitcodiac River and leads through craggy forests and boulder strewn meadows to traverse the northern reaches of the Appalachian Mountains.

From 1,000-foot Hayward Pinnacle, sweeping views of the forested hills you've climbed reward the sweat on your brow and fuel that final push to the park. At the park's northeast border, the Dobson Trail joins the park's trail network on the 2-mile **Forks Trail.** ■

Avian Mosh Pit

In late summer and early fall, the Bay of Fundy's tremendously low tides expose a feast for millions of migrating shorebirds: miles of runny, reddish brown mudflats containing billions of tiny marine creatures. Especially enticing is the half-inch-long mud shrimp (*Corophium volutator*), found here in densities as high as 60,000 per square yard. Fattening up for their long, non-stop flight to South America, the birds devour as many as 20,000 mud shrimp a day.

To see birds in such rare profusion, head south of Moncton on Hwys. 114 or 915 at low tide and find an overlook with views of the bay. (Many birders consider the stretch of Hwy. 915 between Mary's Rock and Cape Enrage particularly productive.) Common sightings include semipalmated plovers and sandpipers, turnstones, yellowlegs, snipes, godwits, curlews, and phalaropes. With the birds bobbing about in such numbers, the flats appear to consist of living cobblestones.

open in winter. Thirty-one miles of groomed trails can be accessed at **Chignecto South.** Most of the routes are rated easy to moderate; warm-up shelters are located along various trails. If you'd like to overnight, a cabin may be reserved for one night's stay by calling 506-887-6000.

Scenic Drives

It's a forgivable bit of hyperbole to call the 25-mile stretch of shore between the village of St. Martins and the western border of Fundy National Park "the last coastal wilderness in North America": It is wild, it is unspoiled, and for those who gaze upon its steep cliffs and plunging waterfalls, it is breathtaking.

The **Fundy Trail Parkway,** which opened in 1999, allows you to drive the 9-mile midsection of this coastline on a low-speed road that parallels a hiking and biking trail. The parkway begins 7 miles east of St. Martins and runs to the mouth of the Big Salmon River. Dozens of scenic lookouts beckon en route, with footpaths leading down to the best beaches. At mile 2.5 on the parkway (parking lot no. 2 or no. 3), don't miss the short walk to pristine **Melvins Beach,** a tidy little cove surrounded by forested cliffs. Here the five-tiered **Fuller Falls** tumbles into the Bay of Fundy. **Pangburn Beach,** reachable by a footpath from the eastern end of Melvins Beach only at low tide, is smaller, more rugged, and even less discovered.

Plans have been drawn up to extend the parkway east, building a bridge over the Big Salmon River in order to link the road to Fundy National Park and Sussex. As of 2001, however, motorists and cyclists must return to **St. Martins** to continue east through New Brunswick. That's no hardship: The town's covered bridges, white clapboard churches, and little red lighthouse make St. Martins a picturesque burg just shy of becoming too cute for its own good. ■

Sunrise over New Brunswick's Cape Enrage

Cape Enrage

■ 65 square miles ■ Southern New Brunswick, south of Moncton at mouth of Chignecto Bay ■ Best season summer ■ Hiking, rock climbing, bird-watching, wildlife viewing ■ Contact Cape Enrage Adventures, 12 Thomson Dr., Allison, NB E1G 4G9; phone 506-887-2273

JUST A 5-MILE DRIVE FROM ALMA at the southeast corner of Fundy National Park (see pp. 158-164) lies Cape Enrage, a grim name for a grand place *(Hwy. 114 to Riverside-Albert, then Hwy. 915 and follow signs to Cape Enrage)*. Here towering cliffs overlook Chignecto Bay and afford views of Nova Scotia beyond. The lighthouse at Cape Enrage has been on station since 1838; the current light tower, being restored by a high school in nearby Moncton, is more than 150 years old. The students' work is not exclusively historical: In summer they operate a small restaurant in the lightkeeper's house and conduct courses in rappelling down the vertiginous cliffs—an adventure not for the faint of heart.

Nearby is the **Cape Enrage Marsh Nature Preserve** *(506-457-2398)*, 65 acres of coastal woods and marshes donated to the province by a local couple. The preserve, a good example of a Fundy salt marsh, includes such rare plants as the Adder's tongue fern. Also on view are interesting red shale and sandstone cliffs containing layered sedimentary deposits. ■

Grand Manan Island

■ 70 square miles ■ At mouth of Bay of Fundy, 22 miles east of Maine coast
■ Year-round ■ Hiking, rockhounding, biking, bird-watching, whale-watching,
wildlife viewing ■ Access by ferry from Blacks Harbour ■ Contact Grand
Manan Tourism Association, 130 Rte. 776, North Head, Grand Manan, NB E5G
4K9; phone 506-662-3442 or 888-525-1655. www.grandmanannb.com

THOUGH ROUGH AND BOGGY at times, Grand Manan's western-shore cliffs
and eastern-shore beaches merit the 90-minute ferry trip from the mainland. This is some of the finest hiking in Atlantic Canada, and the island's
traditional fishing villages afford a picturesque base of operations.

The western shore of Grand Manan is a wall of rock 18 miles long and
300 feet high. The only haven along this coast is Dark Harbour, so called
because the cliffs surrounding the cove keep it in shadow throughout the
morning. All other villages and roads—except the Crossing to Dark Harbour—lie along the bucolic eastern shore, with its 200-year history of
small-holding farmers and fishermen.

The interior is covered with marshes, heaths, and forests of birch,
poplar, and spruce. It is also cut by deep ravines and laced with hiking
trails, most of which cross the island's spine to reach the cliffs on the

Fishing sheds, Castalia, Grand Manan Island

western side. These trails were blazed from the early 1800s on, not for seeing sights but for saving lives: The perilous shoals and unpredictable currents around the island caused dozens of shipwrecks. That many of the trails boast spectacular views across the bay to New Brunswick and the bosky coast of Maine is a bonus for modern hikers.

The name "Manan" is a corruption of the Maliseet-Penobscot Indian word *man-an-ook,* meaning "the island." Indians visited Manan to collect birds' eggs and dulse—coarse red seaweeds that they dried and ate—but they never settled here permanently. The first European visitor was Stephen Bellinger in 1583, who stepped ashore during a trading voyage. The local tourism association suggests that Norse explorers "might" have visited Grand Manan, and that Sebastian Cabot "likely" saw the island, but it also admits the utter lack of documentation for these deeds. One generally accepted event is that Samuel Champlain sheltered on nearby White Island during a storm in 1606.

Grand Manan's first permanent settlement took shape in 1784, when 50 families loyal to the British crown received land grants on little Ross Island, just outside Grand Manan's Grand Harbour. Perhaps out of spite for this slight, the United States claimed the island until 1817, when it finally ceded Grand Manan to Great Britain. In return the U.S. got a small string of islands, including the site of present-day Eastport, Maine.

Purse seining boat, Grand Manan Island

What to See and Do

Bird-watching

After scoping out Grand Manan's abundant birdlife in May of 1833, John James Audubon penned a glowing report that precipitated a stream of enthusiastic visitors. The torrent continues today, as birders make their way here to spy some of the island's 250 species. Two-thirds of that number are seen regularly; nearly 125 species have breeding colonies in the archipelago.

A sizable puffin colony nests on **Machias Seal Island,** 12 miles off **Southwest Head** (Manan's southernmost point). Razorbills, terns, eiders, guillemots, and storm-petrels also nest on Machias Seal Island, one of the few places on the East Coast with a manned—not computerized—lighthouse. **Red Point,** about halfway between Grand Harbour and Southwest Head, is another primo birding spot. To reach it, take the boardwalk trail that originates in **Anchorage Provincial Park** *(506-662-7022)* on the shores of Long Pond Bay. And for the ultimate ornithological indulgence, seek out the bird-watching blinds that have been set up in **Long Point** and **Great Pond.**

Rockhounding

In a meadow on the east side of Southwest Head stand some odd glacial erratics, dubbed **Flock of Sheep** by local fishermen for their appearance from offshore. Passing glaciers smoothed and rounded these large rocks, then left them high and dry in a field when the ice sheets receded 15,000 years ago.

The jagged ledges and striated rocks that menace small boats off the eastern shore of Grand Manan, by contrast, are volcanic souvenirs: They oozed as magma through cracks in the seafloor bedrock, then cooled into their present hull-shredding configurations. Those hexagonal pillars of basalt you'll see near **Dark Harbour** are likewise the vestiges of volcanism.

Just north of North Head—past the old wooden Swallowtail Lighthouse and beyond **the Sawpit** (a natural depression that separates the lighthouse from the island)—is **Hole in the Wall** (Adm. fee), a rock arch carved by storms and tidal erosion. Finally, try to visit the magnificent white quartz cliff on **White Head Island,** the only other inhabited island, reached by a car ferry from Grand Harbour about six times daily in summer.

Wildlife Viewing

Seaborne excursions to the puffin colonies and whale-watching stations of the Grand Manan archipelago are a top draw. Companies such as Grand Manan SeaLand Adventures (506-662-8997) and Island Coast Boat Tours (506-662-9904) both host such outings. They also ferry visitors on scheduled or custom trips around the dozen or so islands east of Grand Manan, notably Wood, Green, White Head, Ross, Thoroughfare, and Nantucket Islands. (The latter, privately owned, discourages drop-in visits with a bad-tempered resident bull.)

The nutrient-rich waters of the Bay of Fundy mean that whale-watchers are likely to see passing finbacks, humpbacks, sperm whales, and seis, as well as the occasional endangered right whale or porpoise. Keep an eye peeled for these creatures during the ferry ride from Blacks Harbour to the Grand Manan community of North Head. On the island itself, the best areas to spot sea mammals are **Swallowtail Lighthouse, Whale Cove** at Hole in the Wall, the **Whistle at Long Eddy** (the island's northernmost point), **Castalia Marsh** (a provincially owned picnic area excellent for bird-watching), Dark Harbour,

A View to a Krill

Whale-watching with a twist is possible off the coast of Grand Manan Island thanks to a small company called Grand Manan Divers and Adventurers (506-662-3211). One of the proprietors dives beneath the tour boat with a video camera, feeding back to visitors images of whatever he finds: scallop beds, sea urchins, herring weirs, lobster nurseries.

As the occasional whale or shark drifts in and out of view, the effect is that of a hallucinatory vision—particularly when the boat is becalmed in a thick fog. On very rare occasions, a great white shark may be seen around the island. After all, Grand Manan holds the record for the world's largest great white shark, a 37-foot-long specimen caught in a weir off White Head in 1930.

Southern Head, Grand Manan Island

Southwest Head, Machias Seal Island, and **Deep Cove Beach.**

Hiking

In many ways, the trip across Grand Manan Channel is a journey back in time to a way of life whose rhythms and relaxed attitudes evoke the 19th century more than the 21st. In that spirit, you may want to leave your car in Blacks Harbour and explore the island on foot. Bicycles can be rented on Grand Manan from Adventure High *(83 Rte. 776. 506-662-3563).*

More than 50 miles of marked trails have been laid out on the island; maintained by volunteers, these paths often pass through private lands. A paved road (Rte. 776) leads from Grand Manan's main community of North Head south past Castalia Marsh to Grand Harbour—a walk of some 4 miles that

takes about an hour to complete. From there it's an easy walk of about the same distance southwest to Seal Cove.

Many visitors bike to Southwest Head, then hike for an hour or so up the western cliffs past **Bradford Cove** to **Pandora,** where splendid views across the bay await you. A more ambitious ramble of 11 miles leads from Southwest Head past Pandora all the way to Dark Harbour, then for another 3.5 miles back along the Dark Harbour Road to North Head. Also recommended is the hike north from North Head. Make your way past Hole in the Wall to the Whistle at Long Eddy Cove, and from there down the west coast to Dark Harbour— about 7 miles all told.

Trail maps are available from the Grand Manan tourism offices in North Head. ■

A Whale of a Nursery

The ungainly northern right whale (*Eubalaena glacialis*) is the most endangered giant whale on the planet. Only about 300 may be left in the Atlantic, and perhaps another 200 in the Pacific. Although the global population of right whales once topped 200,000, the fact that they float when killed made them easy to hunt. (This also explains their name; whalers considered them the "right ones to hunt.") Hunted as early as the 11th century, northern right whales had disappeared from European shores by the 16th century and were commercially extinct along eastern North America by the mid-18th century.

The species is now strictly protected, but marine biologists fear their numbers may be too low to restore the right whale to a self-sustaining population. Despite their year-round social/sexual activity (as witnessed in surface groups of 2 to 45 interacting individuals), female right whales can bear only one calf every three years.

The warm waters off Florida are the prime calving ground for right whales, but the Gulf of Maine and the Bay of Fundy serve as the creatures' main nursery in the western North Atlantic. Normally, more right whale mothers with calves are found here than in any other place in the North Atlantic.

During the 1990s, the average calving interval rose to nearly six years. When you combine this trend with the number of incidental mortalities, the result is a declining population—this in contrast to the 1980s, when right whales proliferated by 2 to 3 percent annually.

Canadian and American researchers, conservationists, shipping and fishing industries, and governments are working together to reduce the accidental deaths of right whales. A right whale conservation zone has been established in the Bay of Fundy north and east of the Grand Manan Basin—the area of the Maritime Provinces where right whales are most likely to be found. Combined with a recent right whale "baby boom" (30 calves born in the winter of 2000-2001), these efforts may help arrest the decline of this magnificent species.

Summer whale-watching aboard the schooner *D'Sonoqua*

St. Croix River

■ 114 miles long ■ Southwest New Brunswick, along Canadian border with Maine ■ Best season summer ■ Canoeing, bird-watching ■ Contact Tourism New Brunswick, P. O. Box 12345, Fredericton, NB E3B 5C3, phone 506-789-6522 or 800-561-0123. www.tourismnbcanada.com; or Maine Tourism Association, P.O. Box 2300, 325 Water St., Hallowell, ME 04347, phone 207-623-0363. www.mainetourism.com

FIRST TRANQUIL AND THEN TUMULTUOUS, the beautiful St. Croix River flows through rolling Appalachian hills on its way from the Chiputneticook Lakes to Passamaquoddy Bay. The river's variety makes it a favorite run for canoeists of all abilities and experience levels: The St. Croix passes through placid lakes, meanders past lovely clusters of cardinal flower and viburnum, and descends a number of burbling rapids that are fast enough to thrill the beginner without putting him or her in jeopardy.

The best way to reach the St. Croix River is from the community of St. Croix on Hwy. 4, located on the Maine-New Brunswick border. Intermediate paddlers will find several excellent two-day canoe trips in the area. Take Hwy. 630 north and Hwy. 122 west to **North Lake Provincial Park** *(506-453 2730)* for a 41-mile float back to St. Croix. From St. Croix canoeists can embark on a 40-mile journey to **Grand Falls,** west of the city of St. Stephen. Paddlers making good time, or with an extra day, can portage around the dam (the U.S. side has shorter portage) and continue 18 miles to St. Stephen. Novice canoeists should head to **North Lake** to get their paddles wet. ■

Grand Falls Gorge

■ 1 mile long ■ Northwest New Brunswick, 150 miles northwest of Fredericton on Trans-Canada 2 ■ Best season spring-early summer ■ Hiking, boat tour, waterfalls ■ Contact the visitor center, 25 Madawaska Rd., Grand Falls, NB E3Z 2R2; phone 506-475-7788. www.grandfalls.com/english/tourism.htm

ONE OF EASTERN CANADA'S GRANDEST, longest, and most picturesque waterways, the St. John River harbors many natural curiosities along its 418-mile length. One such spectacle is the aptly named **Grand Falls,** where the river abruptly funnels into a gorge and plunges 75 feet over a rocky ledge into the basin below. At high water in the spring, the freshet crashes down in a throaty roar.

To glimpse the St. John below the falls, pick your way down the 250-step stairway from the observation deck at the head of the falls. The plunge pools of Grand Falls, dubbed the **Wells in the Rocks,** are worth closer inspection. On summer nights they are illuminated—a gilding of the lily. Several short (less than 1 mile) **walking trails** along the river and above the falls bid you to view the cascade from closer range. You can also take a 30-minute **pontoon-boat ride** to the base of the falls. ■

Rock-top stop en route to summit of Mount Carleton

Mount Carleton Provincial Park

■ 43,000 acres ■ Northern New Brunswick, 50 miles west of Bathurst via Hwy. 180 west and Hwy. 385 south ■ Best season summer ■ Camping, hiking, backpacking, mountain climbing, boating, canoeing, cross-country skiing ■ Adm. fee ■ Contact the park, Natural Resources and Energy, 11 Gagnon St., Saint-Quentin, NB E8A 1N4; phone 506-235-0793. www.gnb.ca/0078/Index.htm

A HARD SCRAMBLE AFTER AN UNHURRIED HIKE, the last few hundred yards of the trail to Mount Carleton's 2,690-foot summit—the highest point in the Maritime Provinces—are well worth the effort. From the viewing platform of the fire tower you'll find clinging to the craggy peak, views extend in every direction over Mount Carleton Provincial Park. You can take in the Nepisiguit Lakes to the east, Mount Head and Sagamook Mountain to the north, Mount Bailey to the northwest, and the Serpentine Mountains and Sisson Branch Reservoir to the southwest.

The park encompasses several of the highest mountains of northern New Brunswick's Appalachians. Seven lakes lie in the valleys among them, not to mention the headwaters of two different river systems: The Tobique River rises in the northwest corner of the park and then flows southwest to join the St. John, while the Nepisiguit River debouches from the Nepisiguit Lakes and eventually empties into Chaleur Bay. Forests of white birch, white and black spruce, and balsam fir are mixed with pockets of red maple at lower elevations, giving the mountain views a different texture in each season: green to black in summer, jeweled with red in fall, white on black in winter.

Equally startling are the views from the crest of 2,550-foot-high Sagamook Mountain. Having slogged your way to the summit, you can rest on a rocky cliff and look almost straight down at Little Nictau Lake.

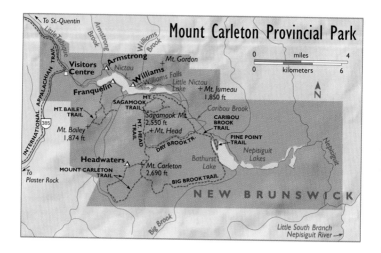

What to See and Do

Hiking

One of the park's two easiest paths is the half-mile (round-trip) **Williams Falls Trail,** a wheelchair-accessible stroll through old mixed forest to a pleasant view of the falls. The second untaxing trek is **Pine Point Trail,** a 1.4-mile loop that starts at the parking area west of Bathurst Lake. It ambles along the lakeshore, passing through a magnificent stand of old red pine and then another of white birch.

Another moderate path, the 4-mile **Caribou Brook Trail** (*access via S shore of Little Nictau Lake*), follows the waterway of the same name as it flows from the south flank of Sagamook Mountain into Little Nictau Lake. Along the way you'll be using part of an aboriginal portage route between the Nictau and Nepisiguit Lake systems. No woodland caribou live in the region anymore, but moose and deer are plentiful, and the handiwork of beavers is everywhere.

More challenging are the trails to mountain tops. **Mount Carleton** itself occupies the junction of two such trails. The 3-mile (one way) **Eastern Trail**—reached by driving south on the park road from Nictau Lake for 8 miles to a parking lot on the mountain's south side—follows an old supply road culminating in a hard, 300-yard scramble over rocks to the fire tower. The **Western Trail,** a bit longer, starts at the same parking lot and winds through the trees to reach a backwoods campground called Headwaters. The two ends of a loop trail lead from the campsite to the summit: The sheltered route climbs through the woods before breaking out into the open for the final rocky scramble to the top. From here you can return to the campsite by descending along the loop's other branch, which is rockier and more exposed to the wind.

The **Mount Bailey Trail,** a 6-mile round-trip beginning near the park headquarters at Nictau Lake, climbs steadily but not steeply through sugar maples and beeches, which give way to white birch and mountain ash higher up. About 2.5 miles along the Mount Bailey Trail, a clearly signposted half-mile side trail strikes off for **Mount Bailey.** The most difficult hike in the park is the 5-mile (round-trip) slog to the summit of **Sagamook Mountain** from Little Nictau Lake. Spectacular views of the Nictau lakes await you en route, but the path can be treacherous on rainy days.

Cross-country Skiing

Winter comes early to the mountains of New Brunswick: Snow falls in October and lingers on the slopes until June, when spring is in full swing in the valleys. In fact, the area is free of frost only 60 days a year. The best skiing can be in March, when fresh snow forms a carpet six feet deep on slopes and trails and the lake ice is still a yard thick.

Several easy groomed trails start at park headquarters (*W end of Big Nictau Lake*). One is a 4.5-mile loop that begins and ends at a heated cabin; shortcuts allow you to cinch the loop to 3 miles or just 1. All three circuits yield splendid views of Franquelin Hill and Mt. Bailey. Experienced skiers will want to test themselves on the 10-mile swing around **Nictau Lake,** or the 19-mile round-trip to the top of Mount Carleton. The park roads, unplowed in winter, must be shared with snowmobiles. ∎

Hit the Track, Jack!

Mount Carleton Provincial Park is a way station on two highly ambitious hiking paths. The 687-mile **International Appalachian Trail** passes through the park on its way to—and from—Cap Gaspé, Quebec. The 1,243-mile-long **Sentier NB Trail** (www.sentiernbtrail.com) is the New Brunswick stretch of the proposed Trans Canada Trail system, which will stretch 10,453 miles from Newfoundland to Yukon Territory, with a branch to British Columbia. About 5,770 miles have been registered but not necessarily completed; many segments have been surveyed but not yet blazed.

The Sentier NB Trail includes several sections that have yet to be linked: the **Acadian Coastal Trail,** the **Miramichi River Trail,** the

Paper-birch bark, Mount Carleton PP

Fundy Coastal Trail, the **River Valley Scenic Trail,** and the **Appalachian Range Trail.** By the summer of 2001, the province had completed 430 miles (or 90 percent) of the proposed **Trans Canada Trail** in New Brunswick.

Restigouche River

■ 100 miles long ■ Northern New Brunswick, from the highlands northeast of Edmunston to Dalhousie on Chaleur Bay ■ Best months June-Aug. ■ Fishing, canoeing ■ Fishing permit reqd. ■ Contact Tourism New Brunswick, P. O. Box 12345, Fredericton, NB E3B 5C3, phone 506-789-6522 or 800-561-0123. www .toursimnbcanada.com

MORE THAN 60 SALMON POOLS make the Restigouche one of North America's premier salmon-fishing rivers. With many of the pools under the stewardship of private lodges and angling clubs, they have attracted some of the best—and some of the wealthiest—anglers on the continent.

The Vanderbilts erected a grand lodge designed by Stanford White on the Restigouche, as did other wealthy American families. The lodges are still there, privately owned. The government of New Brunswick operates one such, called Larry's Gulch, but it is almost always booked solid by cabinet ministers and their guests.

You need not be one of these swells to enjoy the river today. You can get a catch-and-release salmon permit in a number of places along the river (see below), and more than 200 miles of the Restigouche and its tributaries (**Falls Brook, Kedgwick River, Whites Brook, Patapedia River**) are accessible to canoeists.

Whereas the river itself stretches more than 100 miles, the section that has been declared a Heritage River runs only 34 miles, from Jardine Brook *(near jct. with Kedgwick River)* to Million Dollar Pool *(jct. with Patapedia River)*. The upper section, known locally as the Little Main Restigouche, is virtually inaccessible. The heritage portion can be reached at only one point, Hwy. 265 to the little community of Kedgwick River. A campground called Echo Restigouche *(1397 Rte. 265. 506-284-2022)* on the river at the end of Hwy. 265 will arrange canoeing packages, fishing expeditions, and guided hikes into the surrounding forests.

This portion of the Restigouche passes through pristine forest: mature white spruce, white cedar, balsam fir, and yellow birch, mostly, with occasional stands of lofty white pine. The topography is gentle, and the river winds placidly from pool to pool. Canoeists who leave early in the morning (an optimum time to see wildlife) will often find the river shimmering with dew fog, and the salmon feeding in silvery flashes. With luck you will glide past a great blue heron standing in the shallows or catch the thrilling treble of a white-throated sparrow trilling to its mate.

Increasingly popular in summer is the two- or three-day canoe trip along the southeastern border of the **Kedgwick Game Management Area.** The float begins in the town of Kedgwick River and descends to the **Chaleur Bay**—dubbed "one of the most beautiful areas of the whole gulf of St. Lawrence" by French navigator Jacques Cartier in 1534. It still is.

For fly-fishing excursions on the **Lower Restigouche,** contact Craswell's Salmon Fishing Guide Service *(506-759-9890)*. All Atlantic salmon fishing on the Restigouche River is catch-and-release. ■

Fishing for salmon in the Miramichi River

Southwest Miramichi River

■ 120 miles long ■ Central New Brunswick; Juniper, 60 miles northwest of Fredericton, to Miramichi Bay ■ Best months June-Aug. ■ Fishing, canoeing, scenic drive ■ Contact Tourism New Brunswick, 800-561-0123, or City of Miramichi Community Development and Tourism, 506-623-2150

PERHAPS THE MOST FAMOUS New Brunswick salmon river is the Miramichi, which rises in hilly woodlands in the province center and flows first south, then east and northeast into Miramichi Bay. The 37 tributaries and 7,000 streams of the Miramichi system drain 13,000 acres of mostly pristine forest and fish habitat that have made it the world's major river for Atlantic salmon. On the stretch west of Boiestown, tradition inspires many owners to leave their lodges unlocked for passing canoeists.

The 120-mile segment starting near Juniper, on Hwy. 107 (access via small, unnumbered road E of town) offers peaceful wilderness travel through wide, shallow pools amid New Brunswick's trademark white spruce and balsam fir, mixed with yellow birch and the random copse of paper birch. The river is busy with moose; ospreys and eagles are common. Some 12 miles after the river swings away from Hwy. 107, rapids intervene; intermediate paddlers can negotiate them but should scout them out first. At Hayesville the river meets an unnumbered road running south to Boiestown; the Hayesville Bridge is a popular take-out.

For a driving tour of the river, head north from Fredericton on Hwy. 8 to Boiestown, where the road begins to parallel the water. Drive northeast through Doaktown (visit the **Atlantic Salmon Museum** at 263 Main St., 506-365-7787) and Blissfield for good views of the river. At Upper Blackville, take the unnumbered road east to Howard; this scenic detour follows a river bend rather than heading due north on Hwy. 8.

Dozens of small outfitters and campgrounds offer canoeing and day angling all along the river. Tourism New Brunswick has a complete list. To try your luck fly-fishing, contact Upper Oxbow Outdoor Adventures (888-277-6100. www.upperoxbow.com). A good bet for canoeing and fishing is Country Haven Lodge and Cottages (877-359-4665). ■

Kouchibouguac National Park

■ 58,880 acres ■ Central-eastern shore of New Brunswick ■ Best season summer ■ Camping, hiking, kayaking, canoeing, swimming, biking, cross-country skiing, bird-watching, wildlife viewing ■ Contact the park, 186 Rte. 117, NB E4X 2P1; phone 506-876-2443. www.parkscanada.pch.gc.ca/parks/new_brunswick/kouchibouguac

DESIGNED TO PROTECT THE DELICATE NECKLACE of beaches and barrier islands that stretch 15 miles along the warm-water shores of Northumberland Strait, Kouchibouguac (kooch-ee-BOO-gwak) National Park forms a shifting panorama of sandbars, lagoons, and bogs—a delight to naturalists and a bedevilment to offshore fishermen. On the landward side, remnants survive of the Acadian forest primeval; a few wonderful white pines, overlooked by lumbermen, still tower above an intricate landscape of cedar swamps, sea meadows, and bogs.

The countryside is flat—the 30-foot observation tower located on the Bog Trail will be the highest climb of your visit—and the placid waters of the Kouchibouguac, Black, and St. Louis Rivers unwind lazily through the park, keeping the bogs filled and nurturing an explosion of avian life: horned larks, osprey, and dozens of species of waterfowl—especially mergansers and such shorebirds as the piping plover.

The name Kouchibouguac comes from a Mi'kmaq word meaning "river of long tides." Indeed, Kouchibouguac National Park is so level that the ocean tides roll slowly inland for several miles. Though now classified as wilderness, the land encompassed by the park was stripped of most of its forest by Acadian farmers in the late 1800s. For decades after that, farmers freely wandered through the area, hunting wildfowl and cutting the marsh grasses to feed to their cattle.

The park was finally established in 1969, but it came with a price: Some residents were forcibly relocated, rekindling painful memories of an earlier expulsion—the 1755 exile of Acadians to Louisiana—and sparking furious local opposition. Today those passions seem to have died down, and it is generally accepted that the park and its many visitors have been a boon for the local economy. Tourists, for their part, are delighted to find the surrounding villages a rich repository of Acadian music, language, and food.

Most visitors come for the park's beaches and swimming but leave as accidental naturalists. That's because reaching Kellys Beach—the most popular of the white-sand beaches fronting Northumberland Strait—entails a walk through a stretch of forest that is dense in summer with trilliums and trout lilies and lively with thrushes, warblers, and woodpeckers. The beach trail leads over a boardwalk, through bogs and lagoons, and across sand dunes to a seaside expanse that is more than 4 miles long. Interpretive signs along the **Kellys Beach Trail** explain the evolution of barrier islands. Gray seals are commonly seen bobbing in the gentle swells just offshore.

Sunrise on Kellys Beach, Kouchibouguac National Park

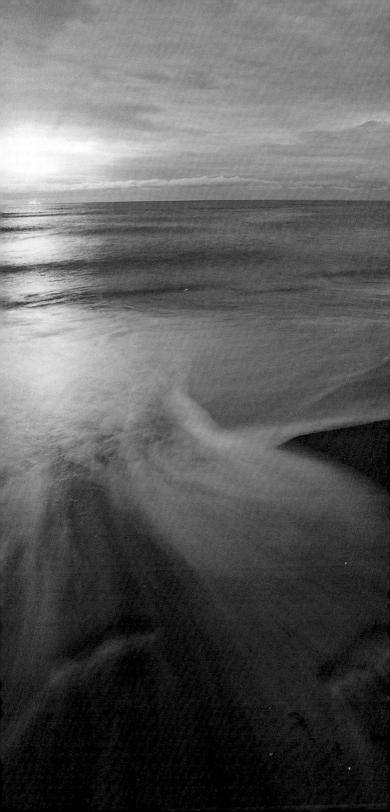

What to See and Do

Hiking

Ten trails of a quarter mile to 15 miles—none of them taxing—have been laid out in Kouchibouguac park. They are often supplemented by boardwalks and interpretive signs. For example, the half-mile **Salt Marsh Trail** (*access via Beaches Rd., 6.2 miles from visitor center*) offers lovely views of the dunes; the **Cedar Trail,** roughly the same length, starts at the Callanders Beach picnic area and takes you on a tour of marshes, lagoons, and dunes. The 1-mile **Kellys Beach Trail** (*access via Beaches Rd., 6.7 miles from visitor center*) leads to its namesake strand. The 2-mile **Bog Trail** (*access via Beaches Rd., 11.4 miles from visitor center*) features an observation tower and platforms for spotting ducks, herons, beavers, and muskrat. At 18 miles round-trip, the park's longest path—the **Kouchibouguac River Trail** (*access at end of Beaches Rd., 11.5 miles from visitor center*)—wanders along the river but may be closed by beaver damage.

Swimming

Warm, sheltered beaches line Kouchibouguac's inland sound; cooler ones are along Northumberland Strait. **Kellys Beach** is supervised from late June to late August; the swimming at **Callanders Beach** and other locations is unsupervised but legal.

Biking

Twenty miles of paved, flat-as-a-fritter biking trails make cycling a wheely good way to see this park. Bikes are available at the Ryans Recreation Equipment Rental Center (*506-876-3733*) near the South Kouchibouguac Campground.

Canoeing

With eight flat-water rivers flowing through the park, a canoe is an ideal way to reach one of its three backcountry campsites. Reserve a site at the visitor center near the park entrance. Canoes, kayaks, rowboats, and paddleboats can be rented at Ryans. ■

Whatever Boat You Float

From June to September, Kouchibouguac National Park operates the "Voyageur canoe" (*506-876-2443. Fee; reserve three days in advance*), a guided ride to offshore sandbars for up to nine people. Seals often swim alongside for a closer look; visitors may spot the occasional osprey or bald eagle while gliding by nesting sites of the common tern.

Local outfitter Kayakouch (*506-876-1199. www.kayakouch.com*) guides kayak tours along the St-Louis River as well as offshore. Tours range from a few hours of paddling through gray seal colonies to four- or five-day excursions among dunes and lagoons, with a chance to see thousands of seabirds up close.

For those who are less self-locomoted, Kouchibouguac Cruise (*506-876-4212*) leads two-hour offshore tours in a 30-person motor cruiser.

Sunset at Hopewell Rocks

Hopewell Rocks Provincial Park

■ 45 acres ■ Southeast New Brunswick in Shepody Bay, 20 miles southeast of Moncton on Hwy. 114 ■ Best season summer ■ Bird-watching, tide-watching ■ Contact Hopewell Rocks Ocean Tidal Exploration Site, 131 Discovery Rd., Hopewell Cape, Albert County, NB E4H 4Z5; phone 506-734-3534 or 877-734-3429. www.hopewellrocks.com

HEAD FOR CAPE HOPEWELL to see what people look like when turned to stone by an angry whale. That's how Mi'kmaq legend explains the existence of the Hopewell Rocks—curious flowerpot stone formations, erosional pillars, and freestanding sea stacks eaten away by the voracious tides in the nearby Bay of Fundy. At high tide, the Hopewell Rocks appear to be unexceptional small islands, each capped by dwarf spruce and fir. By low tide, however, when the water has dropped away—as it does here at an extraordinary 6 to 8 vertical feet per hour—the true shape and scope of the rocks are exposed: They tower as tall as five-story buildings sitting on the ocean floor.

Hopewell Rocks, billed as The Ocean Tidal Exploration Site, has interpretive guides available to lead ocean-floor walks from May to early October, but you are free to explore on your own—at low tide, naturally. Tide tables are posted in the reception center. The beach, reached via a staircase from the reception center's observation deck, is accessible for a few hours on either side of low tide.

As at so many other spots along the Bay of Fundy shore, the Hopewell Rocks area is a critical stop for millions of migrating birds, which pause here each spring and fall to feast on mud clams, periwinkles, and marine worms. Any time from July to October is optimum for spotting a variety of shorebirds, including plover, sandpipers, curlews, and godwits. Low tide is the best time to spy them feeding; at high tide they tend to roost in the cliffs, out of sight of the visitor center and its deck. ■

Newfoundland

Bird Rock, Cape St. Mary's Ecological Reserve

THE LANDSCAPE OF NEWFOUNDLAND enchants visitors. Precipitous sea cliffs, alpine mountains, and Arctic barrens beckon even as the weather turns wild and the winds elemental. This harsh, blustery land, where shearwaters and kittiwakes swirl and quarrel along the cliffs, will get under your skin.

The Island of Newfoundland lies off the east coast of Canada, with the Gulf of St. Lawrence to the west and the Atlantic Ocean to the north, east, and south. Once part of

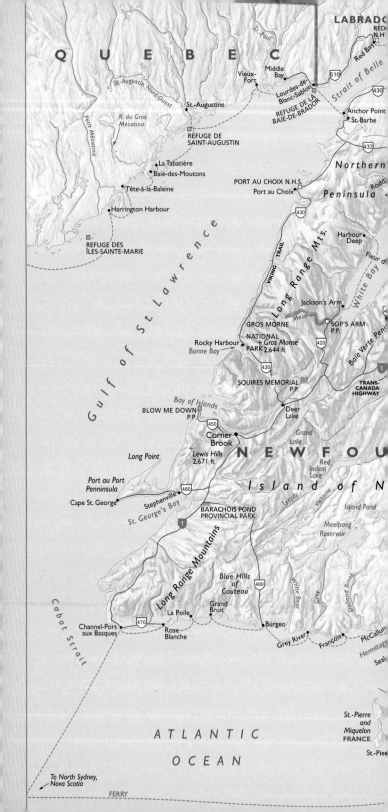

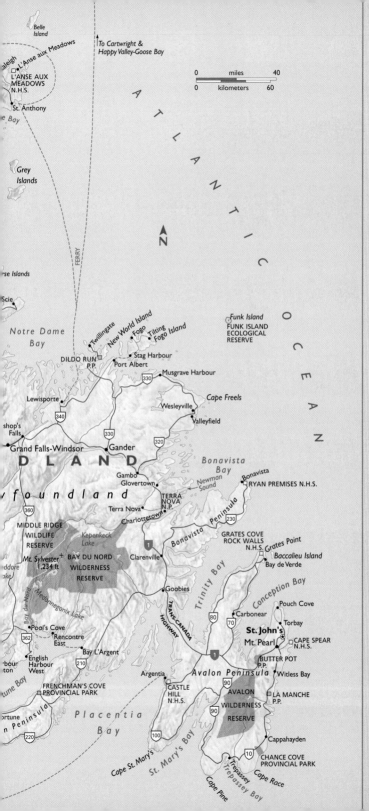

Belle
Island

Raleigh
L'Anse aux Meadows
L'ANSE AUX
MEADOWS
N.H.S.

To Cartwright &
Happy Valley-Goose Bay

e Bay

St. Anthony

ATLANTIC

0   miles   40
0   kilometers   60

Grey
Islands

N

se Islands

FERRY

Scie

Funk Island
FUNK ISLAND
ECOLOGICAL
RESERVE

O   C   E   A   N

Notre Dame
Bay

Twillingate
New World Island
Fogo
Tilting
Fogo Island

Stag Harbour

DILDO RUN
P.P.
Port Albert

Musgrave Harbour

330

Lewisporte

340

Cape Freels

Wesleyville

shop's
Falls

330

Valleyfield

Grand Falls-Windsor

Gander

320

L A N D

Bonavista
Bay

Bonavista

RYAN PREMISES N.H.S.

foundland

Gambo
Glovertown

Newman
Sound

360

TERRA
NOVA
N.P.

MIDDLE RIDGE
WILDLIFE
RESERVE

Kepenkeck
Lake

Terra Nova

Charlottetown

Bonavista
Peninsula

230

GRATES COVE
ROCK WALLS
N.H.S. Grates Point

Mt. Sylvester
1,234 ft

BAY DU NORD
WILDERNESS
RESERVE

Medonnegonix Lake

Clarenville

1

Baccalieu Island
Bay de Verde

Goobies

Trinity Bay

Conception Bay

oddore
Lake

Bay du Nord

360

Pool's Cove
Rencontre
East

362

Bay L'Argent

210

Pouch Cove

Carbonear

80

70

St. John's

Mt. Pearl

Torbay

CAPE SPEAR
N.H.S.

harbour
ton

English
Harbour
West

TRANS-CANADA HIGHWAY

1

BUTTER POT
P.P.

Witless Bay

FRENCHMAN'S COVE
PROVINCIAL PARK

Argentia

CASTLE
HILL
N.H.S.

Avalon Peninsula

90

AVALON
WILDERNESS
RESERVE

LA MANCHE
P.P.

e Bay

n Peninsula

220

Placentia

Bay

100

90

Cape St. Mary's

St. Mary's Bay

10

Cappahayden

CHANCE COVE
PROVINCIAL PARK

Fortune

Cape Pine

Trepassey
Trepassey Bay

Cape Race

Channel-Port aux Basques

a supercontinent, the bulk of the island is geologically an extension of the Appalachian Mountains. Tiny Avalon Peninsula, the easternmost portion of North America, is a remnant of the Eurafrican continent, a pre-Pangaea formation that existed 570 million years ago.

Sitting at the confluence of the cold Labrador Current and the warm Gulf Stream, Newfoundland is subject to some wild weather patterns; fog habitually hangs over the island's eastern and southern coasts. Although it's quite possible to have balmy weather in summer, it's wise not to count on it. You'll enjoy your visit much more if you prepare for rapid changes, dress for squalls, and accept gales as a natural condition of island life.

Newfoundland's animal population is rich but hardly diverse. Fewer than 20 mammals—including lynx, beaver, mink, and fox—are native to the island, though many introduced species—snowshoe hare, moose, and caribou among them—have flourished. Moose, introduced to the island in 1878 and again in 1904, are common throughout Newfoundland; their roadside presence is notorious. Woodland caribou, numbering over 60,000 in several herds, roam the island. Several whale species frequent the waters offshore, especially along the eastern seaboard.

Newfoundlanders fondly call their island the "Rock" because so much of it is exposed, but pockets of lush (if stunted) vegetation abound. Barrens of peat, heath, and marsh cover much of Newfoundland. Black spruce and balsam fir make up the majority of the boreal forest found on the island; stands of larch, alder, paper birch, and aspen are also common.

Wildflowers—among them pitcher plant, fireweed, and harebell—bloom profusely in the summer months, turning the land into a riot of color.

Though outdoor enthusiasts find delight throughout the entire island, Gros Morne National Park, wedged between the starkly beautiful Long Range Mountains and the Gulf of St. Lawrence, is unquestionably Newfoundland's gem. The geology and scenery is exceptional, even by Newfoundland standards.

If you want boreal forest and a shore deeply indented with fjords, try Terra Nova National Park. If you're interested in rocky shores, great bird colonies, tundra barrens, caribou, whales, and icebergs, you need go no farther than the Avalon Peninsula. Cape St. Mary's and Baccalieu Island Ecological Reserves, as well as the stunning Avalon Wilderness Reserve—home to a large caribou herd—all lie within a few hours of St. John's, the capital of Newfoundland. Whatever your preference, Newfoundland will not disappoint you. ▪

Capelins hung out to dry

Cape St. Mary's Ecological Reserve

■ 2,473 acres ■ Southwest tip of Avalon Peninsula ■ Best months May-Aug. Center open May–mid-Oct. ■ Hiking, bird-watching, whale-watching ■ Adm. fee ■ Contact the reserve, St. Bride's, Placentia Bay, NF A0B 2Z0; phone 709-277-1666 or 800-563-6365. www.gov.nf.ca/parks&reserves/capestmarys.htm

"YOU MAY NEVER COME CLOSER to knowing what it is to be a bird," claims a reserve brochure about Cape St. Mary's spectacular Bird Rock. There is some truth to it: The birds are so close, in such numbers, and pay so little heed to visitors that you genuinely feel as though you are somehow participating in the colony's life.

Located at the southwest tip of the Avalon Peninsula, the reserve covers one of the most southerly expanses of subarctic tundra. These heathlands—expanses of barren and bog—lie smothered in dense mosses, lichens, grasses, and low-lying shrubs. White spruce and balsam fir, stunted by the constant battering winds, form an impenetrable mass called tuckamore. Boulders abandoned by the retreat of the last ice age lie scattered everywhere.

Bird Rock, an isolated sea stack 45 feet lower than the surrounding 400-foot-high cliffs and only several feet offshore, is the standout attraction of Cape St. Mary's. It acts as a high-rise apartment building for thousands of nesting birds. The largest northern gannet colony in Newfoundland, the world's most southerly colony of thick-billed murres, and myriad black-legged kittiwakes, razorbills, black guillemots, herring gulls, and great and double-crested cormorants make Cape St. Mary's their home. The nesting area stretches for more than 2.5 miles along the coast, but the birds nest on Bird Rock in such profusion that they "swirl past the cliff face like a blizzard of snow," according to naturalist and ornithologist Roger Tory Peterson.

Aside from the throngs of nesting birds, the reserve seems desolate of wildlife, but the red fox, ermine, masked shrew, meadow vole, willow ptarmigan, and small bands of caribou roam the barrens. Bald eagles, ravens, and other predatory birds routinely appear. Flocks of American pipits and horned larks settle on the barrens. In summer, migrating shearwaters and large numbers of plover stop over in the barrens to feed on berries. In winter when the other birds have left, flocks of common eiders, oldsquaw, black scoters and surf scoters, and eastern Canada's largest wintering population of the endangered eastern harlequin duck populate the reserve.

In summer, morning fog—a product of the cool, damp climate—frequently socks in the reserve. Some say it adds a magical touch. There's nothing quite like listening to the raucous calls of the nesting birds echoing through the fog. And gannet will swoop out of the air, almost within touching distance, before vanishing once again into the mist. (Even in fog, the colony is visible from the lookout area.) The climbing sun will soon burn off the fog and reveal the thousands of flitting birds.

Northern gannet colony, Bird Rock, Cape St. Mary's Ecological Reserve

Northern gannets, Cape St. Mary's Ecological Reserve

What to See and Do

Most visitors begin at the **interpretive center** located at the end of Cape Road, the reserve's access. It offers a wonderful, if rather distant, view of **Bird Rock.** A scale model of the reserve will help orient you; there are regular lectures on the life history of seabirds, and guided walks and nature hikes can be arranged *(709-277-1666).*

The Ocean's Bounty

Let me fish off Cape. St Mary's
Where the hagdowns sail
and the foghorns wail....

One of the richest fishing grounds in the world lies just a few miles off Cape St. Mary's. Much of the historically important inshore cod fishery centered on this area; fishermen who did poorly in other areas around the island could usually count on a decent catch in Cape St. Mary's waters. The cod fishery collapsed because of overfishing and has not recovered, but the waters are still rich in marine life.

Thanks to converging ocean currents (the warm Gulf Stream and the cold Labrador Current), the area has huge concentrations of plankton, which form the basis of a complex marine web. For instance, feeding off the plankton, the small, sardine-size capelins attract scores of seabirds (they devour around 250,000 tons of capelins per year) and whales. Pods of minke—the smallest of the North American baleen whales—humpbacks, and immense fin whales appear in great numbers during July.

The reserve's main attraction is the nesting colonies of Bird Rock. The towering rock is just 30 feet or so off the coast and virtually at eye level, so visitors can come very close to the nests without disturbing them. A half-mile **trail** from the interpretive center leads over rough terrain to the cliff side with views of Bird Rock. Be careful at the cliff's edge: It is very high, and no guardrail or warning signs alert those who stray off trail or too close to the edge. ∎

Mistaken Point Ecological Reserve

▨ Less than 2 square miles ▨ Southeast tip of Avalon Peninsula, 10 miles southeast of Portugal Cove South, along road to Cape Race ▨ Best season summer ▨ Bird-watching, fossil viewing ▨ Contact Newfoundland and Labrador Department of Tourism, Culture and Recreation, P.O. Box 8700, St. John's, NF A1B 4J6; phone 709-729-2424 or 800-563-6353. www.gov.nf.ca/parks&reserves/ecolres.htm

THE IMPRESSIONS OF 620-MILLION-YEAR-OLD soft-bodied creatures—probably the ancestors of jellyfish and sea anemones—have been found off the southeastern coast of the Avalon Peninsula. Volcanic activity fossilized in great detail millions of marine organisms. The tiny Mistaken Point Ecological Reserve protects them and a host of fossils that represent perhaps 20 different kinds of deepwater creatures. These impressions are among the oldest multicell fossils in the world and are of such scientific import that efforts are being made to have the site declared a World Heritage site.

Fossils show only the hard parts of an animal—those tend to survive the volcanic disruption that led to their fossilization. Presumably the volcanic ash settled here gently enough—and solidified quickly enough—to delicately encase the soft-bellied creatures; imprints of their bodies were made before the creatures decayed. Some are so detailed that even the slender threads the creatures used to anchor themselves to the rocks show up. The impressions range in size from a few inches in length to a foot or more and reveal spindle-shaped, leaf-shaped, and dendrite-like—branching or treelike—organisms.

The reserve is about 3 miles long, but the critical portion of it—the one where the densest concentrations of fossils are found—is not much bigger than a couple of basketball courts.

There are no hiking trails, but a well-worn unmarked path leads 1.2 miles from the gravel access road *(about 9 miles S of the community of Portugal Cove South)* to the fossil beds. You can walk around and find a picnic spot with a scenic view on the nearby headlands. For bird-watchers, gannets, gulls, and kittiwakes sport on the cliffs and a variety of ducks play in the water. ∎

Wildflowers in bloom, Avalon Wilderness Reserve

Avalon Wilderness Reserve

■ 264,000 acres ■ South-central Avalon Peninsula, 30 miles south of St. John's ■ Best season late summer/early fall ■ Hiking, backpacking, canoeing, fishing, wildlife viewing ■ Permit required (free from Parks and Natural Areas Division 709-729-2424) ■ Contact Newfoundland and Labrador Department of Tourism, Culture and Recreation, P.O. Box 8700, St. John's, NF A1B 4J6; phone 709-729-2424 or 800-563-6353. www.gov.nf.ca/parks&reserves

PROVIDING SANCTUARY FOR PLANT and wildlife species normally found much farther north, the Avalon Wilderness Reserve protects one of North America's most southerly unspoiled barrenlands. Also sheltered here is the Avalon woodland caribou herd. Illegal hunting once reduced the herd to fewer than 100 animals, but it now numbers close to 2,500.

Not much more than 330 feet above sea level, the terrain is generally flat, but the occasional peak tops 650 feet. Scattered across this gently rolling plateau are giant erratics—boulders left over when ice age glaciers receded 10,000 years or so ago. The glaciers also carved out hundreds of ponds and created parallel moraines—gravelly ridges of rock and debris deposited as the ice retreated.

Dense heaths of partridgeberry, Labrador tea, sheep laurel (known to Newfoundlanders as the deliciously named "goowitty"), and peat bogs rich with pitcher plants blanket the reserve. Lichens are plentiful as well: Straggly old-man's beard decorates black spruce tree trunks and branches, while sponge-like mats of reindeer moss, the caribou's main food, hug the ground. The caribou also eat mushrooms and green plants. Their diet and other factors contribute to the robustness of the herd, which outshines the well-being of caribou herds elsewhere on the island. Because they are so healthy, the males can spend massive amounts of energy producing record-size sets of antlers—a spectacular sight when fully grown in fall.

Though Avalon is best known for its caribou, many other animals live here: Moose, lynx, fox, snowshoe hare, weasel, mink, red squirrel, shrew, and meadow vole make the barrens their home, while otter, beaver, and muskrat swim in the reserve's many waterways and ponds. In summer great numbers of waterfowl—Canada goose, ring-necked duck, green-winged teal, northern pintail, and others—take refuge in the reserve.

What to See and Do

The recreationist will find Avalon a wonderful place to get away and enjoy the solitude. Ringed by Hwys. 10 and 90, the reserve is accessible by foot from a string of coastal communities.

Canoeing

A lovely three- to five-day paddle over approximately 25 miles can be made between Cape Pond and Peak Pond. (You can do the trip in reverse, too, but why battle the current?) You'll need to portage in some places, but you will not encounter any challenging rapids except during high water. The leisurely trip crosses several ponds using connecting streams and affords easy wildlife-watching: Moose are ubiquitous along several stretches of the river, as are caribou and waterfowl.

To access Cape Pond, take the Southern Shore Highway (Hwy. 10) to Cape Pond Road and drive 6.2 miles to the put-in (Cape Pond Road requires a 4WD or high-clearance vehicle). You'll need to arrange a shuttle car or pickup at Peak Pond, which lies off the Salmonier Line (Hwy. 90). Wilderness Newfoundland Adventures (*67 Circular Rd., St. John's, NF A1C 2Z4. 709-753-1432 or 888-747-6353*) can help you set up a multiday trip.

Fishing

Several rivers and streams, including the **Salmonier River** and **North Arm,** provide excellent fishing for smelt and brook and brown trout. The **Peter's River** in particular is popular with anglers hoping to catch salmon. A fishing license is required and nonresidents must be accompanied by a licensed guide when fishing for salmon. Local sport shops and convenience stores usually have a list of names.

Hiking

History buffs and hikers alike will enjoy the **d'Iberville Trail,** which follows the footsteps of French Navy captain Pierre LeMoyne d'Iberville, who led the first mili-

tary crossing of the peninsula's southeast interior from 1696 to 1697. A four-day, three-night affair covering 30 miles, the primitive trail crosses barrens, bogs, coniferous forests, and numerous streams. Pick up the trail in St. Catherine's next to the senior's home off Hwy. 90; you'll end at Horse Chops Road just south of Aquaforte, a short distance from Ferryland on Hwy. 10. ■

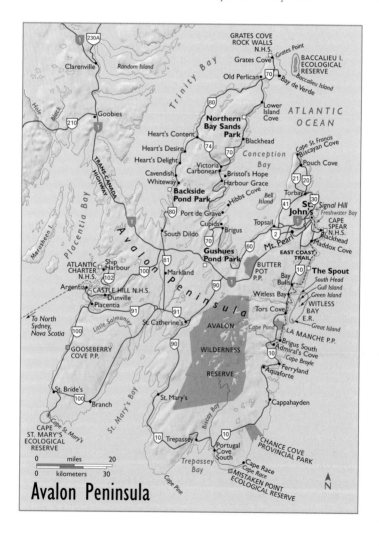

Avalon Peninsula

East Coast Trail

■ 124 miles long ■ Eastern coast of Avalon Peninsula ■ Hiking, swimming, bird-watching, whale-watching, icebergs, geyser ■ Contact East Coast Trail Association, 50 Pippy Place, P.O. Box 8034, St. John's, NF A1B 3M7; phone 709-738-4453. www.ecta.nf.ca

PASSING THROUGH A LANDSCAPE OF GREAT BEAUTY, ruggedness, and variety, the Avalon Peninsula's East Coast Trail follows the most easterly coastline in North America, from St. John's in the north to Admiral's Cove in the south. (Planned additions will extend the trail from Cape Francis in the north to Cape Race in the south.) As the trail rises and falls along the headlands, it traverses barrens dotted with delicate lichen gardens and damp, brooding spruce woods overgrown with old-man's beard. Both whales and icebergs are frequently sighted off the coast.

More than 120 miles long, the East Coast Trail is no day hike. However, the trailbuilders created it as a series of shorter trails, or paths, of manageable distances with numerous access points. For the most part, the trail strings together decades-old (sometimes centuries-old) cliffside paths that connect coastal villages. At present the trail numbers ten paths, beginning in St. John's with the Deadman's Bay Path and concluding in the town of Admiral's Cove with the Brigus Head Path.

Some stretches of the East Coast Trail are easy to hike; others are difficult. You'll walk along high cliffs (some of them over 330 feet above the ocean), ford streams, scramble through great boulder-strewn gullies, and skirt deep coves rimmed with rocky beaches. Detailed maps and descriptions are available from the East Coast Trail Association.

Breaching whale, Witless Bay

What to See and Do

If you have only a day or two to spare, the short paths around St. John's provide excellent opportunities to experience the coastal trail. The East Coast Trail begins at historic **Fort Amherst's lighthouse** on the south side of St. John's harbor.

The first 6.2 miles of the trail, dubbed **Deadman's Bay Path,** lead steeply to the top of the South Side Hills. Pocked with glacial ponds and valleys flooded by beaver dams, these hills offer wonderful views of Signal Hill to the north, the city of St. John's to the west, and Cape Spear to the south. Swimming holes along the summit ridge entice hikers to take an invigorating dip—**Barren Pond** seems to be a favorite with the capital's residents. The path hews to the ridgeline, where you'll see flora such as kalmia heath that is able to survive the windy, exposed conditions.

About 2.3 miles into the hike the trail begins a precipitous descent, following the Ennis River

to Freshwater Bay and the abandoned community of Freshwater. Here a stone walkway bridges a *barachois*—an Acadian term describing shallow pools separated from the sea by sand dunes—at the end of Freshwater Bay.

Continue up the narrow peninsula to Small Point; pause as the path passes Sly Rocks to view the remains of the *Vasco D'Orey*, a ship that sank here in 1977. Although pelagic birds such as black-legged kittiwakes winter at sea, look for their summer nesting colonies among the seaside crags of Small Point. As you scan the sky for this gull, listen for its distinctive, repetitive cry of *kittiwake!* Farther along the path, **Peggys Leg** offers another chance to glimpse cliffside kittiwake nests. From this spit, you'll stroll easily through heath and woods along the remaining 1.7 miles to the parking area in Blackhead.

You can pick up the **Blackhead**

Path here—it links Blackhead to **Cape Spear National Historic Site** *(709-772-5367)*—but many people skip this part of the hike and drive the short distance (2 miles) to Cape Spear. The **Cape Spear Path** starts at the parking area at the eastern end of the historic site's access road. This path can be done as a 6-mile out-and-back walk to North Head. (Or arrange a ride or park a car in Maddox Cove, some 3 miles farther south from North Head.)

Two lighthouses within the first quarter mile alert vessels to the presence of North America's easternmost tip. The remains of shipwrecks just offshore—no fewer than a dozen, the earliest dating to 1850—testify to the hazards of this rocky, windswept shore.

The cape's rugged nature is equally inhospitable to flora. You'll find a combination of bog and low-growing, hearty shrubs commonly called heath marking your journey to North Head. Return the way you came or continue to Maddox Cove.

Hikers with a full day for an excursion will be well rewarded by the trek along the **Spout Path.** The shoreline geyser aptly named **The Spout** is probably the most popular attraction on the East Coast Trail. This is no easy walk in the woods, however, as the shortest route to The Spout is 13 miles round-trip. Access the northern trailhead of Spout Path from the pull-off on Shoal Bay Road *(off Hwy. 10)*; begin at the town of Bay Bulls to hike south to north.

The trail crosses forested headlands of gorges and steep cliffs, home to eagles and nesting kitti-

wakes. The trail winds and twists along craggy shoreline and open windswept meadows before reaching The Spout.

Much like a surfacing whale clearing its blowhole, The Spout blasts water some 200 feet into the air. A rasping, throaty roar accompanies each misty eruption. The waterfall of an underground stream created a funnel-shaped cavity in the rock. When the pounding surf squeezes into this cavity, it drives compressed air through a 2-foot-diameter hole at the surface; the force shoots the fresh water of the waterfall upward as mist. This landmark geyser was noted in ships's logs as early as 1664, but around 1930 a rock within the cavity fell and clogged it. In 2000, engineers removed the nearly three-ton rock from the geyser's throat, restoring its rhythmic pulse. ■

Vanishing Villages

For the 400-plus years that Europeans have lived on Newfoundland, villages have been anchored to the rocks in isolated coves, reachable only by boat or cliffside path. As the fishing industry has waned in recent years, however, this isolated and self-sufficient lifestyle has faded. Many a small village has been abandoned, left to slip unwanted into the sea. Found all along the East Coast Trail, such settlements stand as poignant reminders of a time when fishermen plied the giant swells that roll down the coast.

Witless Bay Ecological Reserve

■ 348 acres ■ Off eastern coast of Avalon Peninsula, between Bay Bulls and Bauline ■ Sea kayaking, bird-watching, whale-watching, boat tours, icebergs ■ Contact Newfoundland and Labrador Department of Tourism, Culture and Recreation, P.O. Box 8700, St. John's, NF A1B 4J6; phone 709-729-2424 or 800-563-6353. www.gov.nf.ca/parks&reserves/witless_bay.htm

VIRTUALLY ABOUNDING WITH NESTING BIRDS, Witless Bay Ecological Reserve is a birder's heaven. The four islands—**Gull, Green, Great,** and **Pee Pee**—that constitute the reserve have sheer cliffs and outcroppings. These features make them ideal for the almost two million seabirds found here in summer. Great and Gull Islands are forested; the others are bare rock.

Several species coexist and nest on the small islands because each has a preferred nesting habitat, so different species inhabit different levels of the islands. Kittiwakes (small gulls) commandeer the cliffs' lower levels. Razorbill auks and common murres nest on ledges above them. Higher

Drifting iceberg, Witless Bay

up, the Atlantic puffin burrows in grassy knolls. Herring gulls and black-backed gulls, the islands' predators, reside on top, seemingly always circling for prey.

The puffin colony—the largest in the North Atlantic, estimated at 216,000 breeding pairs—is nearly three-quarters of the eastern North American population. The world's second largest colony of Leach's storm-petrels, 780,000 pairs, also makes these islands its home.

What to See and Do

Visitors are not permitted on the reserve islands, but that hardly matters. You can still get close enough to experience the screeching chaos of the nesting colonies.

Several tour operators run boats out of Bay Bulls; boats depart every hour or so in summer for leisurely trips around the bay and the four islands. (The reserve is so popular that some ecologists have expressed concern over the effect this benign eco-tourism could have on the bird

Following pages: Iceberg at sunset, Witless Bay

On the Defensive

On a visit to Witless Bay Ecological Reserve you'll see puffins, gulls, guillemots, kittiwakes, and dozens of other birds, but you're unlikely to see a Leach's storm-petrel. Most of a Leach's storm-petrel's life is spent in gull avoidance—frequently to no avail: The discarded wings of thousands of storm-petrels litter Gull Island.

These birds spend much of their time at sea as a defense against gull attacks. They return to their nests under the cover of darkness; very early in the morning—usually around 2 a.m.—they come fluttering in from the open ocean like bats in huge flocks. (Tubular nostrils above the bird's beak expel sea salt from its body, enhancing its pelagic lifestyle.) The storm-petrel also hides its nest as an additional defense. More than half a million conceal their burrows beneath the gnarled and twisted spruces of Gull Island.

populations.) Check out Captain Murphy's Seabird and Whale Tours (P.O. Box 149, Puffin Cove, Witless Bay, NF A0A 4K0. 709-334-2002) or contact the department of tourism for other boat tour operators. Most of the tour boats offer interpretive programs and seabird identification lectures; others have mostly good cheer, storytelling, and Newfoundland music. To find an operator suited to your needs and tastes, ask before you go.

In addition to the thousands of birds, a trip around **Witless Bay** will reveal dolphins, harbor porpoises, whales—especially humpbacks and minkes—sea kayakers paddling about the islands in good weather, and drifting icebergs. To sea kayak, contact Wilderness Newfoundland Adventures (67 Circular Rd., St. John's, NF A1C 2Z4. 888-747-6353). Many of the glaciers, having traveled south from Greenland, run aground in Witless Bay and break up. (Tour operators may get so close to the icebergs that you'll hear the bergs creak and groan.)

The whales, usually present from June to September, are accustomed to humans. The 40-ton humpbacks, in particular, delight visitors when they breach and barrel roll. They often swim close to the boats to get a closer look; the whales sometimes bump the boats, but in general they seem wary of their own power and seldom do even any inadvertent harm.

While in Witless Bay, consider hiking the easy 4.6-mile-long **Micheleen's Path**—part of the **East Coast Trail** (see pp. 195-97)—between Witless Bay and Bay Bulls. Access the trail at the terminus of Bear Cove Road on the eastern edge of town. Wonderful views extend across the bay to the reserve islands—Gull Island is the largest and closest—along the first couple of miles to the rocky promontory of **South Head.** In another 1.5 miles, the path reaches **Island Cove,** which, surprise, has an island in it. The cove is a popular sea kayaking destination. The trail ends in Bay Bulls at the south end of Quay's Road. ∎

Baccalieu Trail

■ 160 miles long ■ Starting point Gushues Pond Park, east of Hwy. 70 on Trans-Canada 1 ■ Best months June–late Oct. ■ Camping, biking, bird-watching, whale-watching, scenic drive, boat tours, icebergs ■ Contact Baccalieu Trail Tourism Association, Unit 1, 4 Pikes Lane, Carbonear, NF A1Y 1A7; phone 709-596-3474

THE GLORIOUS COASTAL BACCALIEU TRAIL hugs the coastline of the Bay de Verde Peninsula. This scenic drive (or trail as it is called in Newfoundland) rises and falls along formidable cliffs and promontories, skirts coves and inlets, and passes rocky beaches. It strings together picturesque small fishing communities, sites of historic interest, and—off the tip of the peninsula—the Baccalieu Island Ecological Reserve. From Trans-Canada 1, the trail follows Hwy. 70 alongside Conception Bay north to the peninsula's tip and returns via Hwy. 80 beside Trinity Bay.

Although you can certainly drive the Baccalieu Trail, it offers an ideal three-day outing for the hardy cyclist. Whatever your preference, the journey will delight you. The first day's 65 miles are the most grueling; the second (65 miles) and third days (30 miles) are not quite as taxing. (This itinerary suggests you overnight at provincial parks, but there are plenty of bed-and-breakfasts, motels, and cottages along the route if you'd rather not camp.)

Begin at **Gushues Pond Park** (*709-229-4003 in season or 709-596-5110 off-season*) on Trans-Canada 1 and head north on Hwy. 70. The road twists and rolls along a ridge, passing meadows, marshes, and ponds. After about 10 miles a short 3-mile detour on Hwy. 60 visits the coastal towns of **Brigus** and **Cupids.** Brigus is the hometown of Capt. Bob Bartlett, a member of Commodore Peary's expedition to the North Pole in 1909; the captain's home, **Hawthorne Cottage** (*709-528-4004 in season or 709-753-9262 off-season. Mid-May–mid-Oct.; adm. fee*), is now a national historic site. Cupids claims to be the first (1610) English settlement in Canada.

Atlantic puffins

Green's Harbour along the Baccalieu Trail

Return to Hwy. 70 and continue north. At Clarke's Beach make a right turn onto Hwy. 72 to cycle up the picture-postcard scenic **Port de Grave Peninsula.** The folksy **Fisherman's Museum** *(709-786-3912. Late June–Labor Day, by appt. rest of year; adm. fee)* at Hibbs Cove depicts typical outport life in the early 20th century. Back on Hwy. 70, cycle through the communities of Bay Roberts, Spaniard's Bay, Tilton, and Riverhead before reaching Harbour Grace, home of the first civilian airport in North America. Amelia Earhart broke barriers when she took off from here in 1932 for her history-making transatlantic solo flight. The **Conception Bay Museum** *(709-596-5465. June–mid-Sept.)* holds exhibits on Earhart, the 17th-century pirate Peter Easton, and the town's history.

Just up the road sits **Carbonear;** try to plan your journey to coincide with the annual **Conception Bay Folk Festival** held here in late July *(for information call 709-596-0345).* It's a celebration of Newfoundland's and Ireland's music, song, and dance. Continue along Hwy. 70, passing a string of tiny communities separated by craggy headlands and towering cliffs popular with photographers. **Northern Bay Sands Park** *(709-584-3465 in season or 709-584-3809 off-season)*, about 24 miles from Carbonear, makes an excellent stopping point for the night.

The second day begins much as the first ends. For 15 miles the trail rises and falls between coves as it hugs the cliffs and passes through several small fishing villages (where whale sightings are common); at Caplin Cove it heads west to reach Old Perlican on the peninsula's west coast. Continue north on Hwy. 70 and follow signs to **Bay de Verde**—first settled in the 1600s by planters from the south trying to escape French raiders—and the spectacular **Baccalieu Island Ecological Reserve** *(709-729-2429).* The **Bears Cove** lookout located on the road into town affords good views of the island.

Tour boats *(Baccalieu Bird Island Boat Tours 709-587-2860. June-*

Sept.) leave from Bay de Verde to ply the waters around the reserve. Baccalieu Island rises sheer out of the Atlantic, its steep cliffs 328 to 980 feet tall. Heath, grassy turf, and stunted old-growth black spruce and balsam fir cover the island, whose only inhabitants are birds and foxes (the latter rarely go hungry). Perhaps as many as 3.4 million breeding pairs of Leach's storm-petrels (see sidebar p. 202)—the world's largest colony and almost 40 percent of the global population—live here. So do thousands of Atlantic puffins, black-legged kittiwakes, northern gannets, thick-billed murres, razorbills, black guillemots, northern fulmars, and black-backed gulls. The cold subarctic waters of the Labrador Current and the warmer waters of the Gulf Stream intersect here; their interaction with the extraordinarily complex coastline cause nutrients to well up and meld together, feeding the marine life that in turn supports the birds.

Return to Old Perlican and pick up Hwy. 80 to head south down the western side of the peninsula; picturesque **Trinity Bay** lies on your right. The road crosses a landscape of rolling hills and forests, with bucolic farmsteads complete with grazing ponies and sod-covered root cellars. Stop at **Heart's Content** to visit the historic cable station *(709-583-2160. Mid-June–mid-Oct.)* where in 1866 the first Morse code signals to Europe were transmitted on a transatlantic telegraph cable. The trail becomes markedly less rugged as it continues south through Heart's Desire, Heart's Delight, Islington, Cavendish, and Whiteway. You may want to stop and camp for the night at **Backside Pond Park** *(709-588-2756).*

The third day is an easy 30-mile ride back to the trail's starting point. Consider stopping at the **Whaling and Sealing Museum** *(709-582-2317. Late June–Labor Day; adm. fee)* in South Dildo. It presents a fascinating account of whaler life and also has some Beothuk Indian artifacts from local archaeological sites. A few short miles later, Hwy. 80 intersects Trans-Canada 1; turn east and return to Gushues Pond Park. ∎

Bay du Nord Wilderness Reserve

■ 714,880 acres ■ South-central Newfoundland, southwest of Terra Nova
■ Best season summer ■ Camping, canoeing, swimming, fishing, wildlife viewing
■ Contact Newfoundland and Labrador Department of Tourism, Culture and Recreation, P.O. Box 8700, St. John's, NF A1B 4J6; phone 709-729-2424 or 800-563-6353. www.gov.nf.ca/parks&reserves/baydwildres.htm

NEWFOUNDLAND'S LAST MAJOR UNSPOILED AREA, Bay du Nord Wilderness Reserve occupies rugged countryside pierced by wild rivers and strewn with massive erratics. Long vistas of peat lands, barrens, and coniferous forests stretch in every direction from the rock drumlin formation of 1,234-foot **Mount Sylvester,** the highest point in the park.

Established in 1990, the reserve sits primarily in the eastern maritime barrens ecoregion (dwarf shrub heaths, bogs, shallow fens). Black spruce, white birch, and kalmia of the central Newfoundland forest dominate the northern edges, with some balsam fir thrown in. Such ecological diversity accounts for the large number of species found in the reserve. Moose, Canada goose, willow ptarmigan, and snowshoe hare are plentiful, but the reserve's most famous residents are caribou. The island's largest herd, the 20,000-head Middle Ridge caribou herd, resides in the reserve.

Anglers will find the lakes, ponds, and rivers of the reserve full of fish, including salmon and brook trout. There are no marked trails in the wilderness, but anglers' trails that fan out from Smokey Falls and from the former village of Bay du Nord itself provide access to the wilderness. No designated campsites exist, but dozens of spots along the river are ideal.

For many visitors, the **Bay du Nord River** is the reserve's main attraction. It rises on the upland area of the reserve some 40-plus miles south of Gander, growing as it flows south through a chain of lakes; eventually the river drains into the waters of Fortune Bay. The 46-mile stretch between Rainy Lake and Fortune Bay is nominated a Canadian Heritage River. The Bay du Nord's exceptional natural beauty and diverse waters—placid lakes, rapids, and waterfalls—make it one of eastern Canada's premier canoeing rivers. Not recommended for beginners, this waterway will challenge even expert paddlers.

The Bay du Nord Canoe Route—the most popular route—takes five to seven days and covers 62 miles. Beginning at **Kepenkeck Lake** *(access via Hwy. 301 and forest trails from Terra Nova, or by floatplane)* you'll pass through a series of small and large lakes, including Jubilee and Koskaecodde Lakes, before reaching **Medonnegonix Lake.** From here the river snakes a channel through a narrow, forested valley; you will encounter rapids and waterfalls en route to 60-foot-high **Smokey Falls.** Afterward, the river runs faster and deeper with long stretches of rapids (Class IV and higher during early spring runoff) and turbulent water—even in late summer—to its terminus at Pool's Cove on Fortune Bay. Medonnegonix Lake to the bay is considered the most difficult part of the route. You can take a floatplane to the lake and make the mouth in two days. ■

Rainbow over Terra Nova National Park

Terra Nova National Park

■ 99,840 acres ■ Northeast Newfoundland, 55 miles southeast of Gander via Trans-Canada 1 ■ Year-round ■ Camping, hiking, sea kayaking, canoeing, cross-country skiing, bird-watching, boat tours, icebergs ■ Adm. fee ■ Contact the park, Glovertown, NF A0G 2L0; phone 709-533-2801. www.parkscanada .pch.gc.ca/parks/newfoundland/terra_nova/terra_nova_e.htm

THE LAST ICE AGE SCULPTED the rugged, forested oceanside landscape of Terra Nova National Park. Located on Bonavista Bay, its idyllic shore-line—an intricate sequence of deep sounds, inlets, sea caves, and head-lands—attracts kayakers and canoeists. Hikers are drawn to the dense forests of black spruce, balsam fir, mountain ash, poplar, and white birch that blanket the rolling hills of the interior.

The sphagnum moss bogs of Terra Nova burst with color with the summer blooming of wild sarsaparilla, pink lady's slipper, bog laurel, and pitcher plant. The alpine bilberry—bog blueberry—bears fruit in late summer; small mammals like the snowshoe hare enjoy its berries while moose browse on the shrub's leaves and twigs.

Black bear, fox, lynx, otter, weasel, and mink populate the interior, but moose is the most common animal. The introduced snowshoe hare has contributed to a growing lynx population in the park; the elusive lynx is sometimes seen in the forested areas where the growth provides cover. The endangered American marten population, fond of mature coniferous and mixed forests, has been reduced to perhaps no more than 16 or 20 animals, but reintroduction efforts are under way.

Bay and harbor seals, Atlantic white-sided dolphins, and various whales live or migrate through the waters off Terra Nova. Sightings of fin, humpback, and pilot whales are particularly common. The unusual depth of Newman Sound (almost 900 feet deep in parts) has produced an interesting mix of species: The arctic red jellyfish lives in the same waters as the false angelwing clam, a more temperate water dweller.

Salton Bay, Terra Nova National Park

What to See and Do

Pick up maps and check out the park's interesting interpretive programs before you begin your exploration of Terra Nova. Start your visit at the **Marine Interpretation Center** (*closed Nov.-April*) at the Saltons day-use area on Newman Sound. Aquariums, exhibits, lectures, videos, and a "touch tank" for kids (and adults!) interpret the aquatic ecology of **Bonavista Bay.** Then it's time to hike one of the park's 14 trails, cruise the sound—sign up at the center for an interpretive tour—or sea kayak along the coast to really experience the park.

Newman Sound

Located in the park's north, the Newman Sound estuary teems with wildlife. Birders and hikers alike will delight in this area. Just north of the Newman Sound Campground, the **Newman Sound Bird Exhibit** details the estuarine web of life. Black ducks, greater yellowlegs, bald eagles, ospreys, and other birds feed off the rich marine life in the shallow waters.

If wading in the estuary is too tame for you, hike the **Outport Trail**—the longest (22 miles round-trip) and most strenuous trail in the park. Alternately winding through deep forest and skirting high bluffs and coves, the trail parallels the coast from the campground to South Broad Cove. If you're feeling hardy, take a 1-mile detour to the top of 630-foot-high **Mount Stamford** for spectacular views of the sound and countryside. Icebergs and whales can be sighted off in the distance during summer. Back on the Outport, Minchin Cove, home to an abandoned village, is roughly 1 mile away, while South Broad Cove lies about 1.5 miles beyond it. Both coves feature primitive campsites (*permit required*). If you prefer to hike the trail one way, scheduled boat tours on the sound will drop you off at either South Broad or Minchin Coves (*trail can be hazardous when wet*).

For a taste of the interior, hike 2.5 miles or so along the **Puzzle Pond Trail;** it branches off the Outport Trail about 1 mile from the campground. It heads into a marshy land of pink-purple flowered sheep laurel and open stands of spruce draped with old-man's beard. The trail continues 1.5 miles past Puzzle Pond to Ochre Hill, its other trailhead.

Ochre Hill and Blue Hill

Ochre Hill, just a couple of miles down a paved road east off Trans-Canada 1, is an ancient conglomerate rock outcropping. The 5-mile **Ochre Hill Trail** leaves from the parking area and loops up and over the hill, then down to a cluster of ponds and back. You'll enjoy the panoramic views of Newman Sound from the viewing platform at the top of the hill.

On the same road, a few short miles to the west, the **Sandy Pond Loop Trail** offers an easy 1.8-mile stroll around the pond. Leave your vehicle next to the trailhead at the Sandy Pond parking area and look for ferns, pitcher plants, orchids, and grouse along your walk.

Blue Hill, 2 miles north of

Saltons Brook, allows you to fully appreciate the park's magnificence. From this point, at about 650 feet the highest in the park, you have spectacular views of the park and Newman Sound.

Sea Kayaking

Sea kayaking is the best way to explore the park's 100 miles of coastline. Terra Nova Adventure Tours (709-533-9797) can arrange guided interpretive kayak tours.

Winter in the Park

Winter—with its relatively moderate temperatures—offers splendid cross-country skiing. Some of the hiking trails are groomed and kept open throughout the season, but the park encourages visitors to break their own trails through the more remote areas of the park. Sandy Pond and Newman Sound Campgrounds have enclosed shelters, with firewood for cooking. ▦

Funk Island Ecological Reserve

▦ 19,200 acres ▦ Northeast Newfoundland ▦ Bird-watching ▦ Summer only ▦ Contact Newfoundland and Labrador Department of Tourism, Culture and Recreation, P.O. Box 8700, St. John's, NF A1B 4J6, phone 709-729-2424 or 800-563-6353

NAUGHT BUT A LOW-LYING BARE ROCK, washed over by the sea in fall and winter, Funk Island—37 miles northeast of Cape Freels—does not even rate an appearance on most maps. In the annals of avian history, however, it is legendary: It was a main breeding ground of the great auk, a large-beaked, small-winged bird of the upper North Atlantic Ocean. Bird-watchers come here to pay their respects to the flightless bird. Worldwide, the great auk was hunted to extinction in the 1800s; the last known were killed in 1844. Defenseless and without guile they were easy prey for hunters. A 17th-century ship's captain wrote, "...as if God had made the innocence of so poor a creature to become such an admirable instrument for the sustenance of man."

Although this ecological reserve is protected against human activity and only approved scientific research expeditions can actually step on to the island, you can circle around it. For a price, fishermen in the communities of Valleyfield and Wesleyville are willing to take visitors on a circuit of the island. (To reach Cape Freels, drive N 74 miles on Hwy. 320 off Trans-Canada 1.)

You'll find yourself contemplating with humility the island's single small patch of grassy turf, lichens, and mosses: This tiny stubborn meadow grows in soil made from the decomposed carcasses of great auks.

Though devoid of great auks, the island still teems with bird life. Canada's largest common murre colony—estimated at 396,000 breeding pairs and representing almost 70 percent of the North American population—nests on the island during the summer breeding season. Northern gannets, puffins, northern fulmars, gulls, and kittiwakes nest here, too. ▦

Reconstructed sod dwelling, L'Anse aux Meadows NHS

Viking Trail

- 267 miles long ■ Northwest Newfoundland, Deer Lake to St. Anthony
- Best months June-Aug. ■ Camping, hiking, fossil viewing, scenic drive, archaeological sites ■ Contact Newfoundland and Labrador Department of Tourism, Culture and Recreation, P.O. Box 8700, St. John's, NF A1B 4J6; phone 709-729-2424 or 800-563-6353

MANY VIKING BUFFS HURRYING toward L'Anse aux Meadows National Historic Site drive the length of the Viking Trail (Hwy. 430) in a day, all but ignoring the glorious and untouched coastal scenery along the way. The 267-mile drive (or trail as it is called in Newfoundland) hugs the Northern Peninsula's west coast, running from Trans-Canada 1 north to the peninsula's tip and then crossing to Red Bay in Labrador. Along the way you'll pass dozens of small, quaint fishing communities and areas of scenic and historic interest. Gros Morne National Park (see pp. 215-223), The Arches Provincial Park, and L'Anse aux Meadows—the settlement for whose residents the trail is named—are all strung along the route.

What to See and Do

The Arches Provincial Park
Just 12.4 miles north of Gros Morne National Park on the Viking Trail (Hwy. 430) lie the interesting arches of The Arches Provincial Park *(800-563-6353)*. A millennia of pounding surf ini-tially carved underwater sea caves; the dolomite rock was later raised above sea level in a geologic uplift and the caves became arches. A short trail leads from the parking area to them. You can climb on or walk under the arches.

Table Point Ecological Reserve

Back on the Viking Trail, drive 25 miles to the tiny Table Point Ecological Reserve *(709-729-2424 or 800-563-6353)*, just north of the community of Bellburns. This coastal reserve protects one of the best known deposits of fossils from the Middle Ordovician period—some 470 million years ago. The fossils, which include specimens of nine different marine animal groups, are well preserved in the limestone. Visitors are allowed on site but only on foot—no vehicles are permitted anywhere in the area.

Port au Choix National Historic Site

Return to the Viking Trail and drive north 40 miles to reach Port au Choix National Historic Site *(P.O. Box 140, Port au Choix, NF A0K 4C0; 709-861-3522. May–mid-Oct.; adm. fee)*. As you motor along, you'll notice the climate gradually becoming subarctic—barren and windswept. The site lies at the southern limit of the limestone barrens ecoregion. Many rare plants, including the tiny, white-flowered Fernald's braya—a member of the mustard family—grow within its boundaries.

Port au Choix protects the archaeological digs in **Phillip's Garden,** which revealed how Newfoundland's prehistoric cultures lived. Excavations in the 1960s turned up Dorset Paleo-Eskimo bone implements, tools, and weapons dating back 1,900 to 2,800 years. An older Maritime Archaic Indian burial ground, estimated at 3,300 to 4,400 years old, yielded bodies buried with their tools and weapons smeared with red ocher.

Begin at the Visitor Reception Centre, where a short film and exhibits explain the prehistoric cultures uncovered in the area. The 4-mile round-trip **Dorset Trail** leaves from behind the visitor center and leads past the archaeological sites in Phillip's Garden. The more scenic 2.4-mile-long **Phillip's Garden Trail** begins on the outskirts of the community of Port au Choix and follows the coastline to the Point Riche lighthouse. The digs are visible from this trail, too; look carefully and you'll see faint outlines of houses in the turf and fossils in the limestone near the point.

Watts Point and Burnt Cape Ecological Reserves

The calcareous barrens of Watts Point Ecological Reserve *(800-563-6353)*, north of Eddies Cove, 60 miles from Port au Choix, border the Strait of Belle Isle. Here, small populations of several rare wildflowers grow in exposed, alkaline gravels. The last ice age isolated these relict flowers on the island. Back on Hwy. 430, go to Hwy. 436 and head in the direction of L'Anse aux Meadows; turn west on Hwy. 437 to reach the Burnt Cape Ecological Reserve *(800-563-6353)*, near Raleigh on Pistolet Bay. The reserve protects a number of rare plants, many of which are endemic to Newfoundland—such as the yellowish green Newfoundland orchid and Fernald's braya. The Burnt Cape cinquefoil flower, on the other hand, grows only here and nowhere else.

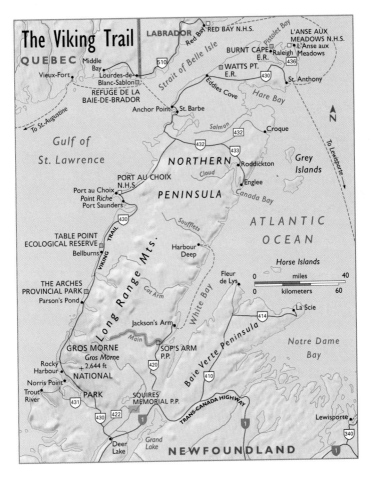

The Viking Trail

LABRADOR
QUEBEC
Middle Bay
Vieux-Fort
Lourdes-de-Blanc-Sablon
To St-Augustine
REFUGE DE LA BAIE-DE-BRADOR
Red Bay
Strait of Belle Isle
RED BAY N.H.S.
BURNT CAPE E.R.
WATTS PT. E.R.
Eddies Cove
Pistolet Bay
L'ANSE AUX MEADOWS N.H.S.
L'Anse aux Meadows
Raleigh
St. Anthony
Hare Bay
Anchor Point
St. Barbe
Salmon
Croque
Gulf of St. Lawrence
NORTHERN
Roddickton
Grey Islands
Cloud
Engle
PORT AU CHOIX N.H.S.
Port au Choix
Point Riche
Port Saunders
PENINSULA
Canada Bay
ATLANTIC OCEAN
Soufflets
TABLE POINT ECOLOGICAL RESERVE
Bellburns
Harbour Deep
Horse Islands
Fleur de Lys
THE ARCHES PROVINCIAL PARK
Parson's Pond
Cat Arm
White Bay
La Scie
Jackson's Arm
Main
Long Range Mts.
Baie Verte Peninsula
Notre Dame Bay
GROS MORNE
Gros Morne 2,644 ft
SOP'S ARM P.P.
Rocky Harbour
Norris Point
NATIONAL
Trout River
PARK
SQUIRES MEMORIAL P.P.
TRANS-CANADA HIGHWAY
Lewisporte
Deer Lake
Grand Lake
NEWFOUNDLAND
To Lewisporte
miles 40
kilometers 60

L'Anse aux Meadows National Historic Site

Return to Hwy. 436 and head north, then drive 20 miles to L'Anse aux Meadows National Historic Site, the only authenticated Viking settlement in North America (*P.O. Box 70, St-Lunaire-Griquet, NF A0K 2X0. 709-623-2608. www.parkscanada.pch.gc.ca. June–mid-Oct.; adm. fee*). Strategically located on the far tip of the great Northern Peninsula, the Norse colony probably served as a base of operations that controlled access to the Gulf of St. Lawrence.

Helge Ingstad, the Norwegian explorer and writer, discovered the settlement in 1960 while searching the North American seaboard for the fabled Vinland of the Norse sagas. A resident of the area told him of a curious collection of mounds that might be signs of ancient buildings. Though the site proved not to be Vinland, excavations here did uncover the remnants of eight 11th-century Norse buildings.

Over subsequent years, an

international team carefully excavated the buildings and determined that although the structures were missing their upper halves—the wood and sod had disintegrated—the remains matched others constructed in Iceland and Greenland around A.D. 1000. Many buildings had only one door, no windows (there may have been smoke holes in the roof), and narrow firepit trenches in the middle of the floor.

L'Anse aux Meadows was a place where ships could be refitted for the voyage back to Greenland. Heaps of slag from ironworking and a dump of iron rivets denote the settlement's active days. It would also have served as a base and winter camp for exploring regions farther south. Butternuts found on site suggest the Vikings journeyed as far south as New Brunswick, the butternut's northernmost range. The settlement was abandoned after fewer than ten years, but researchers are not sure why.

Stop first at the **visitor center,** where a film and scale model give you a good overview of the site. You'll see many of the artifacts discovered during the excavation, including a bronze ring-headed pin of a familiar Norse design, as well as a spindle whorl and a whetstone for sharpening knives and scissors—typical components of a Norsewoman's traveling gear.

A **boardwalk** circles the archaeological site and passes by three full-scale replicas of the sod buildings. In summer, the site offers interpretive lectures and costumed demonstrations of life in the camp of Bjorn, a Norse merchant-adventurer, and his wife Thora. The principals and their campmates use historically accurate implements and artifacts to perform the daily chores of a Viking camp: clothmaking, cooking, and woodworking.

The 30-square mile park also provides some hiking opportunities. The 1.9-mile **Birchy Nuddick Trail,** departing from the visitor center, circles the interpretive site.

To continue on the Viking Trail, return to Hwy. 430 and drive about 10 miles southeast to St. Anthony.

Red Bay National Historic Site

To reach Red Bay National Historic Site (*P.O. Box 103, Red Bay, LAB A0K 4K0; 709-920-2142. Mid-June–mid-Oct.; adm. fee*) on the mainland of Labrador, you'll need to cross the Strait of Belle Isle on the ferry from St. Anthony. Red Bay protects the remains of several 16th-century Basque whaling stations. The profusion of right and bowhead whales in Labrador's waters attracted the whalers to the area and within a few decades a prosperous whale oil industry developed—the world's first oil boom. The protected harbor of Red Bay was the center of activity.

Excavations uncovered three well-preserved galleons and several small boats, among them the whaler *San Juan,* which sank in 1565. The **interpretive facilities** display scale models of work buildings, a reconstructed whaleboat, and original artifacts, including tools, weapons, and clothing. Walk the self-guided trail on nearby **Saddle Island** to see where the Basques lived and worked. ■

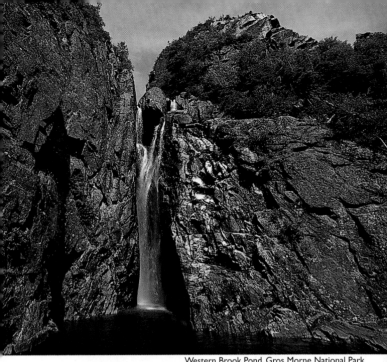

Western Brook Pond, Gros Morne National Park

Gros Morne National Park

■ 445,440 acres ■ Northwest Newfoundland, 19 miles northwest of Deer Lake ■ Best months mid-May–mid-Oct.; Feb.-March for cross-country skiing ■ Camping, hiking, backpacking, mountain climbing, rock climbing, sea kayaking, cross-country skiing, bird-watching, wildlife viewing, boat tours ■ Adm. fee; backcountry permit reqd. ■ Contact the park, P.O. Box 130, Rocky Harbour, NF A0K 4N0; phone 709-458-2417. www.parkscanada.pch.gc.ca/grosmorne

THE GRANDEST, GREATEST, RAWEST landscape in subarctic eastern Canada is exhilarating, occasionally intimidating, and always awe-inspiring. Gros Morne National Park has it all: mountains, headlands, fjord valleys, glacial lakes, wave-carved cliffs, pristine waters, arctic-alpine barrens, and more.

The park's geology stands out in stark relief. Plate tectonics have pushed igneous rock, usually found deep within the crust, to the surface. Recorded here in exposed rock is evidence of the planet's dynamic geological evolution. Some 570 million years ago, the ancient Iapetus Ocean thrived with marine life—graptolites and trilobites flourished on the continental shelf and in the deep water. Then, around 470 million years ago, the plates bearing the future North America and Eurafrican continents collided, eliminating the ocean. The collision formed a supercontinent called Pangaea and pushed up a slice of the Earth's mantle: the mountainous Tablelands of Gros Morne. Much later, the plates shifted again and tore apart the North American and Eurafrican continents. UNESCO added Gros Morne to the World Heritage List primarily because its "rock formations have contributed greatly to the understanding of plate tectonics." The scenic landscape is a mere lagniappe.

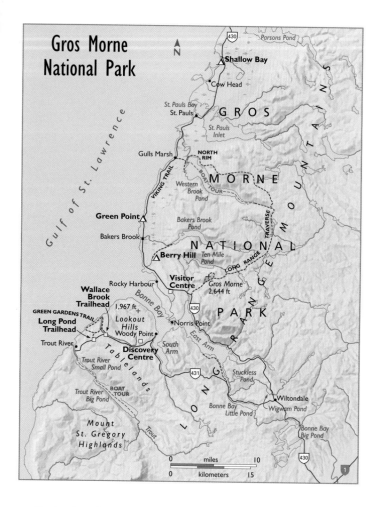

Cutting into the western base of the Northern Peninsula, Bonne Bay virtually splits the park in two. The north and south landscapes differ drastically: The north is dominated by the Long Range Mountains, which rise to the east, and by picturesque cobble or sandy beaches that line the coastline to the west. The south is dominated by the fjord of Bonne Bay and the otherworldly region known as the Tablelands. This dry, brown region of cliffs and boulders is formed of an igneous rock usually found in the Earth's mantle, which was thrust upward by plate tectonics. The high concentration of heavy metals in the peridotite rock impedes most growth, but campion moss and pitcher plants grow in isolated profusion.

Although most visitors discern only two distinct landscapes—the coastal lowlands on the Gulf of St. Lawrence and the alpine plateau of the Long Range Mountains—the park actually encompasses three separate ecoregions: the western Newfoundland forest, the Long Range barrens, and the Northern Peninsula forest. Such diversity results in a vast and unique array of wildlife and flora: Temperate, boreal, and arctic species often coexist in surreal abundance. It's not at all uncommon to stumble upon a common temperate species and find its arctic counterpart nearby. On Gros Morne mountain, for example, snowshoe hare range across the lowlands while arctic hare graze at higher elevations; likewise, the lowland rhododendron grows within a short distance of its arctic cousin, the stunted Lapland rosebay.

There's a good chance you'll see several mammal species on your visit to Gros Morne. Large numbers of woodland caribou frequent the coastal lowlands north of Berry Hill in autumn. Moose roam at will throughout the park; motorists will often encounter them on the roads, especially at dawn and dusk. The Newfoundland black bear—a subspecies larger than its mainland cousin, it averages about 300 pounds—though present, is seldom seen, for it is wary of humans. The red fox, on the other hand, does not share the black bear's cautious nature. A few individuals, having grown accustomed to humans, will wait roadside for handouts from passing motorists; please do not feed them.

More than 230 bird species—from raptors to shorebirds—have been spotted in Gros Morne. Bald eagles and ospreys breed around Bonne Bay. Hosts of shorebirds are plentiful in St. Pauls Inlet during the mid-July to mid-September migration season. Both the rock and willow ptarmigan live on the rocky subalpine slopes and summits of Gros Morne mountain and the Long Range Mountains.

What to See and Do

Begin your visit at one of the park's interpretive facilities at Woody Point or Rocky Harbour. From the park's entrance at Wiltondale *(19 miles NW of Deer Lake on Hwy. 430 off Trans-Canada 1)*, head into the park's southern reaches by taking Hwy. 431 toward Trout River;

Gros Morne Mountain Trail, Gros Morne National Park

Woodland caribou, Gros Morne National Park

to visit the park's northern portion, continue on Hwy. 430 to Rocky Harbour.

The new **Discovery Centre** in Woody Point on Hwy. 431 presents an excellent introduction to the park's geology, flora and fauna, and human history. Exhibits illustrate the forces at work in the park. The **Rocky Harbour Visitor Centre** offers similar exhibits, as well as a host of interpretive programs in the summer. Pick up guidebooks and maps at either location. You can also order them in advance from the Gros Morne Cooperating Association (*P.O. Box 130, Rocky Harbour, NF A0K 4N0. 709-458-3515*).

Any activities should be undertaken with caution. Sudden and treacherous winds blow down from the mountains into the gorges. Active erosion and unstable geology precipitate rock falls. If you plan to backcountry ski, kayak on Western Brook Pond, mountain climb, rock climb, or other such activity, ask the park warden for advice.

Hiking

Gros Morne offers some of the best unspoiled wilderness hiking and backpacking in eastern North America. Despite the park's popularity, on many routes you will see no one at all for days on end. More than 60 miles of trail snake through the park, ranging from half-hour strolls to four- or five-day backpacking routes (*primitive campsites are first come, first served, but you still need a permit*).

Trails at higher elevations may remain closed until July due to snow and wet conditions. To minimize the disturbance to breeding animals, the Long Range Moun-

tains and Gros Morne mountain are usually closed to hikers from early spring until late June.

The very strenuous 21.7-mile (one way) **Long Range Traverse** in the northern part of the park is the most challenging and rewarding hike. This trek—an orienteering adventure over some exceptionally rugged country—is not for the inexperienced. You'll need a map and compass because the trail is unmarked. Park staff will issue you a permit only after you meet with a backcountry specialist for a mandatory pre-trip orientation. Call the visitor center for more information *(709-458-2066)*.

The **Long Range Mountains** form a spine running through the center of the park. From the ridge tops you'll have unparalleled views and the chance to watch and study tundra wildlife and vegetation.

Typically one hikes north to south. Begin by taking the boat to the end of Western Brook Pond; the route follows caribou paths before linking up for the final few miles with the Gros Morne Mountain Trail at Ferry Gulch.

The **North Rim** of **Western Brook Pond** presents an equally strenuous but shorter challenge. From the Western Brook Pond parking lot on Hwy. 430, hike 4.5 miles to Snug Harbour; the 6-mile round-trip North Rim ascent begins here. The trail climbs very steeply through a boreal forest that gradually disappears altogether as the tuckamore and tundra vegetation take over. The trail crosses a plateau to end at the rim of Western Brook Pond's gorge, where dramatic views just open up over the pond, some 2,000 feet below. You can extend the hike by walk-

Sea kayaker off the coast of Newfoundland

Newfoundland by Water

Sea kayaking routes abound in Newfoundland. Popular destinations include the Bay of Exploits on the northern coastline and the stretch along the southwest coast between Channel-Port aux Basques and Burgeo.

Kayaking the complex archipelago in the Bay of Exploits offers the chance to visit dozens of abandoned fishing villages, poignant reminders of an almost vanished way of life. During May you'll be paddling in the company of enormous icebergs.

A paddle along the southwest coast reveals a wild, rugged countryside where villages cling to cliffsides, deep fjords pock the coast, and desolate islands stand sentry.

For information on these and other sea kayaking adventures, contact Coastal Adventurers (P.O. Box 77, Tangier, NS B0J 3H0. 902-772-2774).

ing uphill along the rim.

Generally described as exhausting, the 10-mile (round-trip) **Gros Morne Mountain Trail** scales up and around Newfoundland's second highest summit (2,644 feet). Beginning at the trailhead (*on Hwy. 430, 1.8 miles S of Rocky Harbour Visitor Centre*) the route passes through a number of climatic zones, each with its own distinctive ecology, before reaching Arctic tundra at the summit. Clouds or fog often shroud Gros Morne—the "big dreary" (*be prepared for high winds and rapid temperature changes*).

The first few miles wind easily through boreal forest to a group of small ponds at an elevation of about 1,000 feet; the slope is gradual and there are distant views along the way of Bonne Bay to the south. Less ambitious hikers often stop here to picnic and then head back, which makes for a perfectly satisfying half-day hike.

From here, the pitch steepens sharply and you'll have to scramble a bit to climb a boulder-strewn ravine. Stone cairns on Gros Morne's flattish summit mark the trail to the overlook of the massive bowl of **Ten Mile Pond.** The route down via the northeast slope zigzags for almost 4 miles through Ferry Gulch to connect with the first part of the trail. A primitive campsite in Ferry Gulch can take three tents and is equipped with a pit toilet and bear pole, but campfires are prohibited. You'll need to register and obtain a backcountry permit to use it.

One of the most popular hikes in the park is the moderately difficult 9-mile loop **Green Gardens Trail.** Start off Hwy. 431 at either the Wallace Brook trailhead (*6.8 miles W of Woody Point*) or the Long Pond trailhead (*8 miles W of Woody Point*). A word of warning: In addition to numerous steep pitches, you'll need to ford Wallace Brook a couple of times.

The trail from Wallace Brook begins on the dry, open barrens of the Tablelands then enters a spruce forest. After some rugged terrain you'll reach the clifftop grassy meadows that are the **Green Gardens** of the trail's name. Generations of local residents used these fields as summer pastures for sheep, which still occasionally graze along the trail. From here the trail follows the coast, climbing up and down the headlands to the beach.

The shoreline offers magnificent scenery and plenty of opportunities for exploration: a large wave-carved sea cave, which can be visited at low tide; shallow tide pools that teem with marine life; isolated sea stacks; sandy beaches; and steep cliffs. The Green Gardens Trail loops back toward Long Pond

before heading east and back to the trail alongside Wallace Brook. Although the trail is easily hiked in a day, if you choose to overnight there are three primitive campsites along the coastline.

Boat Tours

A couple different tour operators offer excursions on two of Gros Morne's landlocked fjords (known locally as "fjord ponds"). Tablelands Boat Tours (*709-451-2101. Mid-June–mid-Sept.*) runs on the *Lady Catherine* a 2.5-hour **Trout River Pond cruise.** This 9.3-mile-long former fjord lies in a valley between the barren Tablelands and the steep cliffs of the Gregory Plateau. The tour commentary narrates the geological features and the mechanics of plate tectonics that led to the park's designation as a World Heritage site.

The 2.5-hour tour on **Western Brook Pond** (*Western Brook Pond Tours 709-458-2730 or 800-563-9887. June–mid-Oct.*) is worth the 2-mile hike to the boat dock. The boat takes passengers the length of the park's largest fjord pond. The boat cruises between massive 2,000-foot-high cliffs with cascading waterfalls.

Sea Kayaking

Paddlers find Gros Morne an exhilarating challenge. Ever changeable and sometimes wild winds—particularly easterlies funneling through the fjords—produce turbulent water, while steep breaking waves have been known to come up with disturbing suddenness in shoal waters.

Of the landlocked fjords, **Trout River Pond** is the most accessible and the safest for kayaking. Plenty of landings allow you to explore the Tablelands barrens on one side and the steep cliffs of the **Gregory Plateau** on the other. Launch your kayak at Woody Point, Norris Point, or the Trout River boat launch or day-use area beach. Western Brook Pond, famous for its vertical cliffs, should be attempted only by experts as the wind makes it dangerous. Just reaching it requires a 2-mile portage. The put-in is the Western Brook Pond boat launch.

If you prefer to kayak along the coast, paddle north from Rocky Harbour to Cow Head. This relatively easy route (doable in 2 days) parallels the highway and affords distant views of the Long Range Mountains. Just before Cow Head, **St. Pauls Inlet** pushes inland—it makes for an interesting side trip and may put you smack-dab in the midst of curious harbor seals paddling alongside. The strong tides along this stretch of coast can be a problem, but even relatively inexperienced kayakers should be able to manage them.

Farther south, the one-day paddle between Trout River and Bonne Bay presents an altogether different experience. Kayakers paddle along a rugged coast punctuated by sea caves, 1,150-foot-high cliffs, and sea stacks. This exposed stretch of coast can be hazardous for the inexperienced. Steep cliffs, up to 1,960 feet high, surround the entrance to Bonne Bay's fjord; places to land are limited (you may wish to take out at Woody Point).

Less experienced kayakers will enjoy paddling inner Bonne Bay. The shorelines of the **South** and **East Arms** of **Bonne Bay,** though embraced by high cliffs, are dotted with small communities and coves with landing beaches. A word of warning: The "tickle" (an old Newfoundland word meaning "channel") between outer Bonne Bay and the East Arm experiences the occasional strong current. Rent a kayak or organize an outfitted trip with Gros Morne Adventures *(709-458-2722 or 800-685-4624).*

Cross-country Skiing

Ranging from novice to expert, the park's cross-country ski trails are a Nordic skier's delight. Gros Morne National Park grooms its trails January through March, but the season often extends into April— or even early May during years of high snowfall. Experienced skiers are free to roam off-trail in the unspoiled backcountry *(expect severe whiteout conditions and avalanche situations in mountainous areas).*

Day skiers will find warming huts along some of the trails (**Wigwam Pond** to **Stuckless Pond, Berry Hill** to **Bakers Brook, Trout River Pond Trails,** and **Shallow Bay**). If you plan to overnight, you must register and purchase a backcountry permit.

Two isolated ski huts have been built in the backcountry. One stands in a fir and spruce forest at the edge of Bakers Brook Pond, while the other perches on the forested mountainside of Southwest Gulch and has a view of the Tablelands. The first offers gently rolling hills, the second steep mountain slopes. ∎

Killdevil Mountain, Gros Morne National Park

Main River

■ 35 miles long ■ Northwest Newfoundland, west of Sop's Arm ■ Primitive camping, hiking, white-water rafting and kayaking, canoeing, fishing, wildlife viewing ■ Contact Department of Tourism, Culture and Recreation, P.O. Box 8700, St. John's, NF A1B 4J6; phone 709-729-2424 or 800-563-6353. www.chrs.ca/Rivers/Main/Main_e.htm

OFFERING UNPARALLELED CANOEING, the Main River flows unobstructed from headwater ponds deep in the Long Range Mountains to the sea. It rushes through tundra-like barrens, deep, U-shaped valleys, forests of old-growth balsam fir and black spruce, grasslands of sedges, and a spectacular 14-mile canyon to reach the head of White Bay. This river—the first in Newfoundland to be designated a Canadian Heritage River—is truly an exhilarating ride.

The Main is a challenging journey for the canoeist: Abrupt changes in gradient, channel width, and direction—to say nothing of the river's euphemistic "rock gardens"—contribute to an almost continuously turbulent paddle. In addition, as the Main tumbles through a riverbed that alternates between narrow channels and open, steady stretches, it gradually increases in both volume and gradient, dropping more than 37 feet a mile. Although only 35 miles long all told, each of the river's five sections—**Four Ponds Lake, Upper River, Big Steady, Rapid River,** and **Deep Valley**—offers a distinctly different canoeing experience. For these reasons, the little Main rivals the diversity of many a much longer Canadian river.

A canoe trip down the entire length of the Main will take three to four days. (The river is becoming increasingly popular with kayakers and white-water rafters as well, but because of the river's rocky nature, the latter group can float only from the Kruger Bridge to the river's outlet.) The headwaters are accessible only by floatplane or helicopter. Numerous local and regional outfitters provide fly-in and guide services, as well as

Berry bush along Main River

canoe and kayak rentals. Contact the Department of Tourism, Culture and Recreation for more information.

If you prefer not to fly in, you can leave your vehicle at the Kruger Bridge, where a forest road from the community of White Bay crosses the Main. From here you can either launch your canoe or kayak for the 15-mile paddle to the river's mouth or hike into the Big Steady area. No developed campsites have been established along the river, but plenty of primitive camping sites line the riverbanks and are easily accessible. Hikers can stretch their legs on several unmarked angler trails found around some of the upper ponds and along the river.

Amateur naturalists will treasure a trip down the Main: From the dwarf-shrub barrens to the birch- and spruce-studded grasslands of the Big Steady to the scenic coves and rugged coastal hills of southern White Bay, the landscape teems with wildlife. Healthy populations of moose, caribou, and black bear inhabit the forests, while river otter, beaver, and brook trout cruise the river. The Main also supports a particularly healthy Atlantic salmon population; its gravel riverbed and upper ponds are ideal spawning grounds. Angling is permitted, but you need a license *(available locally)* and you must observe the Department of Fisheries and Oceans fishing regulations *(709-772-4423).* ■

Barachois Pond Provincial Park

■ 8,648 acres ■ Southwest Newfoundland, 12 miles east of Stephenville off Trans-Canada 1 ■ Best months summer ■ Camping, hiking, sailing, canoeing, swimming, fishing, ice fishing ■ Contact Newfoundland and Labrador Department of Tourism, Culture and Recreation, P.O. Box 8700, St. John's, NF A1B 4J6; phone 709-729-2424 or 800-563-6353. www.gov.nf.ca/parks&reserves

A WILD AND LONELY LANDSCAPE, this provincial park—the largest in western Newfoundland—is perhaps the most accessible and family friendly of all the island's nature areas. U-shaped glacial valleys characterize the mountainous terrain. Balsam fir and stands of birch, maple, and rare black ash blanket the valleys, while bogs pockmark the higher elevations. Tuckamore—a nearly impenetrable, stunted thicket of entwined fir and spruce—grows upon the ridges.

Several boardwalk trails crisscross the valley and offer gentle hikes that traverse mountain streams and forest. For the more adventurous hiker, **Erin Mountain Trail** climbs 2 miles through the forest to the mountain's barren 1,115-foot-high summit. The views over the Long Range Mountains to the east and of the waters of St. George's Bay and the Gulf of St. Lawrence to the west are splendid. You can overnight at the summit's lone primitive campsite. The trail leaves from the end of the loop road around campsites 1 to 44 on the peninsula; it crosses a bridge over the narrows of Barachois Pond. A sandy freshwater swimming beach lines each side of the peninsula. ■

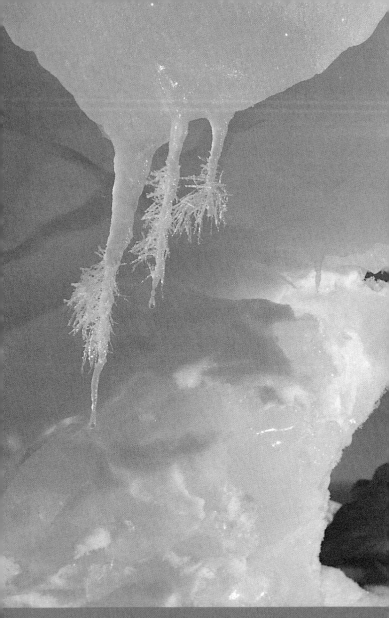

Eastern Arctic

Arctic pressure ridges near Grise Fiord, Ellesmere Island

TO A LAND SO VAST, SO HARSH, so uncompromising, so
ostensibly barren, so prone to weather extremes—why
go? What are the attractions of a destination that some
view as an endless and frozen desolation? The answer lies
in the very questions posed. Although it is true that the
eastern Arctic is harsh and desolate, that statement does
not represent the entire truth. To the Inuit who live here,
it is home—a place that has furnished sustenance and
survival for a very long time. To the many who have

traveled through it, the Arctic is not desolate at all; rather, it is a place of intense beauty and elemental purity, a place where it is still possible to contemplate the very forces that sculpted our planet.

A spectacular realm of ice sheets and glaciers, thrusting peaks of bare rock, ice caverns and glacial cirques, the eastern Arctic as defined in this chapter stretches from Ellesmere Island (just 7° latitude below the North Pole) to the forests of mainland Labrador and the peat bogs southwest of Hudson Bay. This region's three northernmost parks—Quttinirpaaq, Sirmilik, and Auyuittuq—lie within the territory of Nunavut, an Inuit-dominated political entity that was created by the land claim agreement of 1993 and officially established in 1999.

Geology and climate dominate this frozen kingdom, where the "last ice age" is not a distant folk memory but an everyday reality. The Penny Ice Cap in Auyuittuq National Park, for example, is 3,000 feet thick—only half what it was at its height 10,000 to 16,000 years ago, but still substantial enough that its caverns and crevasses provide a laboratory for living history.

Elsewhere in the eastern Arctic, frost, ice, and high winds continue to shape the landscape. In quiet moments you may hear the rumble of a calving glacier or the dull roar of a rockfall. You can also see for yourself how rock flour—the silty residue of still active geologic forces—turns area rivers opaque.

Much of the region's bedrock is ancient, Precambrian rock overlaid with strata of sedimentary rocks

from later epochs. Twisted and wrenched by plate tectonics, the landscape features jagged mountain spires and a fractured coastline that is frequently penetrated by deep-reaching fjords.

Just because Canada's eastern Arctic is a polar desert—a region where it seldom snows (and, of course, hardly ever rains, even in midsummer)—doesn't mean that the landscape is devoid of life. Indeed, wild creatures have adapted to this harsh environment in a variety of ways. Polar bears, with their heavily insulated and thickly furred feet, are at home on ice as much as on land. Migrating caribou have evolved an outer layer of hollow hairs that give them the buoyancy they need to swim large bodies of water. Arctic hare have splayed feet that act like snowshoes. Birds have learned to migrate vast distances—the arctic tern, for instance, heads for Antarctica when winter grips these northern climes.

Arctic plants, by contrast, have not had sufficient time to evolve—the period since the last glacial retreat being no more than a geologic eye blink—but they, too, evince some clever survival stratagems. Despite a lack of nutrients, sedges and lichens thrive. They cling to rock faces in the teeth of howling winds, providing food for migrating herds of caribou.

The surrounding oceans, though icebound much of the year, teem with life. This is especially so in the short polar summer, when whales make their way up the coast to rear their young in northern waters. Belugas, orcas, and humpbacks, not to mention walruses and seals, congregate in fjords and inlets and around pockets of open water that supply plankton and capelin. (The seals, in turn, attract polar bears.) Seabirds by the hundreds of thousands nest in the cliffs edging Ellesmere and Baffin Islands, where they feed in the nutrient-rich waters offshore.

If all these enticements constitute your own personal call of the wild, be aware that the logistics of Arctic travel are formidable. The weather can be fierce and unpredictable year-round, so you must possess not only the proper gear but also a thorough understanding of precisely what the hazards are. Even at the height of summer, for example, Arctic streams can be ferociously cold and unpredictably deep. By the same token, glacier crossings demand extreme caution and lots of experience. Springtime ice melt can create conditions unpleasantly akin to those of quicksand.

In order to reach most eastern Arctic regions, visitors must rely on chartered aircraft. The pilots are experienced wilderness fliers, but foul weather and frequent delays are both inevitable and costly. And with Arctic tourism still only nascent, you may find yourself marooned in a town whose travel facilities range from sparse to bleak.

Some Arctic landscapes, however, can be toured in comfort and style. You might cruise up Iceberg Alley along the Labrador Coast, or take a drive—not necessarily in summer only—across southern Labrador. This is a far cry from the frozen north, to be sure, but it's rewarding just the same: The landscape seems to gain beauty as it empties of people. Here you may meet a few hardy locals who exalt winter with snowshoe and dogsled races, sometimes over immense distances. Not once, curiously, does the word "harsh" enter their vocabularies. ∎

Campsite on Ellesmere Island

Glacier-born Ruggles River, Quttinirpaaq NP

Quttinirpaaq National Park

■ 14,585 square miles ■ Nunavut, northern tip of Ellesmere Island ■ Best months June-Aug. ■ Hiking, backpacking, rockhounding, bird-watching, wildlife viewing ■ Adm. fee. Check-in required at Pangnirtung or at Tanquary Fiord (open June-Aug.) or Lake Hazen warden stations ■ Not for amateurs; search-and-rescue services rare and costly ■ Contact the park, P.O. Box 353, Pangnirtung, NU X0A 0R0; phone 867-473-8828. www.parkscanada.pch.gc.ca

PERCHED AT THE NORTHERNMOST tip of North America, Quttinirpaaq National Park (known as Ellesmere Island National Park until 1999) is stripped to the bone: Elemental and stark, its dramatically massive mountains, glaciers, fjords, rivers, and horizons compose a prodigious land. Little snow falls in winter, which can start in late September and last into May or even later, but the gales are frequent and often sustained. Winter temperatures may climb to 0°F or higher; more typically they linger between -40° and -50°F for long stretches.

In the thin Arctic summer *(June-Sept.)*, the temperature varies from 20°F to 60°F. Sudden savage storms with driving snow have been known to occur in July. During those summer months the sun never sets, throwing one's sense of time off-kilter and exacting a disorienting—sometimes hallucinatory—effect.

The landscape of Quttinirpaaq National Park differs radically from any in the south. The Inuit name for the place means "top of the world"—a fitting appellation for a place that crosses 83° north latitude, less than 500 miles from the North Pole. Much of the park's acreage is polar desert; some areas receive less annual precipitation than the Sahara Desert. The absence of trees hits you right away. And with little plant life to trip the wind, there is no sound; it may take some time to adjust to the silence, especially after a noisy flight in a Twin Otter from **Resolute.**

Even more intense is the combination of intimate perspectives with immense ones. Close up you'll find rocks riven with frost cracks; blankets of tiny yet hardy wildflowers saturated with pinks and yellows and mauves; and willow shrubs just 20 inches high. Look up from these minutiae to discover an infinite backdrop where, thanks to the extraordinary clarity of the air and the lack of focal points, far-off boulders and gleaming glaciers seem no more distant than the hand at the end of your arm.

Towering over the park's northern realm are the **Grant Land Mountains,** forbidding and difficult to access (it's best to see them by air). Rocky peaks called *nunatak,* many of them rising over 6,500 feet, poke through a vast ice sheet that measures 3,000 feet deep in places. One of these, **Barbeau Peak,** stands 8,543 feet high—the tallest mountain in eastern North America.

Hundreds of active glaciers—remnants of the last continental glaciation some 18,000 years ago—cross these icy mountains and extend 25 miles in length. Many have never been traversed by modern man. Ice shelves on the island's northwest coast create a serrated coastline with clinging ledges of sea ice hundreds of feet thick. The largest of these, **Ward Hunt Ice Shelf,** juts 10 miles into the Arctic Ocean.

To the south and east, the landscape drops steeply to the rolling uplands north of the **Lake Hazen** area, the most popular destination for visitors. Fifty miles long and with a surface area of 210 square miles, Lake Hazen is one of the largest bodies of fresh water above the Arctic Circle. The lake is a thermal oasis in the surrounding polar desert—an unusual far-northern hot spot created by several factors, including the south-facing **Garfield Range,** a ring of mountains that acts like a giant solar collector. As a result, there is more vegetation—and thus more wildlife—here than elsewhere on Ellesmere Island. In summer dense concentrations of sedges, arctic grasses, and stunted willows push their way into leaf and flower, along with carpets of lichens and patches of purple saxifrage, mountain avens, and arctic heather. This new growth nurtures populations of small prey animals such as lemmings and arctic hare, which in turn attract arctic foxes and the occasional wolf.

Thanks to the thermal oasis, the **Ruggles River**—the only outflow for Lake Hazen and its drainage basin of more than 3,000 square miles— never freezes over completely. It continues to flow even on the coldest winter days, which can drop to -60°F. Rising southeast of the lake, the **Hazen Plateau** eventually meets the sea at the 2,300-foot cliffs of **Archer Fiord** and the **Robeson Channel;** from either of these on a clear day, you can see Northeast Greenland National Park across the channel.

The Tanquary Fiord warden station in the park's southwest corner maintains a small but informative resource library. The station personnel can provide visitors with a checklist of mammals and birds to see.

Empty though it seems, there is life on this land. Glacier meltwater and the lake itself feeds the sedges, willows, and lichens that sustain Ellesmere Island's wild creatures. Musk oxen—little changed from the days when they walked among mastodons and mammoths—lumber across the landscape. Peary caribou, smallest of their breed (adult males weigh less than 400 pounds), feed on the lichens. Because the park is fairly land-bound, there are fewer polar bears here than in Sirmilik and Auyuittuq parks (see pp. 238-47 and pp. 250-57) to the south. Still, individual bears have been known to hunt the ice floes of Robeson Channel. The droppings of animals such as foxes, oxen, and caribou provide scarce nutrients for the region's thin soil, giving rise to patches of bladder campion, mouse-ear chickweed, and sorrel.

The summer waters contain all manner of sea creatures, including walruses, four species of seal, whales such as beluga, bowhead, and killer, and the fabled narwhal. The world's 35,000 narwhals—whose long, spiral tusks once caused them to be mistaken for unicorns—are found only in the waters off Arctic Canada and western Greenland.

Hundreds of birds patrol the coastal waters, including gyrfalcons (the world's largest falcon), jaegers, and owls, several sandpipers, loons, geese, eiders, and other waterfowl. During the summer, 30 species of birds nest in the area. Like the park's human visitors, some of them must travel huge distances to get here: The arctic terns flies in from Antarctica.

Getting There

The park is reached through Resolute (population 191), one of Canada's northernmost communities. First Air flies into Resolute Bay from Yellowknife (N.W.T.), Ottawa (Ont.), and Nunavut's capital, Iqaluit. These flights fill months in advance, so book early. From Resolute, you'll have to charter a plane (about $10,000 U.S. one way for a ten-passenger craft). Bradley First Air *(867-252-3981)* and Kenn Borek Air *(867-252-3845)* fly into the Tanquary Fiord or Lake Hazen warden station.

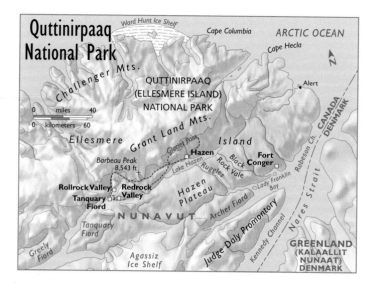

Pilot's-eye view of Ellesmere Island

What to See and Do

Hiking and Backpacking

Most of Quttinirpaaq's visitors—a grand total of 150 each year—come to the park seeking a no-trace backpacking experience in an ultimate wilderness environment. Almost without exception, they find it: You need not trek very far from either warden station to enter a realm of absolute solitude.

The most popular hike—a one-way trip that consumes 10 days while covering roughly 80 miles—connects the two warden stations of Lake Hazen and Tanquary Fiord. This is far from a casual walk in the park: This is orienteering. No trails are marked, and even the easiest route demands that you cross at least one glacier, not to mention dozens of chilling streams and rivers whose water level can

change drastically within minutes.

Two manageable circuits start at the Tanquary camp and lead past old Inuit campsites, giving you extended views of the fjord. Longer two-day circuits, likewise originating at Tanquary, take you through the **Rollrock Valley** and the **Redrock Valley;** both skirt impressive cliffs and offer good views of distant glaciers.

From the Lake Hazen warden station (midpoint on the lake's north shore), popular but difficult trails lead northwest to **Glacier Pass** and northeast to **Blister Creek.** Both unmarked trails yield glacier views that justify all that tundra tromping.

If the park wardens seem leery of recommending additional treks and trails, it's because they do not want visitors to wear permanent paths in the tundra.

Historic Sites

Ellesmere Island was probably first settled by humans about 4,000 years ago, when a group of Paleo-Eskimos from Siberia arrived on the island after crossing the frozen ice cap. Roughly 400 years later, however, they picked up and moved on, leaving only a few campsites and hearths.

Then, about 3,000 years ago, a second wave of Paleo-Eskimos migrated across the Arctic islands. These so-called Dorset people lived in the Quttinirpaaq area from A.D. 800 to A.D. 1000, when they were replaced by the Thule—ancestors of the modern Inuit. Quttinirpaaq was abandoned again during the little ice age starting about 1600.

Rockhounding

The park's striped sedimentary rock will galvanize the amateur geologist. With little vegetation and no soil concealing the area's rock patterns, both historical and ongoing geologic processes can be observed at close range. Indeed, the Ice Age that ended elsewhere on Earth between 16,000 and 10,000 years ago still seems to hold the park in its grip: Immense boulders can be glimpsed through their sheaths of shifting glacier ice.

The presence of so much past is not without peril. Rent by moving ice, the cliffs frequently disgorge their trapped rocks and send them crashing to the valley floors below.

Here's another glacial by-product that's a boon for park visitors:

Intricate ice caverns, carved in glaciers by their own meltwater, glitter in the sunshine like outsize gemstones. The footing in these frostbitten palaces is treacherous—crevasses constantly open in their floors—so seek the advice of a park warden before exploring any of them.

The park's easily bruised ecosystems mean that the movements of humans long gone can still be traced today. Campsites dating back 4,000 years are easy to pick out in the fjord area. Ask park wardens how to identify the stone fox traps, rock cairns, caches, and tent rings used by early inhabitants and explorers.

About 30 miles east of Lake Hazen to the north of Archer Fiord stands **Fort Conger,** an intriguing historic site. Fort Conger was established by the sister ships *Enterprise* and *Alert*, part of an 1875-76 British Arctic Expedition under Sir George Nares. His party explored the north coast of Ellesmere Island and Greenland on sledges hauled not by dogs but by expedition members themselves. A few years later, American Adolphus Greely used the fort as a base for probing Ellesmere's interior during the International Polar Year (1882-83).

Today Fort Conger, like so many other sites in Quttinirpaaq National Park, is accessible only by plane or on foot. Charter aircraft will fly you there by prearrangement, or you can hike in from Lake Hazen. If you choose the latter option, follow **Black Rock Vale**—a grand valley with rolling mountains—to Lady Franklin Bay, then make your way up the coast to Fort Conger. Once there, you'll find a few signs guiding you to three winter shacks built by Edwardian-era explorers, including Robert Peary in 1909. As you gaze upon their expedition exuviae—tin cans, barrel staves, pieces of broken glass—the enduring environmental damage of adventure travel starts to sink in.

Wildlife Viewing

Guides and outfitters offer day- to week-long tours to view wildlife. Remember that the sparse wildlife is not habituated to human company; as a consequence, animals may be more curious than cautious about human intrusions. Even small prey animals such as lemmings pause to examine visitors. Many bird species will circle overhead, peering down at these unaccustomed animals (that's you) to make sure they don't approach ground nests.

Lemmings represent no threat, nor does the occasional arctic wolf or fox—unless, that is, rabies has taken hold. Though uncommon, rabies does occur. You should therefore never allow wolves or foxes to get too close.

Musk oxen are curious too, but they're another story. They may charge, so don't come within 300 feet of one (especially a lone bull).

You may encounter an occasional polar bear in coastal areas. Because park visitors are not permitted to carry guns, avoidance or retreat is the only recourse (see sidebar pp. 248-49 for hints on safe travel in polar bear country). Wardens can supply up-to-date information on polar bears in the area.

Polar bear track

Staying Safe

Few park staffers are on hand to look after visitors to this immense wilderness. No medical help is available. Search-and-rescue efforts (usually paid for by the rescued party) are available only sporadically. Nursing stations (but not necessarily a doctor) are found at **Grise Fiord** (370 miles away) and Resolute (560 miles). For their own safety, all visitors should carry a first-aid kit and a single-side-band radio (rentable in Resolute).

Despite being bathed in the continuous daylight of an Arctic summer, Quttinirpaaq's glacier-fed streams and rivers are ferociously cold. Their depth and speed can change without notice. Glaciers are even more hazardous; proper gear and glacial trekking experience are needed to cross one. Hidden crevasses are a life-threatening menace, especially at higher altitudes. ■

Relaxing after a hard day's work

Sirmilik National Park

■ 8,571 square miles ■ Nunavut, northern Baffin Island ■ Open year-round; travel difficult during freeze-up and breakup ■ Hiking, rockhounding, kayaking, fishing, snowmobiling, dogsledding, bird-watching, whale-watching, archaeological site ■ Fee ■ Check-in required at Pond Inlet or Pangnirtung ■ Access by snowmobile in winter, kayak in summer ■ Contact Park Warden, Box 353, Pangnirtung, NU X0A 0R0, phone 867-473-8828; or Pond Inlet park office, Box 300, Pond Inlet, NU X0A 0S0, phone 867-899-8092. www.parkscanada.gc.ca

WITH ITS 6,560-FOOT-HIGH MOUNTAINS that erupt in sheer slabs from Baffin Bay and its massive glaciers that slip-slide into the sea, Sirmilik National Park is as dramatic as the cerulean sky that stretches over the Canadian Arctic on a seemingly endless summer day. Sirmilik—the name means "glacier" in Inuktitut—was created by the Inuit and the Canadian federal government in 1999 to limit the petroleum industry's plans to begin exploring for oil in Lancaster Sound. Located about 430 miles north of the Arctic Circle and approximately 1,000 miles from tree line, the park is divided into three portions, described below. All of them are best visited from Pond Inlet, a small community across Eclipse Sound to the south.

The park's **Bylot Island Migratory Bird Sanctuary** is a mountainous isle of ice fields and glaciers, famous for its enormous populations of nesting seabirds. **Oliver Sound** is a deep and picturesque fjord, while the **Borden Peninsula** is a stream-crossed plateau that can be comfortably traversed by hikers (who find its abundant riverbanks ideal for camping).

Though Baffin Island is the northern terminus of the Precambrian or Canadian Shield, the ancient rocks here are overlain by several layers of newer, sedimentary rock. The park's southerly regions—mainly peat bogs, wetlands, and coastline—keep a low profile. From there the land rises sharply to a flat, lifeless plateau that ends in the north and east in immense cliffs lining a coast riven by fjords. On the Borden Peninsula, erosion has carved out fantastic rock shapes called hoodoos.

Winters in Sirmilik National Park are long and cold. In January the average high is only -10°F, and temperatures customarily drop to -50°F and lower. At the height of the short summer season in late July, daytime temperatures may soar as high as 50°F, but even then freezing is not out of the question.

These harsh temperatures join forces with the region's thin soil and scarce moisture to keep plant life small, tenacious, and sparse; flora also hugs the ground to avoid the freezing gales. Visitors therefore treasure the little vegetation that does exist, especially in the well-drained soil of the park's uplands. In summertime, broad-leafed willow herb transforms the normally colorless flatlands into a garish carpet of pink, purple, and fuchsia. Arctic poppies flourish even in the most inhospitable areas. The most important plant—one that sustained the Inuit for countless generations—is the arctic willow, dubbed "northern forest" even though it seldom grows more than 18 inches high.

Parts of Sirmilik—notably the interior plateau of Bylot Island—are too barren to support much wildlife, but the coastal lowlands and the marine waters surrounding the island teem with life. Peary caribou, wolves, and foxes inhabit the Borden Peninsula. Lemmings—small rodents with short snouts and stubby tails—are common; because they follow cycles of boom and bust, however, visitors may see them everywhere one year but not at all the next. Curious in the extreme, lemmings rarely hesitate to poke about visitors' tents.

Arctic hare, too, hop about campsites, providing homespun entertainment for campers. The hare turn white in the winter; Inuit seal hunters once used their fur to camouflage the sails on their boats. Also spotted

Qamutik Quests

Just as it did for Inuit ancestors 4,000 years ago, a dogsled (qamutik) is one of the best ways to explore the area above tree line. Preparation is key, so choose a government-licensed guide; call Nunavut Tourism (800-491-7910) for approved outfitters. And because multiday trips entail traveling 5 mph for 8- to 12-hour days on a hard wooden sled at temperatures below freezing, know your limits.

Expect your qamutik to be pulled by 8 to 15 Inuit Sled Dogs, mostly male, weighing 70 to 85 pounds apiece. Instead of the tandem (side-by-side) hitch used in the Iditarod, the dogs are harnessed in a fan hitch: Single tug lines allow individual dogs to jump openings in the ice without pulling down the entire team—and sled! Together they can pull 1,000 pounds and 3 people throughout a nine-day trip.

Each team has two key dogs. The lead dog takes direction from the driver and finds the best path. The boss dog keeps the peace among team members throughout the trip. These are working dogs, so get the guide's permission to approach one.

Arctic Oases

In Baffin Bay, a large polynya —that is, an area of open water that stays ice free year-round—attracts marine animals that feed from it in spring. A polynya takes shape through the interaction of local winds, tidal currents, and water welling up from the shallow ocean floor.

Because it does not freeze over in winter, a polynya is effectively an oasis in the middle of the frozen sea. Plankton and small fish thrive there, providing food for predators such as seals, walruses, beluga whales, narwhals, and polar bears. These areas, therefore, made for good hunting; indeed, they may explain the arrival in this area of ancient Arctic hunters.

throughout the park is the arctic fox. Like the lemming, it is white in winter but turns gray or brown in summer. Caribou, commonplace on the Borden Peninsula, remain a source of food for the local Inuit, who also use caribou bones to fashion artifacts.

Lancaster Sound is a summering area for seals (bearded, ringed, harp, hooded, and harbor), whales (beluga and orca), and walruses. The rare bowhead whale is frequently seen here as well.

The oddest wildlife sighting you're likely to experience is a glimpse of an ivory-tusked narwhal. Often referred to as the unicorns of the sea, these whales possess a spiral tusk up to 10 feet long that grows from their upper lip.

Bylot Island, in addition to its birds, is a summer retreat for polar bears, whose population reaches 150 at times.

Getting There

The park is generally accessed through Iqaluit, the capital of Nunavut territory. First Air *(867-473-8960)* offers scheduled service to Pond Inlet, a small Inuit town of just over 1,100 people that serves as Sirmilik's staging post. From Pond Inlet local outfitters will take you to Bylot Island (about $400 per person; see p. 282), the Borden Peninsula, or Oliver Sound.

What to See and Do

Bird-watching

A bleak realm of glaciers, snow, and ice fields located north and east of Baffin Island and bordering Lancaster Sound, Bylot Island is a seemingly inhospitable place most of the year. Between May and September, however, the island's coastline comes alive with a multitude of marine and land animals, as well as 50 species of birds. The birds—a fascinating mix of North

American and European, low-Arctic and high-Arctic species, often in huge numbers—are the reason most people visit here.

Immense colonies of seabirds nest on the cliffs at **Cape Hay** on the north side of the island and at **Cape Graham Moore** on the east. They are drawn there by nearby polynyas (see sidebar above). The southwestern portion of the island, blanketed by tundra

Fur seal

lowlands, attracts waterfowl and waders.

Perhaps the most impressive sight of all is the colony of thick-billed murres—more than one-tenth of that bird's Canadian population—and the 50,000 kitti-wakes (small gulls) that nest on the capes' cliffs. Both the murre and the kittiwake are pelagic species: They spend most of their lives at sea, returning to the cliffs only to breed. Murres—cousins to puffins and their larger relative, the extinct great auk—are perfectly suited to a marine environment: They can dive more than 300 feet below the water in pursuit of small prey.

About a quarter of the world's population of greater snow geese (some 75,000 birds) can be found on Bylot Island's lowlands at the end of the Arctic summer, around mid-August. They are the headliners in a story of ecological success verging on excess: Between 1900 and 1998, Earth's embattled snow goose population grew from its nadir of just a few thousand birds to more than 600,000—and possibly as high as 1,000,000. One cause for this impressive rebound was the increase in agricultural and refuge development along the fly-ways that the geese use to migrate from the Arctic tundra to the Outer Banks twice a year. Another was the 1916 international treaty banning the hunting of migratory birds between March and September. Together these two factors inflated the bird population to the point where wildlife managers are now seeking ways to drastically reduce their numbers.

The northern and eastern cliffs of Bylot Island are difficult to reach from the landward side; the best way is to arrange a boat excursion from Pond Inlet. Several Pond Inlet outfitters offer tours to the cliffs and the nearby polynyas, giving you an excellent opportunity to see not only the bird colonies but also the seals, walruses,

Following pages: Hoodoos, south coast of Bylot Island

belugas, orcas, and narwhals that are attracted to the open water. The snow goose colonies on the southwest of the island can also be visited by boat from Pond Inlet.

Other birds on Bylot include at least three European or Eurasian species: the common ringed plover, the northern wheatear, and the knot. Pectoral sandpipers and sandhill cranes nest alongside white-rumped sandpipers and turnstones, while the cliffs lining **Eclipse Sound** are home to hawks and peregrine falcons. Also on hand are such upland species as the buff-breasted sandpiper, the snow bunting, the horned lark, and the Lapland longspur.

Birders are not the only ones who savor Bylot. The island is also popular with hikers; though there are no marked trails, the **interior valleys** offer treks that are demanding but far from impossible for the well-prepared backpacker.

Those valleys also attract geologists, both amateur and professional, for the simple reason that glaciation is easy to trace in the sharply etched mountains. Dozens of cirques—high-altitude, bowl-shaped depressions that give birth to glaciers—litter the mountainsides. Some of them are easily accessible; others require you to cross rock litter, boulder mounds, or glacial moraines (ridges) left behind by the ice as it retreated.

Oliver Sound

Perhaps the most popular area in the park for hiking and boating, Oliver Sound—the fjord south of Pond Inlet—is huge, scenic, and spectacular. Because its waters are protected from the prevailing

winds, it is also much safer for boating than Lancaster or Eclipse Sounds. Oliver Sound also happens to be relatively ice free.

With no trails laid out here or anywhere else in the park—the mere act of marking them would be regarded as harmful—hiking paths are nonetheless obvious, and good campsites abound on both shores. Local guides from Pond Inlet (see p. 282) can show you the easiest and most agreeable routes, some of which trace the edges of grand cliffs with immense views. The boundaries of the numerous medium-size glaciers nearby make popular (and easily accessible) places to explore.

Borden Peninsula

Located between Admiralty and Navy Board Inlets, the Borden Peninsula (Tiuralik) is a softer, gentler landscape by Arctic standards. Although the high plateaus are still rugged enough to satisfy those with a taste for the extreme, the lowlands are often carpeted with summer wildflowers such as white arctic heather, purple saxifrage, and eight-petaled white mountain avens. This startling intensity of color can look flamboyantly tropical.

As a consequence, the Borden Peninsula is a good place for hiking and camping. The **Mala River Valley,** midway down Navy Board Sound, appeals to backpackers because of its birds and to geologists because of its "open system" pingos—that is, small mounds of earth or gravel with cores of ice.

A curious sight are the peninsula's hoodoos, which attract shutterbugs from far and wide. Found

Inuit at Quttinirpaaq

The Inuit

Eighty-five percent of the 24,700 people living in the new territory of Nunavut—the Canadian political entity created in 1999 that holds three northern national parks—are Inuit, a culture with a rich and re- markable history. Though their ancestors have occupied the region for more than 4,000 years, they did not begin to relinquish their nomadic existence until the 1950s; that's when the Canadian govern- ment—eager to centralize services such as health and education— forced the Inuit to move from their small hunting and fishing settle- ments into established towns such as Pond Inlet (population 1,154 in 1996), which dates only to 1959. All Inuit over the age of about 50 were, therefore, very likely born in a *karmat*—a traditional shelter of stone, sod, and whale jawbones.

"Inuit," the plural form of "Inuk," means "the people" in the Inuktitut language. The Inuit were earlier called Eskimos ("eaters of flesh") by the Algonquian Indians. That name reflected a diet devoid of green plants and vegetables, because all Inuit lived (and still do) north of tree line. They subsisted on high-fat, high-protein animals such as seals, whales, walruses, fish, caribou, polar bears, foxes, hare, and seabirds, eaten cooked, dried, or raw. The treeless environment also required the early Inuit to survive without any conveniences derived from wood: They used seal oil for fuel, bones and stones for tools, and ice blocks for housing.

Today snowmobiles and Twin Otters have replaced the kayaks, umiaks, and qamutiks the Inuit once used. As this region covering more than one-fifth of Canada evolves, Nunavut's leaders will be challenged to find new ways of boosting the economy while preserving the old ways of living off the land.

Traffic sign in Inuktitut language

At the Edge of the World

The picturesque little community of Grise Fiord (Ausuittuq for "the place that never melts"), located on the southern tip of Ellesmere Island, is a popular excursion from the northern parks (Sirmilik or Quttinirpaaq). Canada's northernmost community, with only 150 residents, it perches by the sea at the head of a fjord on the south coast of Cornwallis Island.

Norwegian explorer Otto Sverdrup named the town during his 1899-1903 expedition for the prevalent seal barking, which reminded him of pigs grunting (grise is Norwegian for "pig"). Lodging is at the Grise Fiord Cooperative (867-980-9913). Plane service is from Resolute, 220 miles southwest, twice a week.

shapes by many centuries of erosion. Similar structures are found at the Hopewell Rocks (see p. 181), Mingan Archipelago (see pp. 113-15), and in Fathom Five National Park (see pp. 35-36).

Eclipse Sound

The main water route to Bylot Island and the Borden Peninsula, Eclipse Sound is often covered with pack ice until midsummer. Because the sound is subject to gales, strong currents, and high waves, boaters generally avoid it. Icebergs are common, and the larger ones have a pesky tendency to ground themselves in shallow water. An iceberg may loiter in the sound for years before moving out into Baffin Bay.

For whale-watchers, however, the sound is worth exploring when weather conditions permit. Outfitters from Pond Inlet know the area well and can arrange a visit to the sound, weather permitting, where you're likely to spot a narwhal, an orca, a beluga, or a bowhead whale. You might also spy a polar bear patroling the shore or hunting on the pack ice.

Navy Board Inlet

Dangerous and unpredictable, glacier-ringed Navy Board Inlet (Nalluata Imanga) harbors all kinds of whales and marine mammals. If conditions are favorable, have an outfitter take you out to see the pods of beluga that feed in the inlet.

Lancaster Sound

An open and often hazardous body of water between Devon Island to the north and Sirmilik National

in many places within a few days' hike of Navy Board Inlet, on the eastern side of the peninsula, these isolated stacks of sedimentary rock have been sculpted into fantastic

Park, Lancaster Sound furnishes a rich marine home for seabirds and marine mammals, including walruses, polar bears, seals, and whales. Among mariners, it is known as the eastern entrance to the Northwest Passage, that elusive shortcut to the Pacific Ocean that entranced and entangled so many explorers for so many decades.

Button Point

A tiny peninsula on the southeast corner of Bylot Island—attached by nothing more than a narrow land bridge—Button Point (Sannit) was named after British Arctic explorer Sir Thomas Button. Its location near year-round open waters attracted Danish archaeologist Therkel Mathiasson in 1923. Since then Button Point has yielded a substantial collection of artifacts used by the Dorset people; these descendants of Siberian nomads occupied Arctic Canada for more than 3,000 years before being chased off by the invading Thule.

Father Guy Mary-Rousselière (1913-1994), a Pond Inlet archaeologist and anthropologist who is fondly remembered in the area as Father Mary, spent six decades—from the 1940s to the 1990s—combing the sites. He discovered that the frozen landscape had functioned like an icy vault, perfectly preserving such Dorset cultural treasures as drums and flint blades.

His most stunning find was a pair of carved driftwood masks, circa A.D. 500 to 1000, which now reside in the Canadian Museum of Civilization in Hull, Quebec. You can view other Father Mary finds and read some pages from his journals at the **Nattinnak Visitor Center**

(867-899-8225) in Pond Inlet.

Other Activities

The landscape and the wildlife are the main draws, of course, but Sirmilik park's dozens of peaks—bare of snow in the extended sunshine hours of summer—have begun attracting climbers. Most of the good climbing is on the Borden Peninsula; any Pond Inlet outfitter (see p. 282) should be able to describe how to reach these sites.

Pond Inlet outfitters offer a range of other services as well, from tidewater fishing for arctic char along Oliver Sound in summer to dogsledding excursions across the Borden Peninsula in winter. For those with a taste for the exotic, outfitters will take you to "live off the land" as the Inuit did.

Staying Safe

Visitors to Sirmilik and the other Canadian Arctic parks are expected to be self-sufficient and to possess self-rescue capabilities. Despite the hazards presented by polar bears, park visitors are not allowed to carry guns. There are no designated campsites—you may camp anywhere, as long as you don't light a campfire. Also strictly prohibited is the gathering of vegetation, rocks, antlers, fossils, or artifacts. Litter and garbage—including used toilet paper—must be carried out of the park; nothing can be buried or thrown away.

Now, back to those polar bears: They are a definite danger, so don't camp along the shoreline, where they patrol in search of food. When you pitch your tent, make sure it affords a view of any approaching bears (see sidebar pp. 248-49). ∎

Bearly Speaking

POLAR BEARS LOOK CUTE and cuddly on film—mother-cub affection magnifies the effect—but they are not to be taken lightly. In addition to being North America's largest land carnivores, they are among its most dangerous.

In summer, when most humans see them, the animals suffer from overheating and must rest often to cool off. For that reason, polar bears are usually seen lolling about or ambling along at their average walking speed of 3.5 miles per hour, fanning the misconception that they are slow or easily eluded. In fact, adult polar bears are strong and fast. They run well up or downhill and can reach 30 miles an hour for short bursts, meaning you cannot outdistance a bear unless you have a large lead and can quickly reach an impregnable stronghold.

Don't count on escaping a polar bear's notice, either. They have good hearing, a sharp sense of smell, and excellent vision.

At 17,000, there are more polar bears in Nunavut than in any other Canadian political jurisdiction. The global polar bear population is estimated at 25,000 to 40,000 animals—far more robust than in the 1960s, when their numbers sank to 10,000. This conservation success story resulted from international cooperation: Russia and Norway ban any hunting of the creatures, while Canada and the United States strictly regulate it.

The bears seldom range above the 80th parallel—too little food, too little open water. Their southern range hinges on the movement of sea ice, their preferred conveyance. When the ice extends into southerly latitudes in severe winters, they have shown up in Iceland and Newfoundland.

A polar bear will eat reindeer or caribou, seabirds and ducks, fish, kelp, or human garbage, but its favorite food is seal, preferably bearded or ringed seals. It may stalk seals that have hauled out onto the ice, but more commonly the bears engage in "still hunting": Waiting motionlessly by a breathing hole until a seal pops up, the bear drags its victim onto the ice and kills it with bites to the neck or head. This is why the polar bear's ideal hunting ground is a patch of sea ice pocked with pools of open water.

Polar bears are solitary animals. They gather only in April or May to breed, which customarily takes place (after scuffles between competing males) on sea ice near good seal-hunting locations. The growth cycle of the embryo is about four months, yet the cubs are not born until some time between November and early January. Delayed implantation is the reason for this curious timetable; to ensure that the female puts on enough weight while she gorges on summer seals, the fertilized egg stops growing from April through July. During this stage, impregnated females may increase their body fat to 50 percent or more, amassing a five-inch layer around the thighs and rump—a caloric storehouse when food is scarce.

Starting in July, when the pregnant females return to land to den, they eat almost nothing at all—a state of privation dubbed "walking hibernation." Thus begins an eight-month fast in which a breeding female may shed as much as 45 percent of its weight. Heat retention and energy conservation therefore become key. To achieve both, the female carves out a cozy den in a snowbank (or occasionally a mud-

Female polar bear encircling her cub

bank) not more than about 10 miles from shore.

The cubs (a female generally gives birth to twins) weigh just a pound or so when they are first born, but they grow rapidly. By the time they venture out of the den at five to six months, they weigh 33 pounds. At about 30 months the mother chases them off, a sign that she is ready to breed again.

A polar bear stays warm thanks to its dense fur coat. Oily "guard hairs" allow the bear to shake off water before it freezes. These clear hairs reflect light, creating that white effect; strip the fur away and you would find black skin that absorbs the sun's rays. Bears in the wild often have a yellowish cast caused not only by oxidation but by bloodstains (no one ever accused a polar bear of fastidious feeding).

Because polar bears occasionally stalk humans, and because a bear attack is usually fatal, people must exercise extreme caution when traveling in polar bear country. If a bear comes near and you can't reach safety, try to get upwind of the creature so it can smell you clearly; humans are not high on the animal's list of desirable foods, so this often suffices to quash the bear's interest. If it does not, use

deterrents such as flares, air horns, cracker shells, Capsaicin, or red-pepper spray. Failing that, Parks Canada advises, use whatever comes to hand: a ski, a knife, a block of ice (non-Inuit are not allowed to carry guns in Nunavut parks). If you're in a group, make as much noise as you can.

Parks Canada further counsels the following measures:

▪ Avoid areas with bear tracks, scat, openings dug in the snow at seal holes, seal carcasses, or polar bear dens.

▪ Do not travel when visibility is poor. Terrain features such as boulders or pressure ridges may conceal a bear.

▪ Seeking carrion or easier footing, polar bears prowl beach edges in summer. Whatever the season, set up camp at least a mile from the shore.

▪ Avoid camping on points of land next to large features such as icebergs; on islets just offshore; and near pressure ridges. All of these areas attract polar bears.

▪ Travel in a group; carry a high-frequency radio to contact help in an emergency.

▪ Erect a warning system around your tent at night. Ask Parks Canada about portable trip-wire alarm systems. ▪

Capturing Weasel Valley on film, Auyuittuq NP

Auyuittuq National Park

■ 7,606 square miles ■ Cumberland Peninsula, east-central Baffin Island
■ Travel difficult during freeze-up and breakup; boat travel possible only when
fjord is safely ice free (mid-July–mid-Oct.) ■ Camping, hiking, backpacking,
mountain climbing, kayaking, fishing, ski touring, glaciers, ice caves ■ Adm. fee.
Check-in required at Pangnirtung (south side of park) or Qikiqtarjuaq (north
side) ■ Contact the park, P.O. Box 353, Pangnirtung, NU X0A 0R0; phone 867-
473-8828. www.parkscanada.gc.ca

JUTTING OUT TOWARD GREENLAND from Baffin Island's spectacular Cumberland Peninsula, Auyuittuq National Park contains some of the most
magnificent scenery in the north: crashing ice, precipitous fjords, glacier-
sculpted mountain valleys, knife-edged peaks, and the massive Penny Ice
Cap, a looming relic of the last ice age. The park's name, pronounced ow-
YOU-ee-tuk, means "the land that never melts." That's a fitting moniker
for a landscape where summer snowstorms are not uncommon and gales
have been known to exceed 110 miles an hour.

Baffin Islanders are fond of joking that God didn't rest on the seventh
day; instead, he spent it throwing rocks at Baffin Island. Indeed, the buck-
ling of bedrock into brutally high mountains is a basic part of the park's
geology. Nevertheless, Auyuittuq is, for Arctic parks, fairly accessible; its
southern corner is a two-day, 18.6-mile hike from the town of Pangnirtung, northeast of Iqaluit across Cumberland Sound.

The highlights of the local landscape are the handiwork of passing glaciers, which dropped large, angular boulders (or erratics) that show little of

the roundness of water-tumbled stones. The rocks' degree of lichen cover is a clue to the date they were deposited: The darker boulders are the oldest; they were probably left behind during the last "mini ice age" three centuries ago. The lighter boulders signal more recent deposition—perhaps within the last few years, or as recently as that rock slide you just heard.

The bedrock beneath the park is Precambrian (Baffin Island forms the northeastern margin of the Precambrian, or Canadian Shield), with later overlays of sedimentary rock. Although tectonic forces have buckled and twisted the land, far more evident is the effect of glaciers: In addition to erratics, receding glaciers have left behind end moraines, lateral moraines, and other massive piles of rubble.

Fork Beard Glacier, accessible to hikers, is studded with massive boulders that can be clearly seen from the trail. Watch long enough and you'll see and hear a virtual rain of debris tumbling down the glacier's vertical face.

Dominating the park's less visited north side are the Penny highlands, whose peaks of Precambrian granite reach 6,890 feet. Most of the highlands are covered by the solid ice of the Penny Ice Cap, 1,000 feet thick and 1,969 square miles, a remnant of the continental glaciers of the last Ice Age. Today, the ice cap still spawns active glaciers. The longest, the Coronation Glacier, is almost 2 miles wide and slides downhill for 20 miles before ending in a massive ice cliff looming over the water at the head of Coronation Fiord.

The Penny Ice Cap also provides a stage for innumerable studies on climate change and global warming. Like tree-ring dating, bore holes drilled hundreds of feet down into the ice reveal the history of the ice cap, including the temperatures in effect during the formation of various layers. No life can survive on the desolate Penny Ice Cap; the park's only vegetation is found at lower elevations. There, red mountain sorrel, white starwort and arctic heather, pink moss campion and broadleafed willow, and purple saxifrage grow in a burst of colors that attract photographers from around the world.

The tundra's limited plant life restricts its wildlife population, yet somehow arctic hare, lemmings, and foxes find a way to subsist. Polar bears and caribou are now rare, but the former still den in the park's remote northeastern sections.

Along the coast, by contrast, animal life abounds. It includes several varieties of seals, beluga whales, narwhals, and the occasional walrus. Bowhead and

Warden's cabin, Weasel Valley, Auyuittuq NP

Moonrise over Thor Peak, Auyuittuq National Park

humpback whales are sometimes spotted too. More than 40 species of birds summer in the park (only four are year-round residents), including ptarmigan, snowy owls, eider ducks, peregrine falcons, and gyrfalcons. Snowy owls can be aggressive during nesting season. If you see one, it's best to keep your distance.

Getting There

From Iqaluit, you can arrange air travel to Qikiqtarjuaq (Broughton Island) or Pangnirtung with First Air *(867-473-8960)* or Kenn Borek Air *(867-979-1919)*. You'll have to travel with a local outfitter (see p. 282) to reach the North Pangnirtung trailhead (on Davis Sound) from Qikiqtarjuaq. Similarly, most people use an outfitter to reach the Overlord trailhead from Pangnirtung, but undertaking that two-day trek yourself is not out of the question. In winter, most visitors prefer to travel in the company of an outfitter equipped with snowmobiles, but certain routes can be skied on your own.

Outfitters know the local winds, so don't assume that an outfitter who balks at setting off in calm weather is being overcautious. The head of the fjord can be tranquil while 55-mile-per-hour winds are howling at Pangnirtung, and vice versa. Tides, too, pose a problem. To avoid rocks exposed by low tide, boats must set out within two hours of high tide. During breakup (last week of June to first week of July) boat or snowmobile travel is impossible, but you can still hike in from Pangnirtung. From Qikiqtarjuaq, however, the park cannot be reached during breakup.

What to See and Do

Hiking

Most visitors come to Auyuittuq for the 41-mile, 6- to 10-day trek that starts in the park's southeast corner at Overlord, a one-hour boat ride north of Pangnirtung. After threading **Akshayuk Pass** (formerly Pangnirtung Pass), the hike circles Summit Lake and returns to Pangnirtung.

The pass—an ice-free defile that is one of the wildest and most dramatic valleys in this wild and dramatic place—winds between upthrust mountains carved into otherworldly shapes. Cutting across Baffin Island's Cumberland Peninsula from Pangnirtung Fiord in the south to Davis Strait in the north, Akshayuk Pass owes its deep, U-shaped profile to the glaciers that once filled it. A few of

these boreal behemoths still venture down to the floor of the pass on the north side. Be prepared, therefore, to cross frequent rubble mounds (the debris from glacial moraines) and several rivers.

A longer (60-mile) version of this hike, for experienced travelers only, extends 40 miles beyond Summit Lake to the trailhead at North Pangnirtung Fiord, near the town of Qikiqtarjuaq. If you decide to tackle this epic trek, consider starting it from Qikiqtarjuaq (an outfitter will have to ferry you to the park); given the area's frequent ice delays, it's better to be stranded in the south than at the trail's lonely northern terminus. If you find yourself similarly marooned at the trail's southern end (Overlord), you can always make

Pangnirtung resident, Baffin Island

the two-day walk from there to Pangnirtung.

To begin the **Summit Lake circuit hike** from the south, pick up the main trail at the Overlord warden station at the head of Pangnirtung Fiord. Look southeast from here and you'll spot 4,888-foot **Overlord (Pangniqtup Qingua)**, a peak guarding the southern entrance to Akshayuk Pass. To the west, the **Weasel River** empties into Pangnirtung Fiord, which falls as much as 30 feet from high tide to low, exposing tidal flats that provide a rich habitat for plover and phalaropes.

As you strike out on the trail, you'll come across curious beach-like dunes—piles of fine sand ground by glaciers and sorted by the winds—that rise nearly 100 feet high. For the first few miles the path leads over sandy flats, fords several glacial streams, and crosses a footbridge spanning a sizable tributary of the Weasel. Circular **Crater Lake (Aqulutaqrusiq)**, on the west side of the Weasel but hidden from the trail by the ridge that forms the end moraine of Tumbling Glacier, is a startling greenish-blue. That's because no silt-laden waters flow into it. The Weasel River, by contrast, has been turned milky and opaque by "glacial flour"—fine particles of glacier-crushed rock.

Just north of Crater Lake is your next landmark, a 2,165-foot-high cascade called **Schwartzenbach Falls (Qulitasaniakvik)**. The Inuit name for these falls means the "place to get caribou"; Inuit hunters once climbed above the waterfall to pursue caribou in the valleys beyond. A trailside cairn marks the Arctic Circle's location of about 66°33.5' north latitude.

Just over 2 miles past the falls, **Mount Odin**—the loftiest summit between the Carolinas and Ellesmere Island—towers 7,043 feet above the valley's west side. Another summit inspired by the Aesir, **Thor Peak,** looms 5,495 feet above the valley floor to the east (your right) of the trail. Like the Norse god of thunder, it possesses great power: a leaning, mile-high slab of sheer granite that is the planet's highest continuous cliff face.

Summit Lake, which you finally reach after about 20 miles of hiking, marks the highest point in Akshayuk Pass: Glacial waters from the lake flow north in the Owl River and south in the Weasel. Both waterways drop a total of 1,650 feet before debouching into the Arctic Ocean.

Summit Lake makes a good base for day trips. One of the most popular hikes from the lake is the **King's Parade Route,** a 15-mile (round-trip) trek that leads to splendid views of three glaciers: the Caribou, the Parade, and the Turner. (The terminal moraine of the latter nearly pinches Glacier Lake off the northern end of Summit Lake.) Both the Turner and its cousin, the Highway Glacier to the north, flow down from the Penny Ice Cap; they are reachable by hikers but should be attempted only by the experienced.

Mount Asgard (Sivanitirutinguak), 6,610 feet tall, commands the surrounding glaciers. Since the 1950s, when it was first scaled by a three-man team sponsored by the Arctic Institute of North America, the flat tops of its twin towers have attracted world-class climbers from dozens of countries.

East of Glacier Lake stands 3,500-foot **Mount Battle.** The reward for climbing it is long views of the pass, both to the north and to the south. From its flanks you may also be able to see the edge of the Penny Ice Cap itself.

Most backpackers skirt the north end of Glacier Lake and begin heading back to Overlord on the lake's western shore. Continuing north on the main trail rather than turning around is an unwise course of action because sections of the Owl River bed thaw deeply in summer, forming waist-deep quagmires that can snare the unwary. It's best not to hike on the river's muddy banks. And no matter where you end your hike, you'll need to arrange for pickup there.

Finally, after a total of 60 miles, you'll reach the coastline at Davis Strait. Here glaciers have incised the valley floors below sea level, creating deep, narrow fjords with vertical walls up to 3,000 feet high. In summer, as the many active glaciers along the trail continue their retreat, you can hear geology in action: Meltwater torrents roar, windblown grit scours the rock in frequent gales, rocks tumble from the ice face, and Coronation Glacier slides inexorably toward the sea.

Bowhead whalebone frame for storing sod

Inuksuit, Weasel Valley, Auyuittuq NP

Inuksuit

Inuksuit, the stone markers laid out by Inuit in many parts of the Arctic, are similar to the stone cairns that dot the Sahara: They can save a traveler's life by pointing the way; they can lead a hunter to food; and they can offer solace to a seeker of spirits. To the Inuit, they "act in the capacity of a human."

Norman Hallendy, an old Arctic hand known among the Inuit as Apieqsukti ("the inquisitive one"), has written extensively about the Arctic for 35 years. In *Inuksuit: Silent Messengers of the Arctic*, he describes the following kinds of inuksuit, found throughout the Arctic:

Iqaluqarniraijug Red and black stones along the water's edge indicating a good place to fish.

Kattaq Two rock slabs standing upright that mark the entrance to a revered place.

Niungvaliruluit A cairn in the shape of a window, used for aligning and indicating direction.

Tammariikuti A small stone placed on an existing inukshuk, usually by a hunter, to inform those following that he changed direction.

Tikkuuti A directional pointer constructed of various size rocks graded from largest to smallest.

Tuktunnutiit A cairn with antlers, marking a caribou-hunting area. May also indicate a cache of meat nearby.

Usukjuaq A phallic symbol of fertility that points out a rich area for fishing and spawning.

Mountain Climbing

Akshayuk Pass is busy by Arctic standards, but venture out of the valley and you will encounter far fewer people. Dozens of sheer peaks and their rough granite cliffs make for challenging and strenuous climbing. Favorite summits include Mount Odin, Thor Peak, **Mount Northumbria, Tyr Peak, Tête Blanche,** and Mount Asgard.

Because of the degree of skill required to scale these peaks, many climbers in this region do not use an outfitter. Likewise, most outfitters are loath to escort beginners.

Ski Touring

April, May, and June are the best times to go ski touring in Auyuittuq. Only those experienced in glacier travel, however, should undertake this activity, which can be quite dangerous. Favorite day trips include the 12-mile circuit around Mount Battle and the 3-mile ascent of the Tyr Peak glacier, which lies southwest of Summit Lake. You can also ski-tour the King's Parade Route.

Two- and three-day routes crisscross the area near **Rundle Glacier** and the **Caribou-Norman Glacier Loop.** The warden station in Pangnirtung has brochures describing and mapping these trails; ask there how to visit the park's fantastically exquisite ice caves.

Other Activities

In the less visited northern portion of the park, backpacking and hiking are for seasoned outdoorspeople only. Instead, consider taking a guided snowmobile or dogsled trip.

The **Angmarlik Visitor Centre** in Pangnirtung *(867-473-8737)* contains an interesting small museum and library. Local people may be willing to arrange guided tours of Pangnirtung—and, if you so desire, a visit to a "blubber station": **Kekerten Island Whaling Station** is now a national historic site. You can also arrange fishing and whale-watching expeditions on Cumberland Sound.

Staying Safe

Visitors must be self-reliant and capable of self-rescue. If they are not, the expense of a search-and-rescue mission may fall on the extricated party. ∎

Hikers' Haven

Though the valley floor is clear of snow (and thus accessible to hikers) between May and September, most visitors hike the pass between late July and mid-August. Devotees of true wilderness may find the pass overcrowded; that is, you might run into as many as two or three other parties in a typical day. If you prefer to avoid such encounters, try the hike in the long days of June or early September.

Approaching Summit Lake and along the trail's more difficult sections, you'll find the path marked by human-shaped rock cairns erected to guide hikers to safe routes across moraines and rivers. An emergency hut (no camping allowed) containing a radio appears about every 20 miles along the trail.

Dewey Soper Migratory Bird Sanctuary

■ 2 million acres ■ Nunavut, southwest Baffin Island ■ Best times spring-fall
■ Bird-watching ■ By chartered plane from Iqaluit or Pangnirtung ■ Contact
Canadian Wildlife Service, P.O. 1714, Iqaluit, NU X0A 0H0; phone 867-975-4637. www.mb.ec.gc.ca/nature/index.en.html

ESTABLISHED IN 1957 AND DESIGNATED a Wetland of International Importance by the Ramsar Convention in 1982, this two-million-acre bird sanctuary stretches 155 miles from Foxe Basin in the southwestern part of Baffin Island to the vast tidal flats and coastal tundra of the **Great Plain of the Koukdjuak.** Nunavut's capital, Iqaluit, lies 217 miles to the southeast. The sanctuary's name honors Dewey Soper, a Canadian government biologist who found the eggs and nests of blue phase snow geese here in 1929. Today the wetland provides nesting grounds for almost one-third of Canada's lesser snow goose population.

An ideal habitat for water birds, the Great Plain consists mostly of marshy wet and dry tundra saturated with shallow ponds, lakes, and hundreds of slowly flowing streams. The beaches along Foxe Basin stretch nearly nine miles wide at low tide.

Only 43 bird species have been recorded in the sanctuary, yet the numbers of each are immense: An estimated two million geese may be found foraging on the Great Plain from May to mid-September. Among them you'll spot lesser snow geese, Canada geese, and the Atlantic Brant, which prefers tidal flats and brackish or salt waters. Other common species include oldsquaw, Sabine gulls, king and common eiders, and red phalarope.

Although Inuit are permitted to hunt in all Nunavut sanctuaries, the Dewey Soper bird sanctuary is so isolated that little of this activity takes place here. ■

Oldsquaw

Soper River

■ 60 miles long ■ Nunavut, Meta Incognita Peninsula, Baffin Island ■ Camping, hiking, white-water rafting and kayaking, canoeing, dogsledding, bird-watching, wildlife viewing, ski touring ■ Access through Iqaluit to Kimmirut ■ Contact Nunavut Tourism, P.O. Box 1450, Iqaluit, NU; phone 867-979-6551 or 800-491-7910. www.nunatour.nt.ca

MEANDERING FROM ITS HEADWATERS on the Meta Incognita Peninsula of southern Baffin Island to Soper Lake 60 miles away, the Soper River—a Canadian heritage river—weaves a ribbon of green through a land that is bleak and brown. Located within **Katannilik Territorial Park,** it offers a 30-mile stretch of navigable water—a rarity for rivers in the Arctic islands. The Inuit, who use the Soper for transportation in both winter and summer, call it Kuujjuaq—"the place where water falls."

Vegetation thrives along the river, where a microclimate spurs willows to grow 6 to 10 feet tall. Drawn by these tender greens, animals such as arctic hare, lemmings, and caribou (and therefore foxes and wolves) gravitate to the riverbanks. You stand a remarkably good chance of spotting a caribou or even a wolf from your canoe; their range here is fairly narrow, and the visibility is good. In the sky above wheel peregrine falcons and gyrfalcons, hawks, snow buntings, horned larks and plover, guillemots, terns, murres, and loons. Hikers and campers can take it all in from tiered riverside terraces that reveal the water's stages.

Summertime canoe, rafting, or kayaking trips promise comfortable and fairly safe paddling through Class II and III rapids; the occasional waterfall requires a portage. Many paddlers start at the Soper River's confluence with the Joy, where the water flow picks up enough to allow some floating. For most of its boatable run, the Soper flows through a steep, narrow valley. As you approach the coast below the Livingstone River, old fire rings—reminders of the area's ancient inhabitants—begin to appear. Evidence of more recent human activity presents itself near Big Bend in the form of old mica and lapis lazuli mine pits. (*For canoe or kayaking trips, contact the Chewonki Foundation, 485 Chewonki Neck Rd., Wiscasset, ME 04578, 207-882-7323, www.Chewonki.org; or NorthWinds, P.O. Box 820, Iqaluit, NU X0A 0R0, 867-979-0551, www.northwinds-arctic.com*).

In winter, the valley takes on an entirely different but no less breathtaking look. Though the days are short and quite cold, you can ski-tour up the snowy valley or hire a dogsled to skim across the icy landscape.

From Iqaluit, served by First Air (*800-267-1247*), flights leave weekdays for Kimmirut; the Soper is accessible on foot or by boat from there. Two landing sites—at Mount Joy and Livingstone Falls—have been designated on the river itself. It's easy to canoe downstream from either one to the Inuit community of Kimmirut. For a challenge, tackle the nine-day, 65-mile hike along the **Itijjajiaq Trail,** which leads from Iqaluit to the Soper River and then all the way to Kimmirut. You'll need an experienced guide, plus boat transport across Frobisher Bay to the trailhead. ■

Parc de Conservation de Pingualuit

■ 278,000 acres (proposed park) ■ Northern Quebec, 1,100 miles north of Montreal, on Péninsule D'Ungava ■ White-water rafting and kayaking, bird-watching, wildlife viewing, meteor crater ■ Access by snowmobile, skis, or on foot only ■ Contact Société de la faune et des parcs du Québec, Édifice Marie-Guyart, 675 boul. René-Lévesque Est, 10e étage, Quebec, QC G1R 5V7, phone 800-561-1616. www.fapaq.gouv.qc.ca; or Communications Office, Management, Planning and Development for Quebec Parks, phone 418-521-3845

SOME 1.4 MILLION YEARS AGO, a meteorite 400 feet in diameter slammed into the Earth's crust at 55,800 miles per hour, releasing energy equivalent to 8,500 Hiroshima bombs. This explosion gouged out the Cratère du Nouveau-Québec, which is 2.1 miles in circumference—a landmark the Inuit call **Pingualuit,** or "where the land rises." In 2003 the crater will become the focal point of Quebec's first far northern provincial park.

Photographed by the crew of a U.S. Army Air Forces weather plane on June 20, 1943, and first explored by Canadian prospector and frontiersman Frederick Chubb in early 1950, the crater brims with water of a rare purity: colorless, tasteless, and virtually devoid of mineral content. This rarefied reservoir is fed exclusively by rainwater and snow, and it lacks any natural outlet. The crater's lake would take some 330 years to renew itself, making the water extremely vulnerable to pollution.

As many as ten mammal species, including lemmings, caribou, arctic foxes, rare musk oxen, and perhaps 25 types of birds, roam the crater—a dramatically giant pockmark in otherwise barren tundra.

The proposed park will also comprise the nearby **Puvirnituq River Corridor Sector,** which contains the Puvirnituq River and **Lamarche Lake Canyons.** Unlike other Ungava destinations, the river provides opportunities for white-water enthusiasts. Summer birders may spot nesting pairs of gyrfalcons and rough-legged hawks along its banks.

Arctic fox

A third section of the upcoming park, the **Plateau,** encompasses a network of lakes—Rouxel; Vergons; Nallusarqituq, a part of Rivière Vachon; and Saint-Germain—linked by a string of waterways called the Great Lakes Necklace.

The nearest settlement—the Inuit hamlet of Kangiqsujuaq, about 50 miles away—will be linked to Montreal by plane. Plans call for park access from Kangiqsujuaq to be by snowmobile, skis, or foot only. ■

Caribou meat air drying, near Nain

Torngat Mountains

■ 3,474 square miles (proposed park) ■ Northern tip of Labrador and Quebec between Ungava Bay and Labrador Sea ■ Year-round ■ Hiking, mountain climbing, sea kayaking, bird-watching, whale-watching, wildlife viewing, archaeological sites ■ No roads or scheduled flights; access by outfitters from Nain or other northern towns ■ Contact the Labrador Inuit Association, P.O. Box 70, Nain, NF A0P 1L0, 709-922-2942; or Parks Establishment Branch, Parks Canada, 25 Eddy St., Hull, QC K1A 0M5, phone 888-773-8888. www.parkscanada.gc.ca

ECOLOGY, HISTORY, CULTURE, ornithology, wildlife biology, and even mineralogy all dovetailed in the late 1990s to make the Torngat Mountains a Canadian park reserve-in-waiting. The push to protect the Torngats stemmed from the desire to create an environmental showcase for a region that has never been seriously marred by commerce or industry. Extending 120 miles from Cape Chidley at the very extremity of Labrador down to Hebron Fiord on the Atlantic coast, the Torngat Mountains also constitute a historical and spiritual legacy for the Inuit of Labrador.

In addition, the Torngats harbor breeding and nesting sites for such endangered species as the peregrine falcon and the eastern Harlequin duck. The mountains stand astride the migratory path of the George River caribou herd—the world's largest, at half a million animals (see sidebar p. 264)—and encompass the entire range of the Torngat Mountain caribou herd. Black bears, musk oxen, wolves, polar bears, and eagles also populate the range.

With the discovery of massive nickel deposits in Labrador's Voisey Bay in the mid-1990s, the mining industry lobbied to open the area to development. Newfoundland & Labrador Province stepped in, creating a special management area that placed a temporary freeze on industrial and commercial use. The national park boundaries will approximate those of the Torngat Mountains, ranging from **Saglek Bay** (of interest for its 3.6-billion-year-old rocks) to **Killiniq Island** at Labrador's northern tip.

What to See and Do

Torngat comes from the Inuit word Torngasok, the god of wind and storms. In this rugged landscape, steep and craggy mountains rise directly from the sea, and deep fjords pierce the coast. There are virtually no inhabitants or vegetation. It is not a place for the timid, the unfit, or the inexperienced.

The difficult access makes visitors dependent on outfitters to reach the area. This is not such a bad thing: There are a variety of worthwhile options available, from cruises up the coast to rugged hikes across the mountains from Ungava Bay in Quebec. Nain, a town 250 miles south of the proposed park, offers a regular coastal steamer in summer, scheduled flights to Happy Valley-Goose Bay on Air Labrador or Innu Mikun, and a raft of outfitters eager for your business (see p. 282).

Take a flight-seeing trip in a Twin Otter or floatplane to get a fix on the grandeur of the bare mountains and the precipitous fjords. It also enables you to take in the massive scope of the glaciers and track the procession of icebergs making their stately way south on the cold Labrador Current. And who knows? From the air you may even be able to spot the George River caribou herd.

Boat travel, by contrast, gives you a more intimate view of the Torngat Mountains. A typical boat trip from Nain takes place in a sturdy vessel with an Inuit crew: You'll wind among islands and glistening icebergs, perhaps diverting up a few fjords for close-up views of their stark cliffs. And with the rich waters of the Labrador Current attracting dozens of marine mammals, you may have a chance for whale-watching en route.

Trails and markers in the park-to-be are nonexistent, and the plan is to keep it that way. Hikers must therefore make their own way,

Bald eagle

scrambling through corridors carved out by earlier glacial action and following the paths of migrating caribou through rock-strewn valleys, around moraines, and across icy rivers.

If you'd like to make an overland crossing between two fjords, seek out an outfitter with marine access from Nain. They may be willing to put their boat to work as a floating base camp, dropping you in one fjord and then moving on to collect you at the end of your day hike in the next. Other possibilities include a trek inland to the Quebec Labrador watershed or (from the Quebec side) an excursion up the **Rivière George** or an overland trip from **Obloviak Fiord** to the watershed and back.

A popular trek leads 40 miles north from Saglek Bay to **Nachvak Fiord,** passing through the rich tundra of the **Ramah region.** (Ramah was the name given to an old Inuit settlement founded in this area by Moravian missionaries in 1871.) Along the way you'll have opportunities to climb **Cirque Mountain,** with its characteristic bowl-shaped depression, or Newfoundland & Labrador's highest peak, 5,420-foot **Mount Caubvick,** which straddle the border between Labrador and Quebec. As you scale Caubvick, note the change from early Precambrian metamorphic rock to younger sedimentary rocks such as Ramah chert—prized by prehistoric Inuit for use in trading and tools.

Many visitors use Saglek as a staging point for two- or three-day forays to the watershed and beyond. These hikes lead through numberless alpine valleys and cross tundra, mountain passes, and as many as 10 rivers, providing ample chances to spot caribou, black bear, and the incredible profusion of bird species in the subarctic. Because there are no trails through this wilderness, you will need orienteering skills or an outfitter guide. ■

Barren-ground caribou

Herd and Scene

To watch thousands of caribou thunder over the crest of a hill is an awesome sight. So is a glimpse of the animals swimming en masse across a river, their bodies riding so high it appears they're walking on water (air bubbles trapped in their hollow hair buoy them up).

Of North America's 60 or so distinct caribou populations, none is more impressive to behold than eastern Canada's George River caribou herd on its annual migration from summer tundra to winter taiga. Numbering 400,000 to 700,000 animals, this herd performs one of the last epic migrations—nearly 5,000 miles—on the continent. The animals follow routes established by their ancient forebears, divertible from their course only by such natural occurrences as fires, extreme weather, or mosquitoes. Equally remarkable is their range: The caribou roam an area of Labrador and Quebec that covers some 190,000 square miles.

The herd's continued health is anything but guaranteed. Threats come from several sources. For example, the Canadian Forces base at Goose Bay, Labrador, stages several thousand low-level flights a year, many of them only 100 feet high; the engine noise may distress and disrupt the caribou's breeding population. Logging, mining, and hydroelectric development further endanger the George River herd: In the 1980s, more than 10,000 animals drowned in an area along the Caniapiscau River flooded by Hydro Quebec.

Worst of all, the caribou's food source seems to be disappearing. The animals eat a slow-growing lichen that can take more than 50 years to recover. This troubles wildlife biologists, who know that the caribou population is historically subject to wild fluctuations. Between 1890 and 1920, the herd fell to nearly none, while between 1976 and 1996 it ballooned from 178,000 head to more than 700,000. According to Innu lore, one sure sign of a coming crash is when caribou trails grow more and more distinct; this signals overuse—and therefore imminent depletion—of a single food source.

Mealy Mountains

■ 1,930 square miles (proposed park) ■ Central Labrador, southeast of Lake Melville ■ Year-round ■ Hiking, mountain climbing, canoeing, fishing, bird-watching ■ Contact Labrador Lake Melville Tourism Association, P.O. Box 148, Station C, Happy Valley-Goose Bay, NF A0P 1C0; phone 709-896-3489. www.happyvalley-goosebay.com

SOARING SKYWARD from the southern shores of Lake Melville, the Mealy Mountains stretch nearly 120 miles into the heart of Labrador. The 3,000-foot-high peaks form islands of arctic tundra in a region of boreal forests and ocean coast. For wilderness types, the area represents not just spectacular scenery but some of Labrador's best canoeing and salmon fishing. The **Eagle River,** which begins as snowmelt runoff high in the Mealys, is one of the finest wild rivers remaining in North America.

The status of the mountains the Innu call Akamiuapishk is in some flux. With logging and mining interests exerting pressure to extend the Trans-Labrador Highway into the valuable interior, the Innu have joined federal and provincial governments in calling for the establishment of a park that would preserve the region's ecology and cultural heritage.

Large populations of moose, black bear, red fox, lynx, and snowshoe hare share habitats with the small resident herd of caribou. Along the coast of the Labrador Sea, birders can flesh out their life lists with sightings of Atlantic puffins, murres, petrels, gannets, Canada geese, eider ducks, black ducks, and the endangered Harlequin duck.

From the unprepossessing and military-dominated town of Happy Valley-Goose Bay, the western Mealy Mountains are but a snowmobile run, a boat ride, or a 30-mile hike away. Alternatively, you can access the eastern Mealys and the Eagle River system from Cartwright or from communities on Sandwich Bay such as Separation Point and Paradise River.

The 152-mile **Turnigan Trail** *(709-896-8750)* cuts through a part of the proposed park, linking Goose Bay to Cartwright. Its snowmobile trail gives winter access to otherwise unreachable villages and camps, while in summer the trail affords fishermen a land route into the uplands of such wilderness rivers as the **Kenamu,** the Eagle, and the **Paradise.**

So wild are the Mealys that none of the peaks have names. With not a trail or a lodge in sight, visitors must hire guides in Happy Valley-Goose Bay or Cartwright— or rely on their own wilderness skills. But even with their summer snowcaps many mountains are easy to climb, and the views from on high are truly seldom scenes. ■

Razorbill

Iceberg Alley

FROZEN SAPPHIRES OF THE SEA, newly calved icebergs make their stately but deadly way from Greenland to the Maritime Provinces between July and mid-October each year. After crossing the mouth of the Hudson Strait from Baffin Island to the northern tip of Labrador, they pick up the Labrador Current and continue to drift southeast past the Island of Newfoundland. About 250 miles southeast of the isle, in the Grand Banks of Newfoundland, some bergs cluster in a pelagic processional that is often referred to as "Iceberg Alley." This icy gauntlet has long posed a navigational hazard to passing ships—most notoriously the R.M.S. *Titanic,* which sank on April 15, 1912, less than three hours after ramming an iceberg in the alley.

By the time a berg materializes within sight of the harbor entrance to Newfoundland's capital, St. John's, it has spent roughly two years afloat. About 85 out of 100 bergs in the alley get their start in one of the tidewater glaciers that hug the western coast of Greenland. Another 10 percent are calved—that is, broken free of their parent glacier and dropped into the sea—on Greenland's east coast. The remaining 5 percent come from northern Ellesmere Island.

Not every calved iceberg finds its way south, however. While some run aground on the ocean bottom, others drift into a fjord and stall there, slowly melting, for years. Each year, an average of 2,000 bergs pass Cape Chidley, at Labrador's northern tip; of that number, 1,400 make it across the Strait of Belle Isle separating Labrador from the island of Newfoundland. Only 400 to 800 survive as far south as St. John's.

In the century since the *Titanic* disas-

Icebergs off Grey Islands, Newfoundland

ter, new detection methods devised by the Ice Patrol Service have drastically curtailed the risk of deadly run-ins between ships and bergs. Founded in 1914 and now funded by 19 European and North American nations, the patrol *(www.uscg.mil/lantarea/iip/iip.html)* uses computers, satellites, and special aircraft to track the movements of the 22 (in 1999) to nearly 2000 (in 1991) icebergs that drift south of 48° North each iceberg season (February to September).

To get a glimpse of Iceberg Alley yourself, head for the harbor of St. John's or any other vantage point along the east coast of Newfoundland or Labrador. The town of St. Anthony, for example, prides itself on its iceberg count, which is often posted on the town's website *(www.town.stanthony. nf.ca/)*. Perhaps the most dramatic sightings of all can be had from the summer Cruising Labrador ferry *(passengers only; vessels do not carry vehi-*

cles). Operated by Coastal Labrador Adventure Cruises, the ferry travels from St. Anthony, Newfoundland, to Nain, Labrador, with numerous ports of call. Twelve-day excursions on the *Northern Ranger,* the working supply vessel, begin in early July and end in mid-October; prices range from $2,300 (CN) to $3,400 (CN), depending on the time of year and the type of accommodations. For more information contact Newfoundland and Labrador Department of Tourism *(P.O. Box 8730, St. John's, NF A1B 4K2, 800-563-6353. www.gov.nf.ca/ferryservices)*.

Blasts from the Past

More than mere tourist magnets, iceberg sources—that is, glaciers—attract scientific scrutiny because they reveal weather conditions 15,000 years ago; that's when the snow fell that constitutes today's icebergs. Additionally, sea ice and icebergs can both reveal the long-term changes in ocean temperatures that have been brought on by global warming.

As centuries passed and more snow accumulated, it compacted into exceedingly dense ice. Eventually this ice cap became so heavy that it began to flow as glaciers down mountainsides and valleys toward the coast. Easing (and speeding) their passage was spring runoff, which allowed the glaciers to move as much as 65 feet a day. Where they met the sea, the glaciers were weakened by tides, waves, and warm spring temperatures. Smaller pieces of ice, or icebergs, eventually calved into the sea.

Analysis of this ice has shown that it is pure fresh water. Most bergs look white, however, because air bubbles are trapped in the ice. Startling blue streaks indicate places where meltwater has refrozen with few air bubbles. ■

Labrador Frontier Circuit

■ 700 miles on Quebec Hwy. 389 and Newfoundland Hwy. 500 from mouth of St. Lawrence River to Happy Valley-Goose Bay ■ Year-round; avoid outdoor activities during blackfly months of June and July ■ Camping, hiking, fishing, snowmobiling, cross-country skiing, wildlife viewing, scenic drive, dam tour ■ Contact: for road conditions in Labrador, Provincial Department of Works, phone 709-896-7840 or Royal Newfoundland Constabulary, phone 709-944-7602; for road conditions in Quebec, Quebec Ministry of Transport, phone 418-589-2065 or Quebec Provincial Police, phone 418-296-2324; for information, Labrador West Tourism, 709-944-7631

HARD-CORE ROAD WARRIORS, TAKE HEART: In 1992 it became possible to undertake an epic loop of 1,700 land miles and 45 hours of sea crossings that treats you to a positively heroic swath of natural real estate in four eastern Canada provinces. This Odyssean scenic drive starts in **Baie-Comeau** on the St. Lawrence River and makes a beeline north to Labrador City and Wabush in western Labrador, then heads east across central Labrador to reach **Happy Valley-Goose Bay.** From there you have two choices: Retrace your route, or hop the ferry *(June-Nov.)* to Lewisporte in Newfoundland, then drive across Newfoundland to either Argentia or

Fishing dories and coastal ferry, Labrador

Channel-Port aux Basques and board another ferry for Nova Scotia. Finally, you can drive through New Brunswick and rejoin the St. Lawrence at Rivière-du-Loup for the ferry crossing to St.-Siméon on the North Shore.

Portions of the drive through northern Quebec and western Labrador are on gravel, but they are perfectly feasible in an everyday sedan. With proper planning and frequent checks on road conditions, it is also possible to make the drive in winter, when each northern community stages its own particular snow festival, snowmobile race, or dogsled race.

Western Labrador bills itself as the Last Frontier. That sobriquet is apt for those portions of the landscape that remain unspoiled and untouched, but it unravels when you get an eyeful of the abandoned mining community of Gagnon or get buzzed by a low-level military flight out of Goose Bay.

Taking the Plunge

Murres—*Uria aalge*—are extraordinary in many ways. Take the behavior of the three-week-old chicks: Even before they can fly, they fling themselves off cliffs and glide to the ocean below, where the father awaits. The birds then set off on a swimming migration that takes them 600 miles into the Atlantic, where they winter, grow up, and finally learn to fly.

The Labrador Frontier Circuit starts in Baie-Comeau and heads out of town on Quebec Hwy. 389, charitably described by initiates as "partially paved." For the next 360 miles to the Labrador border it passes through wild, rugged, beautiful countryside dominated by deep river valleys, boreal forests of black spruce, and clear lakes. If you put your mind to it, you can reach the Quebec community of Fermont in about nine hours. But why would you want to do that? Attractive roadside stops along the way invite you to pull over and soak in the view of Quebec Province's characteristic lakes and fishing streams.

About 10 miles after crossing the Labrador border you'll come to the towns of Labrador City and then Wabush, the self-styled "heart of industrial Labrador." Indeed, the residents proudly point out, North America's largest open-pit mining, concentrate, and pelletizing operation lies just a few miles away. Yet there are natural compensations galore for these wilderness depredations: Angling is unsurpassed for the area's Ouananiche (land-locked salmon), speckles (trout), and northern pike, and both communities have carved out hiking trails that pass pristine streams and crystal waterfalls. Labrador City boasts more than 300 miles of groomed snowmobile trails that weave through birch-covered valleys, giving winter visitors an outside chance of spotting members of the George River caribou herd (see sidebar p. 264). Outfitters in Labrador City (see p. 282) will custom-design an expedition such as the popular three-day canoe venture down the Churchill River to Muskrat Falls.

If you pass this way in March, check out the Labrador West Winter Odyssey or the Labrador 120 (a dogsled race from Labrador City to Steers River and back). Also in March there's the Great Labrador Loppet, a cross-country ski event that attracts hundreds of participants—

Labradorite and whalebone carving

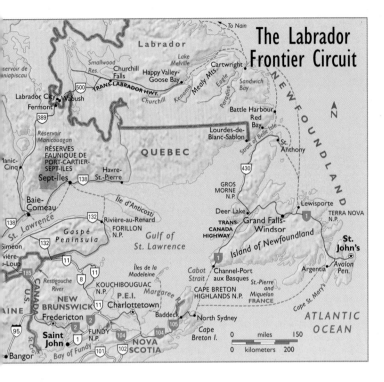

perhaps you'll be one of them? For more information, call 709-944-7631.

From Labrador City the drive veers east on Hwy. 500, an all-weather road that leads to Churchill Falls 150 miles away. No services exist between the two towns, so tank up on both fuel and food before undertaking this leg of the scenic drive. The trip will take a rushed traveler about three hours, but that would mean missing the crystal-clear brooks and tree-ringed lakes at Ossokmanuan River, Churchill Falls, and Bowdoin Canyon, so take your time. To help you identify sites en route, check out the Geology Association of Canada's guide to the geology of the Trans-Labrador Highway (www.geosurv.gov.nf.ca/gacmap/LAB2.html).

East of Churchill Falls, the Frontier Circuit grows steeper, trickier, and altogether more beautiful. Even lead foots may find themselves dawdling on this final stretch of the scenic drive—186 miles (about six hours) to Goose Bay—as they pause to appreciate its rivers, bogs, and mountains.

Goose Bay offers air service to the Island of Newfoundland, Nova Scotia, and Quebec, as well as twice-weekly ferry service to Lewisporte on Newfoundland's north coast. The 500-mile ocean crossing takes 36 hours or so; reservations are a must (Coastal Labrador Marine Services, 866-535-2567). The ferry operates only from mid-June to mid-November. Once you get to the Island of Newfoundland, you'll find that Marine Atlantic ferry services (800-341-7981 or 902-794-8109) has regular sailings from Argentia or Channel-Port aux Basques to North Sydney, Nova Scotia. ∎

Beluga whales in Hudson Bay, near Polar Bear Provincial Park

Polar Bear Provincial Park

■ 9,400 square miles ■ Northeast Ontario, on shores of James and Hudson Bay ■ Best months June-Aug. ■ Camping, hiking, kayaking, canoeing, fishing, bird-watching ■ No facilities. Access by chartered aircraft from Hearst, Cochrane, or Moosonee, Ontario ■ Contact Ministry of Natural Resources, Box 190, Moosonee, ON P0L 1Y0; phone 705-336-2987. www.ontarioparks.com/pola.html

FLY NORTH TOWARD THIS REMOTE PARK from the towns of Cochrane, Moosonee, or Hearst, Ontario, and you'll spy terrain that appears to be flat, monochromatic, and waterlogged—something like an unsqueezed sponge. At lower altitudes, however, it resolves into a subtle and beautiful palette of pinks, browns, mauves, and greens so intense they look black, an intricate mosaic of rivers, shallow lakes, and fens. This is the Great Muskeg country, the world's largest continuous peat bogs, also known as the Hudson Bay lowlands. In Ontario alone, the muskeg (a ground layer of organic material, or peat, 25 to 30 inches thick) covers almost 380,000 square miles, spreading into Manitoba to the west and Quebec to the east. The park itself is but a fraction of this immensity, a section of muskeg selected for formal protection along James and Hudson Bays.

Those two bays, together with the Hudson Bay lowlands, are the remnants of the ancient Tyrrell Sea, created by the meltwaters of the Pleistocene epoch. As this sea slowly disappeared, it left behind impervious clay layers up to 10 feet thick, which provided poor drainage. The resulting sodden land, paired with the cool climate, retarded the decay of dead plants. Each year's growth therefore left behind a waterlogged muck that slowly morphed into peat. In many places, the peat reached a thickness of 13 feet; this base became the "soil" in which new plants took root, but it also meant those roots lost contact with the actual soil beneath. As a result, rainwater became the sole source of moisture and nutrients. This in turn encouraged the formation of bogs, in which flourished such typically acid-resistant flora as gnarly dwarf spruces, sphagnum mosses, bog laurel, and Labrador tea laurel.

Although winter turns the lowlands into millions of tiny frozen peat plateaus, in summer the bogs and fens burst into exquisite bloom—a wondrous rainbow of colors from pale yellows and greens through ochers, umbers, purples, and browns. Prominent blossoms include flame-colored lousewort, purple lousewort, bunchberry, and chickweed.

Averaging only 600 visitors per year, Polar Bear Provincial Park offers no campsites, shelters, boat landings, supplies, or staff. The weather is harsh and unpredictable; in summer it may swing from almost 80°F to not much above freezing in a matter of hours. Visitors must bring tents with a low profile lest they be torn away by the frequent gales. Why, then, do people visit?

Mainly for the birds. The spongy muskeg and endless marsh support dozens of bird species—some common, some exotic—in astonishing numbers. These include the willow ptarmigan, tundra swan, snowy owl, bald eagle, the ungainly godwit, and a long list of others: red-throated loons, king eiders, rough-legged hawks, stilt and pectoral sandpipers, plovers and jaegers, greater and lesser yellowlegs, dowitchers, sandhill cranes, and huge flocks of Canada geese from the Mississippi flyway.

The lowlands are generally an important part of the yearly cycle for large numbers of birds—almost one million Canada geese and upward of 50,000 Atlantic brant. The spring goose migration is eagerly anticipated by the local Cree, who retain unlimited duck hunting rights in the area.

The jewel in this avian crown is the world's southernmost colony of lesser snow geese. During the spring breeding season, the snow goose "homestead" can be heard—and sometimes smelled—miles away as the ganders honk and squawk to protect their nests. This extraordinary gathering place was discovered in 1944, when it was estimated at 100 nesting pairs. (Such early counts were based on anecdotal tallies, whereas today's populations are gauged by aerial surveys.) By the time the next snow goose census was taken in 1973, the count had reached 30,000 pairs. There are now more than 60,000.

A canoe affords the best way to scope out all this birdlife. Short hikes on land are possible, but the sopping ground makes walking a challenge at best: When the muskeg is not sucking at your

Sik sik, or ground squirrel

Pan ice formations near Polar Bear Provincial Park

boots, mosquitoes are sucking your blood. Thanks to the region's flattened topography, wilderness canoe trips here tend to be blessedly free of both white water and portages, making for some pleasantly undemanding paddling. Many rivers offer excellent canoe routes; particularly good are the **Brant, Kinushseo, Lakitusaki, Shagamu, Sutton,** and **Winisk Rivers.**

Even if most people go for the birds, the place lives up to its name with a polar bear population estimated at 400. When the bears return to the water with their cubs after a hungry summer ashore, the coast may be populated by 200 of the huge white beasts, virtually guaranteeing a sighting. Keep in mind that a distant polar bear is a safe one.

Myriad other mammals live around Polar Bear park. Atlantic walrus can frequently be seen loafing offshore. Beluga whales and bearded seals are common. In the muskeg you might spot beaver, otter, gray wolf, arctic fox, red fox and marten, moose, woodland caribou, or black bear.

Getting There

Charter services usually cost about $2,000 per person, including air transport and canoe or kayak rental. Only four landing sites are allowed within the park: Brant River, Shagamu River, Sutton River, and a place simply called Site 415. Scheduled flights *(Air Creebec 705-336-2221)* operate twice weekly from Moosonee to Peawanuck, the Cree enclave in the park's north-central coastal area. You'll need the services of an outfitter if you plan to fish in this remote setting.

Staying Safe

Visitors should bring everything they will need, plus a week's extra rations to accommodate the inevitable delays involved in being extracted. Survival camping—living off the land—is not permitted. In summer the mosquitoes, deerflies, and horseflies can be ubiquitous, relentless, and maddening. ■

Other Sites

GREAT LAKES AND CANADIAN SHIELD

Frontenac Provincial Park

Crisscrossing a diverse landscape of gorges, lakes, and bogs, 105 miles of hiking trails—the Moulton Gorge Trail being the most popular among them—get you out into this rugged 14,500-acre park in eastern Ontario. Frontenac Provincial Park also offers good swimming and canoeing with 48 campsites (none are vehicle accessible). Eagles, turkey vultures, red-tailed hawks, cliff swallows, and many other birds populate the skies. Frontenac is renowned for its innovative instructional programs, such as teaching children to cope with being lost in the woods, moccasin making, and wilderness first aid. Contact the park, P.O. Box 11, Sydenham, ON K0H 2T0; phone 613-376-3489.

Ivanhoe Lake Provincial Park

The so-called quaking bog— a small lake completely overgrown with a carpet of vegetation that quivers visibly when disturbed—is a curiosity of this 3,926-acre park in Ontario's boreal forest area. (You're not supposed to make it quake deliberately, though unfortunately many hikers do.) Three hiking trails will take you through woods and wetlands, where you may spot moose or wild-rice plantings. Open from mid-May to late September. Contact the park, 190 Cherry St., Chapleau, ON P0M 1K0; phone 705-899-2644.

Killbear Provincial Park

This park's glorious combination of rugged and rocky coastline, azure waters, mixed woods (mostly conifers, maple, and birch), and perhaps the best sand beach in the bay attracts many visitors. The 4,340-acre provincial park—like its companion parks Bruce Peninsula and Georgian Bay Islands—is a refuge for the endangered massasauga rattler. A few trails, as well as the shoreline, provide opportunities for exploration; the park is also popular with kayakers. Contact the park, P.O. Box 71, Nobel, ON P0G 1G0; phone 705-342-5492.

Mono Cliffs Provincial Park

Two massive outlying sea stacks—separated from the main body of the Niagara Escarpment by erosion— form the park's most prominent features. With 1,800 acres, Mono Cliffs offers superlative hiking over part of the escarpment. A number of caves penetrate the cliffs; although you can't enter them on foot, you can peer into them from boardwalks and lookout points. In common with the rest of the escarpment, the cliffs virtually drip with ferns and orchids. Cross-country skiing is available in season. Contact Earl Rowe Provincial Park, P.O. Box 872, Alliston, ON L9R 1W1; phone 705-435-2498. www.ontarioparks.com

Ouimet Canyon Provincial Park

Located northeast of Thunder Bay on Lake Superior's north shore, this 1,920-acre nature reserve encompasses the dramatic 490-foot-wide canyon. Two viewing platforms perched on the lip— each with a vertiginous 320-foot drop to the valley floor below—allow visitors to experience its grandeur. Rare arctic-alpine plants (fir-club moss, saxifrage, shield fern, and others) left over from the last ice age survive deep in the canyon, where the sun so rarely penetrates that snow lingers until early summer. The canyon floor itself is off-limits, but walkways, platforms, and interpretive displays enable you to enjoy the natural environment. Open from mid-May to the mid-November. Contact the park, P.O. Box 5000, Thunder Bay, ON P7C 5G6; phone 807-977-2526. www.ontarioparks.com

Presqu'ile Provincial Park

Presqu'ile's 2,170 acres protrude into Lake Ontario, making the park a natural stop for migrating birds and, in the fall, monarch butterflies. The beach area along Lake Ontario and the boardwalk across the park's marsh offer the best bird-watching. More than 320 species have been cataloged at Presqu'ile. The popular Monarchs and Migrants Weekend (Labor Day) takes place most years, but check with the park first. Open spring to fall. Contact the park, R.R. 4, Brighton, ON K0K 1H0; phone 613-475-4324. www.ontarioparks.com

THE ST. LAWRENCE

Parc d'Aiguebelle

Abundant wildlife—moose, beaver, wolf, fox, lynx, and black bear—roam this 65,920-acre park in the Abijévis hill country north of Rouyn-Noranda. More than 18 miles of hiking trails snake through the park. You can cross a nerve-racking 210-foot-long suspension bridge high above Lac La Haie or climb a steep wooden staircase (more than 200 steps) to a limpid lake at the base of a cliff. Cross-country skiing is popular in winter. Contact the park, 1737 Rang Hudon, Mont-Brun, QC J0Z 2Y0; phone 819-637-7322. www.sepaq.com

Parc des Monts-Valin

Located north of the Saguenay River, dramatic mountains (some reaching more than 3,000 feet) steep valleys, spectacular views, and dozens of lakes characterize Monts-Valin's 37,760 acres. Abundant moose and bear inhabit the park. Locals maintain that the park is haunted—perhaps because snow and ice sometimes engulf small conifers, turning them into "mummies." In winter, the park is a haven for cross-country skiers and snowshoers. Contact the park, P.O. Box 68, St-Fulgence QC G0V 1S0; phone 418-674-1200. www.sepaq.com

Parc du Bic

This 8,192-acre marine park protects a complex coastline of coves, headlands, and small islands on the south shore of the St. Lawrence between Montmagny and Ste.-Anne-des-Monts. Seals congregate at Cape Caribou, while a diverse collection of seabirds—especially eiders—populates the coast. Interpretive signs at the visitor center explain the park's natural history and pinpoint its various vantage points. You can explore the park's 8.6 miles of trails on foot or by bike. Open from May to the first snows. Contact the park, P.O. Box 2066, Le Bic, QC G0L 1B0, phone 418-736-5035 (in season); or Committee for the Development of Bic-St. Fabien, phone 418-869-3311.

Réserve Faunique de Matane

Offering wooded mountains, dozens of lakes and rivers, and rugged, unspoiled countryside, this massive, 494-square-mile wildlife reserve is a western extension of the Parc de la Gaspésie (see pp. 116-120). Moose, deer, wolves, foxes, and black bears draw wildlife watchers. Several observation towers along the 12 miles of trails make the viewing easier. Bird-watchers will revel in the reserve's rich avian life—the golden eagle, for one, is on the increase. Wildlife lovers may wish to avoid the reserve, however, during the late fall and early spring hunting seasons. Paddlers can rent canoes on site. Contact the reserve, 257 St. Jerome St., Matane, QC G4W 2A7; phone 418-562-3700.

MARITIME PROVINCES

Cape Chignecto Provincial Park

Overlooking the Bay of Fundy, Cape Chignecto's 10,378 acres include unspoiled wilderness—18 miles of coastline, old-growth forest, protected coves, and cliffs that tower 600 feet high—as well as massive 50-foot Fundy tides. More than 30 miles of coastal and inland hiking trails—some of which cross steep ravines on wooden boardwalks and bridges—have been laid out. Wilderness camping is a key draw of the park. Open mid-May–early Oct. Contact the park, phone 902-392-2085 (in season); or Nova Scotia Department of Natural Resources, Parks and Recreation Division, R.R. 1, Belmont, NS B0M 1C0; phone 902-662-3030.

Herring Cove Provincial Park

Reached via a bridge from Lubec, Maine, this 1,050-acre park lies on the eastern side of New Brunswick's Campobello Island. Six hiking trails, including the 2-mile Rock of Gibraltar Trail, will keep walkers happy; other activities on tap here include bird-watching—bald eagles reside in the area—kayaking, whale-watching, and fishing. Open May–Oct.; cross-country skiing is possible in the winter. Contact the park, Campobello Island, NB E0G 3H0; phone 506-752-7010. www.campobello.com

New River Beach Provincial Park

Offering scenic landscapes and windswept sea cliffs, New River Beach protrudes 1.5 miles into the Bay of Fundy (some 34 miles west of St. John). The 3-mile-loop Barnaby Head Trail crosses coastal bogs—look for dwarf conifers and carnivorous pitcher plants—to reach the spectacular coastline; 0.3 mile is wheelchair accessible. Along the coast you'll find sand dollars, sea urchins, crabs, and eider ducks. The latter are common in the park's waters because a major rookery sits just offshore. Contact the park, 8 Castle St., New River Beach, NB E2L 4Y9; phone 506-755-4042 (summer) or 506-658-2410 (off-season). www.tourismcanadanb.com

Taylor Head Provincial Park

Taylor Head—45 miles northeast of Halifax—juts 4 miles into the Atlantic Ocean and offers picnic areas, interpretive displays, and 10 miles of hiking trails over unspoiled coastline. Stunted spruce, coastal barrens, sand dunes, and stone beaches dominate the landscape. The hiking trails are rough, but they offer splendid opportunities for bird-watching. Open mid-May–mid-Oct. Contact Nova Scotia Department of Natural Resources, Parks and Recreation Division, R.R. 1, Belmont, NS B0M 1C0; phone 902-662-3030.

Thomas Raddall Provincial Park

Located on Nova Scotia's South Shore—just across the harbor from Kejimkujik Seaside Adjunct—Thomas

Raddall offers 1,600 acres of pristine white-sand beaches and a rugged shoreline of rocky headlands crenellated with small coves. Bird-watchers make for this park because it sits on the migratory flyway and because four bird sanctuaries are located nearby. Camping and hiking are possible. Open mid-June–mid-Oct. Contact the park, phone 902-683-2664 (in season); or Nova Scotia Department of Natural Resources, Parks and Recreation Division, R.R. 1, Belmont, NS B0M 1C0, phone 902-662-3030.

NEWFOUNDLAND

Blow Me Down Provincial Park

The Blow Me Down Mountains, which reach elevations of 2,100 feet, surround this 558-acre park overlooking the Bay of Islands in western Newfoundland. Boardwalks and a couple of staircases facilitate the hiking. Be sure to stop at the Governor's Staircase—a quartz rock formation that can appear liquid at first glance—on your hike up to the park's observation tower. The views from atop the tower are spectacular. A short trail from the picnic area leads to a beach. Open in summer. Contact Newfoundland Department of Tourism, Culture and Recreation, P.O. Box 8700, St. John's, NF A1B 4J6; phone 800-563-6353. www.gov.nf.ca/tourism

Dildo Run Provincial Park

A rocky, boulder-studded landscape of rolling hills covered with spruce and fir in the interior and fens and bogs in the lowlands characterizes this park's picturesque 808 acres. Located on New World Island just south of Twillingate, the park

overlooks the bay waters of Dildo Run. Visitors enjoy the shore's tide pools and, in early summer, the drifting icebergs. If you have time, consider touring the bay islands—one of the least developed and most scenic areas of Newfoundland. Contact Newfoundland Department of Tourism, Culture and Recreation, P.O. Box 8700, St. John's, NF A1B 4J6; phone 800-563-6353. www.gov.nf.ca/tourism

Squires Memorial Provincial Park

The scenic Humber River, which rises in Gros Morne National Park, is the featured attraction of Squires Memorial. The river offers excellent salmon angling (Newfoundland fishing permit required). Thousands of salmon head upstream in August, using the fish ladder blasted into nearby rocks. A hiking trail leads to the river's Big Falls—10 feet high but 285 feet wide. Canoeing and rowing (the park rents two-man dories) are permitted. Contact Newfoundland Department of Tourism, Culture and Recreation, P.O. Box 8700, St. John's, NF A1B 4J6; phone 800-563-6353. www.gov.nf.ca/tourism

EASTERN ARCTIC

Ijiraliq (Meliadine) River Territorial Historic Park

On the west coast of the Hudson Bay, Ijiraliq River protects a rich store of Thule and pre-Dorset (1000 B.C.) cultural artifacts and remnants. Interpretive signs explain the park's cultural history. Amateur geologists will find the massive esker—a ridge of sand and gravel left by a glacier—of particular interest; others will simply cherish the wonderful views it affords of the Meliadine Valley. The park is an easy 6-mile hike north of the community of Rankin Inlet, where an

Elder's cabin is available for overnight stays. Contact Hamlet of Rankin Inlet, phone 867-645-2895; or Nunavut Tourism, P.O. Box 1450, Iqaluit, NU X0A 0H0, phone 800-491-7910. www.nunavutparks.com

Mallikjuaq Island Territorial Historic Park

Set on Baffin Island in a bleak and splendid rolling landscape, the park's name—"big wave" in Inuktitut—refers not to the ocean but to the shape of the frozen rock. The park is accessible only by boat, snowmobile, or foot—a sometimes soggy 45-minute hike from the community of Cape Dorset. You'll likely see caribou and foxes in the summer, as well as a wide variety of birds, including the snowy owl. Remnants of the ancient Thule culture, most of them dating back a thousand years, dot the land. Most people visit in July, when nights last only about 4 hours. Contact the park, phone 867-897-8996; or Nunavut Tourism, P.O. Box 1450, Iqaluit, NU X0A 0H0, phone 800-491-7910. www.nunavutparks.com

Sylvia Grinnell Territorial Park

This small park (365 acres) just a stroll away from Nunavut's capital, Iqaluit, offers an easy and worthwhile introduction to the Arctic. The tundra vegetation includes arctic poppies and northern heathers. Caribou (winter or spring) and arctic foxes roam the land. No trails exist; most people hike along the shores of the Sylvia Grinnell River and its falls (not very high and almost submerged at high tide). Anglers will find chances aplenty to catch char (fishing permit required). Contact Nunavut Tourism, P.O. Box 1450, Iqaluit, NU X0A 0H0; phone 800-491-7910. www.nunavutparks.com

Resources

The following is a select list of resources. For the most comprehensive listings for lodging, camping, outfitting, and transportation information contact the provincial tourist bureaus. They all maintain extensive websites as well. For chain hotels and motels in Eastern Canada, see p. 282.

GREAT LAKES AND CANADIAN SHIELD

Federal and Provincial Agencies

Arts in the Wild
Queen's Park
Toronto, ON M7A 2R9
416-314-0944 or
800-ONTARIO
www.artsinthewild.com
In conjunction with Ontario Tourism, Arts in the Wild offers more than sixty outfitters and learning vacations.

Ontario Parks
300 Water St.
P.O. Box 7000
Peterborough, ON
K9J 8M5
416-314-0944 or
800-ONTARIO
www.ontarioparks.com
Information on Ontario's more than 270 natural areas. For campsite reservations call 888-668-7275.

Ontario Tourism
Queen's Park
Toronto, ON M7A 2R9
416-314-0944 or
800-ONTARIO
www.ontariotravel.net
Complete lodging, camping, transportaion, and park information.

Paddling Ontario
Queen's Park
Toronto, ON M7A 2R9
416-314-0944 or
800-ONTARIO
www.paddlingOntario.com
Information on flat-water, white-water, and sea kayaking, and canoeing.

TrailPAQ
30 Stewart St.

P.O. Box 450 Stn. A
Ottawa, ON K1N 6N5
613-562-5101
www.trailpaq.ca
Trail information and recommendations for hiking throughout Canada.

Parks Canada
111 Water St. E.
Cornwall, ON K6H 6S3
613-938-5879 or
800-839-8221
www.parkscanada.pch.gc.ca
For information on national parks in Ontario (descriptions, fees, etc.).

Ontario Private Campground Association
R.R. 5
Owen Sound, ON
N4K 5N7
519-371-3393
www.campgrounds.org
400 privately owned campgrounds, representing 70,000 campsites; accommodating needs from tent camping to RVs.

Outfitters

Bruce Peninsula Outfitters
6798 Hwy. 6
Tobermory, ON N0H 2R0
519-596-2735
www.bpo.on.ca
Guided horseback and extended hiking in the Bruce Peninsula. Specializing in bird-watching.

Canoe Canada Outfitters
300 O'Brien St.
P.O. Box 1810
Atikokan, ON P0T 1C0
807-597-6418
www.canoecanada.com
Fully supported fishing and canoeing in Quetico Provincial Park.

Canoe Frontier Expeditions
Box 38
Pickle Lake, ON P0V 3A0
807-928-2346 or
800-285-8618
www.canoefrontier.com
River and wilderness adventures in the Hudson and James Bay watersheds.

Conservation Nature Tours
R.R. 1
Hanover, ON N4N 3B8
519-364-1255 or
888-301-4268
www.svca.on.ca/naturetours

Part of Saugeen Valley Conservation Authority, CNT offers hiking and paddling trips throughout Bruce and Grey Counties. Offers women-only and family oriented trips.

Killarney Outfitters
Killarney, ON P0M 2A0
705-287-2828 or
800-461-1117
www.killarneyoutfitters.com
Sea kayak on Georgian Bay, paddle a canoe in Killarney Park. Photo tours from Killarney to Algonquin.

Naturally Superior Adventures
R.R. 1
Wawa, ON P0S 1K0
705-856-2939 or
800-203-9092
www.naturallysuperior.com
Outfitting services in Lake Superior Provincial Park and Pukaskwa NP. Sea kayaking of Lake Superior's shoreline and canoeing of nearby rivers. Guided and unguided trips. Certified instruction.

Tobermory Adventure
112 Bay St. S.
P.O. Box 241
Tobermory, ON
N0H 2R0
519-596-2289
www.tobermory.com
Diving, kayaking, and fishing trips around the Bruce Peninsula.

Quiet Water
Box 399
Waubaushene, ON
L0K 2C0
705-538-2343
www.sailboatsales.com
Sailboat rentals in Georgia Bay.

Swift Canoe & Kayak
R.R. 1, Hwy. 11 N.
Gravenhurst, ON P1P 1R1
705-687-3710 or
800-661.1429
www.swiftcanoe.com
Canoe and kayak rentals near Georgian Bay as well as Algonquin Provincial Park. Georgia Bay outlet offers a kayak school.

Woodland Caribou Outfitters
Box 830

231 Howey St.
Red Lake, ON P0V 2M0
807-727-9943
www.woodlandoutfitters
.com
Canoeing and fishing trips
from Red Lake. Centrally
located for easy access to
Woodland Caribou Provincial Park and Atikaki Park.

THE ST. LAWRENCE

Federal and Provincial Agencies

Federation of Quebec
Outfitters
5237 boul, Hamel
Rm. 270
Québec, QC G2E 2H2
418-877-5191 or
800-567-9009
www.fpq.com
Lodging and outfitter information for hunters, anglers,
and families looking for
outdoor holidays.

Fédération Québécoise de
Camping et de Caravaning
(FQCC)
Camping in Quebec
P.O. Box 1000
Montréal, QC H1V 3R2
514-252-3003
www.campingquebec.com
Nonprofit organization
dedicated to campers and
RVs. Travel services, activities, and information on
over 470 campsites in the
province.

Parks Canada
3 Passage du Chien d'Or
P.O. Box 6060, Haute-Ville
Québec, QC G1R 4V7
418-648-4177 or
800-463-6769
www.parkscanada.pch.gc.ca
For information on national
parks in Quebec (descriptions, fees, etc.).

Parks Quebec (Sépaq)
801 chemin St-Louis,
Suite 180
Québec, QC G1S 1C1
(418) 686-4875
www.sepaq.com
For in-depth information
on provincial parks, wildlife
reserves and camping.

Tourisme Québec
C.P. 979
Montréal, QC H3C 2W3

514-873-2015 or
877-BONJOUR
www.bonjourquebec.com
Province-wide accommodation, camping, and park
information. Reservation
service available.

Outfitters

1000 Islands and Seaway
Cruises
263 Ontario St.
Kingston, ON K7K 2X5
613-549-5544 or
800-848-0011
www.1000islandscruises
.on.ca
Cruises of St. Lawerence
Islands National Park.

Horizon Nature Adventures
4165-A, St-Denis St.
Montréal, QC H2W 2M7
514-286-6010 or
888-318-6010
www.hna.qc.ca
Specialized kayaking, canoeing, hiking, dogsledding and
cross-country skiing trips
across Quebec.

New World River
Expeditions
100 Rouge River Rd.
Calumet, QC J0V 1B0
Offers white-water clinics
and rafting and kayaking
trips.

Tuckamor
7123 rue Lac Noir
Ste-Agathe-des-Monts,
QC J8C 2Z8
819-326-3602
www.tuckamor.com
Offers fully outfitted hiking,
skiing, and canoeing trips
to a variety of locations
including La Vérendrye and
Mont Tremblant.

MARITIME PROVINCES

Federal and Provincial Agencies

Nova Scotia Department of
Tourism and Culture
2695 Dutch Village Rd.
Ste. 501
Halifax, NS B3O 4V2
902-425-5781 or
800-565-0000
www.explorens.com
Complete lodging, camping,
outfitter, park, and trans-

portation information in
Nova Scotia. Reservation
service available.

Parks Canada
1869 Upper Water St.
Halifax, NS B3J 1S9
902-426-3436 or
888-773-8888
www.parkscanada.pch.gc.ca
For information on national
parks in Atlantic Canada
(descriptions, fees, etc.).

Prince Edward Island
Department of Tourism,
Parks and Recreation
Box 940
Charlottetown, PE
C1A 7M5
www.peiplay.com
902-368-7795 or
888-PEI-PLAY
Complete lodging, camping,
outfitter, park, and transportation information for
Prince Edward Island. Reservation service available.

Tourism New Brunswick
P.O. Box 12345
Campbellton, NB E3N 3T6
800 561-0123
www.tourismnbcanada.com
Complete lodging, camping,
outfitter, park, and transportation information in
New Brunswick. Reservation service available.

Ferries

Bay Ferries
94 Water St.
P.O. Box 634
Charlottetown, PE
C1I 7L3
888-249-7245
www.nfl-bay.com
Between Bar Harbor, Maine,
and Yarmouth, Nova Scotia
(Late May–late Oct.); from
Woods Islands, Prince
Edward Island to Caribou,
Nova Scotia (May–late
Dec.); from St. John, New
Brunswick to Digby, Nova
Scotia (year-round).

M/S Scotia Prince
P.O. Box 4216
Portland, ME 04101
207-775-5616 or
800-341-7540
www.scotiaprince.com
Operates between Portland, Maine, and Yarmouth,
Nova Scotia early May–
late Oct.

Outfitters

Arpin Canoe Restigouche
8 Arpin Rd.
Kedgwick River, NB
E8B 1R9
506-284-3140 or
877-259-4440
www.canoerestigouche.ca
Canoe rentals, guiding, and
shuttle service along the
Restigouche.

Coastal Adventures
P.O. Box 77
Tangier, NS B0J 3H0
902-772-2774 or
877-404-2774
www.coastaladventures.com
Twenty years of hiking
and paddling experience in
Atlantic Canada. One- to
ten-day trips. Inn-to-inn and
women-only tours offered.
Custom trips by request.

Freewheeling Adventures
R.R. 1
Hubbards, NS B0J 1T0
902-857-3600 or
800-672-0775
www.freewheeling
adventures.com
Locally guided cycling,
hiking, and ocean kayaking
trips in coastal Nova Scotia
and the Atlantic Provinces.
Van-supported inn-to-inn
trips with small groups; also
custom tours, trip planning
services, and equipment
rentals.

FreshAir Adventure
16 Fundy View Dr.
Alma, NB E4H 1H6
506-887-2249 or
800-545-0020
www.freshairadventure.com
Day and half-day sea kayaking in the Bay of Fundy near
Fundy National Park.

**Grand Manan Sea-Land
Adventures**
11 Bancroft Point Rd.
Grand Manan Island, NB
E5G 4C1
506-662-8997
Sailing and whale-watching
in the Bay of Fundy.

**O'Donnell's Cottages and
Expeditions**
439 Storeytown Rd.
Doaktown, NB E9C 1T3
506-365-7636 or
800-563-8724
www.odonnellscottages.com

Lodging and guiding
services in the Miramichi
River Valley. Adventures
include day and multi-
day canoe, hiking, and
biking trips

Outside Expeditions
P.O. Box 337
North Rustico, PE
C0A 1X0
902-963-3366 or
800-207-3899
www.getoutside.com
Fully supported kayak
and biking expeditions
exploring Prince Edward
Island, Nova Scotia,
Newfoundland, and Îles
de la Madeleine.

Scott Walking Adventures
1707 Pryor St.
Halifax, NS B3H 4G7
902-423-9751 or
800-262-8644
www.scottwalking.com
Cape Breton and south
shore Nova Scotia walk-
ing/hiking tours. Other fully
supported trips throughout
Atlantic Canda.

Small Craft Aquatic Centre
P.O. Box 130
Fredericton, NB E3B 4Y7
506-460-2260
Half-day guided tours of
the St. John River and its
islands and streams.

Smooth Cycle
172 Prince St.
Charlottetown, PE
C1A 4R6
902-566-5530 or
800-310-6550
www.smoothcycle.com
Bicycle rentals and self-
guided day and multiday
tours of Prince Edward
Island.

NEWFOUNDLAND

Federal and
Provincial Agencies

Newfoundland and Labrador
Department of Tourism,
Culture and Recreation
P.O. Box 8700
St. John's, NF A1B 4J6
800-563-6353
www.gov.nf.ca/tourism
Complete lodging, camping,
outfitter, park, and trans-
portation information in

Newfoundland. Reservation
service available.

Parks Canada
1869 Upper Water St.
Halifax, NS B3J 1S9
902-426-3436 or
888-773-8888
www.parkscanada.pch.gc.ca
For information on
national parks in Atlantic
Canada (descriptions,
fees, etc.).

Ferry

Marine Atlantic
355 Purves St.
North Sydney, NS
B2A 3V2
902-794-8109 or
800-341-7981
www.marine-atlantic.ca
Service between North
Sydney, Nova Scotia and
Channel-Port aux Basques,
Newfoundland (year-round);
and between North Sydney,
Nova Scotia, and Argentia,
Newfoundland (late
June–early Oct.).

Outfitters

Eastern Edge Outfitters
93 St. Thomas Line
Paradise, NF A1L 2P9
709-782-5925
White-water and sea
kayaking trips throughout
Newfoundland.

Gros Morne Adventures
P.O. Box 275
Norris Point, NF A0K 3V0
709-458-2722 or
800-685-4624
Hiking, backbacking,
ski touring, and sea
kayaking trips. Explore
Gros Morne NP or the
East Coast Trail. Winter
inn-to-inn touring available.
Sea kayaking in Notre
Dame Bay.

**Wilderness Newfoundland
Adventures**
67 Circular Rd
St. John's, NF A1C 2Z4
709-753-1432 or
888-747-6353
www.wildnfld.ca
Half-day to multiday sea
kayaking, canoeing, moun-
tain biking, and hiking trips
on the Avalon Peninsula.

EASTERN ARCTIC

Federal and Provincial Agencies

Newfoundland and Labrador Department of Tourism, Culture and Recreation
P.O. Box 8700
St. John's, NF A1B 4J6
800-563-6353
www.gov.nf.ca/tourism
Complete lodging, camping, outfitter, park, and transportation information in Labrador.

Nunavut Tourism
P.O. Box 1450
Iqaluit, NU X0A 0H0
867-979-6551 or
800-491-7910
www.nunatour.nt.ca
Complete lodging, camping, outfitter, park, and transportation information for Nunavut.

Parks Canada
P.O. Box 353
Pangnirtung, NU X0A 0R0
867-473-8828
For information on national parks in Nunavut (descriptions, fees, etc.).

Air Charters

First Air Limited
General Delivery
Resolute Bay, NU X0A 0V0
867-252-3981
www.firstair.ca
Scheduled flights to Resolute with charter access to all of Ellesmere and Baffin Islands and other far north destinations.

Kenn Borek Air Limited
General Delivery
Resolute Bay, NU X0A 0V0
867-252-3845
or
P.O. Box 1741
Iqaluit, NU X0A 0H0
867-979-0040
www.borekair.com
Scheduled flights to the far north and charter flights to Quttinirpaaq, Sirmilik, and Auyuittuq National Parks.

Ferry

Coastal Labrador Marine Services
P.O. Box 790
Lewisport, NF A0E 3A0
709-535-6872 or
800-563-6353
Serves lower Labrador with auto ferries and passenger service to Nain and some 40 coastal villages from St. Anthony.

Outfitters

Adventure Canada
Lochburn Landing,
14 Front St.
South Mississauga
ON L5H 2C4
800-363-7566
www.adventurecanada.com
Land and sea expeditions exploring Nunavut's national parks, Ellesmere Island, and Baffin Island.

Nature Trek Canada
220 Hillcrest Rd.
Saltspring Island, BC
V8K 1Y4
250-653-4265
www.naturetrek.ca
Specializes in hiking trips into Labrador's mountains and along Newfoundland's East Coast Trail. Nature Trek will also take visitors to the George River, flying in on float plane from Schefferville, Quebec.

NorthWinds
P.O. Box 820,
Iqaluit, NU X0A 0R0
867-979-0551
www.northwinds-arctic.com
All-inclusive dogsledding and backpacking. Ellesmere Island, Baffin Island, and Greenland. Small groups can create their own adventure in the Arctic.

Pikialuyak Outfitting
P.O. Box 88
Qikiqtarjuaq, NU
X0A 0B0
867-927-8390
Provides transportation to North Pangnirtung Fiord trailhead in Auyuittuq National Park. Also offers custom trips.

Polar Sea Adventures
P.O. Box 60
Pond Inlet, NU X0A 0S0
867-899-8870
Provides a variety of trips including dogsledding excursions to the edge of Sirmilik National Park.

Toonoonik Sahoonik Outfitters
General Delivery
Pond Inlet, NU X0A 0S0
867-899-8366
www.pondtour.com.
Owned and operated by the people of Pond Inlet, The company offers a range of Arctic adventure travel trips in and around the Pond Inlet/Eclipse Sound/ Bylot Island area. Sirmilik trips, dogsled tours, whale-watching, fishing, sea kayaking, hiking/trekking, and customized trips.

Wilderness Adventure Company
R.R. 3
Parry Sound, ON
P2A 2W9,
705-746-7048 or
888-849-7668
www.wildernessadventure.com
All-inclusive guided trekking on Ellesmere Island and Devon Islands.

Hotel & Motel Chains

Best Western International
800-528-1234

Clarion Hotels
800-252-7466

Comfort Inns
800-228 5150

Days Inn
800-325-2525

Delta Hotels
800-268-1113

Embassy Suites
800-362-2779

Fairmont Hotel and Resorts
800-441-1414

Hilton Hotels
800-HILTONS

Holiday Inns
800-HOLIDAY

Howard Johnson International
800-446-4656

Quality Inns
800-228-5151

Ramada Inns
800-2-RAMADA

Sheraton Hotels
800-325-3535

Travelodge International
800-578-7878

Westin Hotels and Resorts
800-325-3000

Index

Abbreviations:
National Historic Site = NHS
National Marine Park = NMP
National Park = NP
National Park Reserve=NPR
National Wildlife Area = NWA
Provincial Park=PP

About the Author and Photographer

Marq de Villiers lives in Lunenburg, Nova Scotia, on Canada's Atlantic coast. He is the author of several books on travel, nature, and history, including *Into Africa: A Journey Through the Ancient Empires* (Key Porter Books, 1999) and *Water: The Fate of Our Most Precious Resource* (Houghton Mifflin, 2000).

Michael Lewis has photographed the Rockies, the Midwest, Canada, and Africa for the Book Division of the National Geographic Society. He logged nine ferry crossings, several airplane rides, and 12,000 miles in his truck for this guidebook. He lives in Denver with his wife, Sharon, and their dogs, Carlos and Lucy.

Illustrations Credits

National Geographic Guide to America's Outdoors: Eastern Canada
by Marq de Villiers
Photographed by Michael Lewis

Published by the National Geographic Society
John M. Fahey, Jr., *President and Chief Executive Officer*
Gilbert M. Grosvenor, *Chairman of the Board*
Nina D. Hoffman, *Executive Vice President,*
  President, Books and School Publishing

Prepared by the Book Division
Elizabeth L. Newhouse, *Director of Travel Publishing*
Allan Fallow, *Senior Editor and Series Director*
Cinda Rose, *Art Director*
Barbara Noe, *Senior Editor*
Caroline Hickey, *Senior Researcher*
Carl Mehler, *Director of Maps*

Staff for this Book
Keith R. Moore, *Book Manager*
Robin Currie, Kim Kostyal, Jane Sunderland, *Text Editors*
Joan Wolbier, *Designer*
Marilyn Mofford Gibbons, *Illustrations Editor*
Sean M. Groom, Victoria Garrett Jones, *Researchers*
Lise Sajewski, *Editorial Consultant*
Matt Chwastyk, Jerome N. Cookson, Sven M. Dolling, Thomas L. Gray,
  Nicholas P. Rosenbach, Gregory Ugiansky, National Geographic Maps,
  Mapping Specialists, XNR Productions, *Map Edit, Research, and Production*
Tibor G. Tóth, *Map Relief*
R. Gary Colbert, *Production Director*
Sharon Kocsis Berry, *Illustrations Assistant*
Anne Marie Houppert, *Indexer*
Larry Porges, *Editorial Coordinator*
Deb Antonini, *Contributor*

Manufacturing and Quality Control
George V. White, *Director*; John T. Dunn, *Associate Director*; Vincent P. Ryan, *Manager*;
Phillip L. Schlosser, *Financial Analyst*

Library of Congress Cataloging-in-Publication Data

De Villiers, Marq
  Guide to America's outdoors. Eastern Canada / by Marq De Villiers ; photography by Michael Lewis.
    p. cm.
  Includes index.
    1. Canada, Eastern—Guidebooks. 2. National parks and reserves—Canada,
  Eastern—Guidebooks. 3. Outdoor recreation—Canada, Eastern—Guidebooks. I. Title:
  Eastern Canada. II. Lewis, Michael, 1952 Feb. 5- III. Title.

  F1009 .D48 2001
  917.1304'4--dc21

  2001034565
  CIP

The information in this book has been carefully checked and is accurate as of press date.
However, details are subject to change, and the National Geographic Society cannot be
responsible for such changes, or for errors or omissions. Assessments of sites are based on
the authors' subjective opinions, which do not necessarily reflect the publisher's opinion.
The publisher cannot be responsible for any consequences arising from the use of this book.